Mental Health Policy and Practice

Interagency Working in Health and Social Care
Edited by Jon Glasby

Aimed at students and practitioners, this series provides an introduction to inter-agency working across the health and social care spectrum, bringing together an appreciation of the policy background with a focus on contemporary themes. The books span a wide range of health and social care services and the impact that these have on people's lives, as well as offering insightful accounts of the issues facing professionals in a fast-changing organisational landscape.

Exploring how services and sectors interact and could change further, and the evidence for 'what works', the series is designed to frame debate as well as promote positive ways of interdisciplinary working.

Published titles
Baggott: *Partnerships for Public Health and Wellbeing: Policy and Practice*
Glasby/Tew: *Mental Health Policy and Practice 3rd edition*
French/Swain: *Working with Disabled People in Policy and Practice*
Kellett: *Children's Perspectives on Integrated Services: Every Child Matters in Policy and Practice*
Williams: *Learning Disability Policy and Practice: Changing Lives?*

Mental Health Policy and Practice

3rd edition

Jon Glasby and Jerry Tew

 palgrave

First published 2006
Second edition 2010
Third edition 2015
Published by
PALGRAVE

Palgrave in the UK is an imprint of Macmillan Publishers Limited, registered in England, company number 785998, of 4 Crinan Street, London, N1 9XW.

Palgrave Macmillan in the US is a division of St Martin's Press LLC, 175 Fifth Avenue, New York, NY 10010.

Palgrave is a global imprint of the above companies and is represented throughout the world.

Palgrave® and Macmillan® are registered trademarks in the United States, the United Kingdom, Europe and other countries.

ISBN: 978–1–137–02594–4

This book is printed on paper suitable for recycling and made from fully managed and sustained forest sources. Logging, pulping and manufacturing processes are expected to conform to the environmental regulations of the country of origin.

A catalogue record for this book is available from the British Library.

A catalog record for this book is available from the Library of Congress.

Library of Congress Cataloging-in-Publication Data

Glasby, Jon.
    Mental health policy and practice / Jon Glasby and Jerry Tew. -- 3rd edition.
        pages cm. – (Interagency working in health and social care)
    Revision of: Mental health policy and practice / Helen Lester and Jon Glasby. 2010. 2nd ed.
    Summary: "The third edition of Mental Health Policy and Practice remains a clear and comprehensive overview of UK mental health policy. It includes ideas from a wide spectrum of mental health services, examples of successful evidence-based practice and analyses the impact, and likely impact, of the latest shifts in policy and changes to legislation"– Provided by publisher.
    ISBN 978-1-137-02594-4 (paperback)
    I. Tew, Jerry, 1955- II. Title.
    RA790.5.L45 2015
    362.2–dc23   2015003830

Typeset by Cambrian Typesetters, Camberley, Surrey

This book is dedicated to Helen Lester, a wonderful friend, colleague, researcher and GP. Helen was co-author of the first two editions of this book, before she tragically died, as preparations for a third edition were under way. One of the last things Helen said to us was to make us promise that we would produce this third edition – and we hope that her passion for the role that research can play in improving services and hence people's lives shines through our attempt to honour her wishes.

Contents

List of Boxes, Figures and Tables

Boxes

Figures

Tables

Acknowledgements

The publishers and authors acknowledge the following for kind permission to reproduce material in this book:

Carer's Trust for Box 9.9 'John's Story' (available at www.carers.org);

Paul Hoggett for his permission to reproduce Figure 7.1 'User Involvement', from *Going Local* (1992); and

Sainsbury Centre for Mental Health for permission to reproduce Table 6.1 'Mental Health Needs in Prison', from *Mental Health Care and the Criminal Justice System* (2009).

This book contains public sector information licensed under the Open Government Licence v3.0.

1 Introduction

In this chapter we discuss:

- The importance of partnership between health and social care.
- What we mean by mental health.
- The impact of mental illness.
- Different ways of thinking about mental illness.
- The incidence and prevalence of mental illness.

This revised and updated book is designed as an introduction to mental health policy and practice in the United Kingdom (UK) for students as well as for qualified practitioners, their managers and policy makers. That a third edition is needed so rapidly reflects the rate of change in mental health policy and practice across the four countries of the UK, with an increased degree of diversity as devolved administrations have had the opportunity to set their own policy directions. Our focus is on policy and practice relating to a range of mental health difficulties – including both more common difficulties (such as anxiety or depression) and those that may be seen as more serious and disabling (such as to psychosis) – but generally excluding neuro-degenerative conditions such as dementia which have tended to be dealt with somewhat separately in terms of policy and service provision. We will also consider the emphasis on the promotion of mental health and mental well-being that has become more prominent in mental health policy over recent years.

While mental health has acquired greater policy prominence over time, and a range of new service models and initiatives have been put in place, much remains to do in terms of:

- Developing better primary care-led and community-based models of service provision.
- Continuing to improve specialist mental health services and promoting a more personalised, recovery-oriented approach.
- Reducing stigma and promoting inclusion.
- Balancing concerns about risk and safety with increasing expectations around service user choice, control and self-management.
- Moving away from a focus on the needs of people in crisis to promote positive mental health for all.

It is these issues (although with some significant differences in emphasis), that are setting the context and agenda for policy development across the countries of the UK. However, in all UK countries, after a period of substantial growth in funding between 2000 and 2010, any desire to improve mental health services has now to be envisioned within a challenging financial context in which substantial savings are being required within the National Health Service (NHS) and, often to an even greater extent, within local authority social care services.

In seeking to understand the directions of (and contradictions within) current policy, we also aim to provide some historical perspective – exploring how thinking and practice has continued to evolve over time, and what may have been the more or less obvious drivers for such developments.

Now published as part of a broader series on interagency working for different user groups, this book does not just focus on a particular professional or organisational perspective – but on a wider whole systems approach. However, within this 'whole system', our focus is primarily on specialist mental health and social care services – although we recognise that people with mental health problems are also affected by (and concerned with) the everyday services and supports that are so essential to all of us (for example, housing, employment, income, education, family, neighbourhoods, transport, leisure and community safety) – and we try to reflect this wherever possible.

The importance of health and social care partnerships

Part of the difficulty in providing a holistic response to people with mental health problems derives from the structural barriers built into our welfare state (see Glasby and Dickinson, 2014, for further discussion). This is true across a range of different agencies – but is particularly the case with regard to the relationship between health and social care. Traditionally, the post-war welfare state is based on the assumption that it is possible to distinguish between people who are sick (health needs) and those who are merely frail or disabled (social care needs). This was enshrined in two pieces of 1940s legislation (the NHS Act 1946 and the National Assistance Act 1948) and continues to form the basis of service provision in the early twenty-first century (Glasby and Littlechild, 2004; Glasby, 2012). As a result, two separate systems have developed, each with different ways of working, different structures and different priorities (see Box 1.1). Even in Northern Ireland, where health and social services have been formally integrated, front-line professional practice can still feel very divided (see, for example, Heenan and Birrell, 2006, 2009).

In response, governments have explored different ways to promote more joined-up services and to provide a more efficient and coordinated response to people with complex needs. Over time, responses have ranged from the Joint Consultative Committees, joint care planning teams and joint finance initiatives of the 1960s and 1970s to attempts to ensure greater coordination with mechanisms such as care management and the Care Programme Approach in the 1990s. More recently, we have seen a plethora of approaches, including the creation of

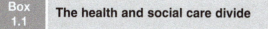

Key features of social care include:

- councillors democratically elected at a local level;
- local government is overseen and monitored by the Department for Communities and Local Government (although the Department of Health has a significant role in the oversight and monitoring of social care);
- subject to means testing and charges;
- based on specific geographical areas;
- traditional focus on social factors contributing to individual situations and on choice/empowerment; and
- strong emphasis on social sciences.

Key features of NHS care include:

- non-executive directors appointed by central government;
- overseen and monitored by the DH;
- free at the point of delivery;
- boundaries are based on GP practice registration;
- traditional emphasis on the individual and on medical cure; and
- strong emphasis on science.

pooled budgets between the NHS and local government, the promotion of joint commissioning, integrated provider organisations, senior joint appointments, joint assessments of local need, the creation of multidisciplinary teams at local level and greater emphasis on information sharing, a single point of access, single assessment and the co-location of different professional groups (see Glasby and Dickinson, 2014, for an overview). Arising out of this partnership agenda, different health and social care professions reading this book will increasingly be working in inter-professional settings and/or integrated organisations, working with a wider range of colleagues from different professional and organisational backgrounds. While this has long been recognised in mental health, it has sometimes seemed a slower process in other settings – and there still remains much to be done even in mental health to ensure people using services receive a holistic and fully coordinated response.

What do we mean by mental health?

According to the World Health Organization (WHO) (2001), mental health is more than simply an absence of symptoms of mental distress – it involves a positive sense of well-being and an ability to lead a full and productive life. Everyone has mental health needs, whether or not they have a diagnosis of mental illness.

Positive mental health includes the ability to understand and make sense of our surroundings, to cope with change and to connect with other people. When mentally well, we are aware of and have control over different strands of our life; we have the will to live life to its full potential; things make sense to us. Mental health is increasingly recognised as an essential component of our general health as exemplified in the key strategy documents such as *Towards a Mentally Flourishing Scotland* (Scottish Government, 2009b) and *No Health without Mental Health* (HM Government, 2011).

Mental well-being

In policy terms, the concept of mental well-being has assumed increasing prominence in recent years, particularly in Scotland, but also in England under the coalition government. Although this concept is subject to different interpretations, it is generally accepted that well-being comprises two key aspects (Ryan and Deci, 2001):

1. *Positive thoughts and feelings.* This is the *subjective* or 'hedonic' aspect of well-being. This has been popularised as 'happiness' (Layard, 2006), drawing on the ideas of positive psychology (Seligman, 1991) – but also encompasses other aspects of subjective experience such as sense of belonging and having meaning and purpose in life.
2. *Flourishing and active engagement in life.* This is the *objective* or 'eudemonic' aspect of well-being. It is predicated on the capacity to exercise agency and choice, and has been described as 'a dynamic state in which the individual is able to develop their potential, work productively and creatively, build strong and positive relationships with others, and contribute to their community' (Foresight Programme, 2008: 10).

Although they are related concepts, well-being is not the same as 'quality of life' which primarily focuses on the circumstances in which people live, rather than on how they respond to those circumstances. Research suggests that well-being is not the 'opposite' of mental disorder: some people with ongoing 'symptoms' manage to achieve high levels of well-being while others do not (Weich *et al.*, 2011), and this may be seen as a critical issue in terms of judging the effectiveness of service provision.

Well-being is seen to be achieved through a combination of personal and social factors – and may be enhanced through policies and practices which:

■ enhance people's ability to be in control of their lives;
■ increase resilience and community assets; and
■ facilitate participation and promote inclusion (National Mental Health Development Unit, 2010).

Although the idea of well-being has been applied at the individual level, it may also be used at the level of social groups, such as families or communities, to describe the degree to which these may or may not be flourishing and be experienced positively.

What do we mean by mental ill-health?

Mental ill-health covers a spectrum from psychosis through to more everyday experiences such as anxiety or depression. It has been understood and defined in many different ways, and meanings have changed across time, and are influenced by geography, discipline and personal perspective. A lawyer will have one definition, a psychiatrist another, a service user another still.

The legal definition under the English Mental Health Act 2007 is 'any disorder or disability of the mind' with similarly broad definitions in the corresponding legislation across the countries of the UK. Psychiatry most commonly conceptualises mental distress in terms of specific mental illnesses, such as schizophrenia, with precise diagnostic criteria. Psychology tends towards the idea of a formulation that describes a person's experiences and behaviours as phenomena in their own right, rather than necessarily as symptoms of an underlying illness. Social work is most concerned with the relationship between people's mental experiences and their wider life circumstances – including factors such as disadvantage, stigma and discrimination.

Providing something of an antidote to professional debates, the writings of people who have experienced mental distress first-hand are invaluable in providing an insight that neither romanticises nor underestimates the meaning, effects and consequences of mental ill-health. William Styron (2001: 46–7) described his depression as:

> a storm of murk … near paralysis, psychic energies throttle back close to
> zero. Ultimately the body is affected and feels sapped, drained … I began
> to conceive that my mind itself was like one of those outmoded small
> town telephone exchanges, being gradually inundated by flood waters: one
> by one, the normal circuits began to drown, causing some of the functions
> of the body and nearly all those of instincts and intellect to slowly
> disconnect.

Users' experience and writings can, however, also demonstrate the ways in which people find value even in the most difficult circumstances. David Karp (1996: 104) records how one of his interviewees, a female freelance writer, aged 41, described her depression as a gift: 'that if we can befriend it, if we can travel with it, that it is showing us things. Somewhere along the line we have got to integrate it into our lives. All of us are depressed someway, somewhere at sometime. If we don't allow it in, it can be disruptive. If we allow it in, it is a teacher.'

Over the years, user organisations, such as Survivors Speak Out and the Hearing Voices Network, have provided fora in which people have shared and started to make sense of their experiences on their own terms (Wallcraft and Michaelson, 2001; Dillon, 2010). As we discuss in Chapter 2, it is largely through the writings of mental health service users that the notion of recovery has become an increasing part of the discourse of mental health – and this is reflected in the range of service user and survivor narratives that are now available through the Scottish Recovery Network website (www.scottishrecovery.net).

Different approaches to understanding mental health difficulties

As Coppock and Hopton (2000) have suggested, there is a tendency for mental health professionals to opt for one particular approach to understanding mental health difficulties, often allied to their training and professional background. We firmly believe, however, that no one approach has all the answers and that the origin of mental health difficulties must inevitably represent a confluence of different factors. This implies that we need to be reflexive in our thinking rather than holding fast to one particular conceptual model. As Tyrer and Steinberg suggest, 'those who imprison themselves within the confines of one model only have the perspective of the keyhole' (2003: 138).

Whatever your belief about the origins and nature of mental illness, the notion of 'madness' is indisputably ancient and ubiquitous. There is probably no society past or present that has failed to acknowledge its existence. Madness became associated with health and sickness through the writings of the early Greeks, particularly Hippocrates (470–410 BC). Hippocratic medicine explained health and illness in terms of the rhythms and shifting balances of humours (juices or fluids). Within this belief system, 'humoral balance' of vital fluids was essential for good health, and illness was the result of an increase or decrease in the humours. In terms of mental illness, excess blood and yellow bile were thought to lead to mania and surplus black bile to melancholy or depression.

Perhaps the next great leap in thinking, at least in terms of rationalising madness, came from the work of René Descartes (1596–1650), who moved away from the more mystical elements of the Hippocratic tradition, towards a theory of particles of matter obeying mathematical laws. Descartes proposed that there are two types of material in the world: the mental or mind, and the physical or body. He equated the mind with the soul and stated that the mind docked with the body at the pineal gland. He also proposed that the mind and body were therefore separate entities (sometimes talked about as 'Cartesian dualism'). This had significant consequences for thinking about madness since, in effect, it implied that mental and physical health are separate entities.

The Enlightenment came to be characterised by the emergence of two very different approaches to mental ill-health, both of which remain influential today. For some, madness was to be seen as the result of a disease process and a bodily malfunction, and this has become a very influential paradigm. In Britain, Thomas Willis (1621–75) coined the term 'neurology', and, as an avid dissector, tried to localise mental functions to particular regions of the brain. However, also integral to Enlightenment thinking was the alternative paradigm of 'moral treatment' as pioneered by William Tuke in the York Retreat in the eighteenth century in England and by Philippe Pinel in France (Porter, 2002; Foucault, 1967). They reacted against the dehumanising and degrading treatment of people who were seen as mad – both in the wider community and in institutions such as Bethlem

Royal Hospital (Bedlam) in London. Instead, they believed in offering a safe, respectful and nurturing environment in which people could learn once again to be moral citizens capable of managing their irrational impulses and exercising self-control. People were subjected within organised routines of productive work, self-improvement and recreation. Positive behaviour was rewarded and coercive sanctions avoided as far as possible.

These two traditions came together, somewhat uneasily, in the large-scale expansion of asylums in the nineteenth century. Initially, these were run by non-medical superintendents, but gradually this changed to a more medically dominated regime. By the late nineteenth century, the main priority for the growing number of psychiatrists was to legitimise their discipline as a hard biomedical science alongside neurology and pathology. Creating a credible knowledge base for psychiatry helped to underpin psychiatrists' claims for their medical authority over 'madness'. Scull (1979) cites an editorial from the *Journal of Mental Science* (the former title of the *British Journal of Psychiatry*) in 1858 that captures this early biomedical professional justification: 'Insanity is purely a disease of the brain. The physician is now the responsible guardian of the lunatic and must remain so.'

A key figure in this movement was Emil Kraepelin (1856–1926), a German psychiatrist who assumed that there was a discrete and discoverable number of psychiatric disorders and argued that each disorder had a typical symptom picture. He also believed that each disorder was associated with a different brain pathology and different aetiology (that is, cause and origin). As Bentall (2003: 13) suggests, 'on Kraepelin's analysis, therefore the correct classification of mental illness according to symptoms would provide a kind of Rosetta stone, which would point directly to the biological origins of madness'. Kraepelin also highlighted the importance of long-term outcomes and of illness trajectories by suggesting that the natural history of psychiatric illness was a better clue to its nature than the symptoms a patient showed at one particular point in time. Kraepelin was therefore responsible for a significant innovation in the conceptualisation and classification of illness, encouraging psychiatrists to describe and taxonomise mental disorders and informing and shaping the dominant disease model in twenty-first century psychiatry (see Box 1.2).

Box 1.2	Central tenets of the disease model

- Mental pathology is accompanied by physical pathology.
- Mental illness can be classified as different disorders which each have characteristic common features.
- Mental illness is biologically disadvantageous.
- The causes of physical and mental pathology in psychiatric illness are all explicable in terms of physical illness.

Source: Summarised from Tyrer and Steinberg (2003: 10)

The notion of mental illness as a biomedical entity was challenged in the 1960s by a number of disparate individuals and groups, including UK anti-psychiatrists such as R. D. Laing and the US psychiatrist Thomas Szasz. Laing, in classic texts such as *The Divided Self* (1960) and *The Self and Others* (1961), claimed that psychotic symptoms are meaningful in themselves and therefore cannot be understood as medical phenomena. Szasz (who vehemently denied any association with the anti-psychiatry movement), claimed that the concept of mental illness is incoherent and that mental illness is not a disease, but a misinterpretation of people's reactions to 'problems of living' (1961). Szasz (1970: 23) stated that:

> The expression mental illness is a metaphor which we have come to
> mistake for a fact. We call people physically ill when their body
> functioning violates certain anatomical and physiological norms; similarly
> we call people mentally ill when their personal conduct violates certain
> ethical, political and social norms. This explains why many historical
> figures from Jesus to Castro and from Job to Hitler, have been diagnosed
> as suffering from this or that psychiatric malady.

Although intellectually influential, Szasz's views have not been widely accepted. Nevertheless they chime with a wider critique of the role played by medicine and the emerging range of 'psy' practices in legitimating and enforcing forms of social control (Porter, 2002; Foucault, 1967). As the US sociologist Irving Zola argues:

> Medicine is becoming a major institution of social control, nudging aside,
> if not incorporating, the more traditional institutions of religion and law
> … this is not occurring through the political power physicians hold or
> can influence, but is largely an insidious and often un-dramatic
> phenomenon accomplished by 'medicalising' much of daily living, by
> making medicine and the labels healthy and ill relevant to an ever
> increasing part of human existence. (Kosa and Zola, 1975: 170)

In parallel with the rising influence of the biomedical disease model in the twentieth century, was the development of psychological understandings of mental ill-health. Although internally divergent, the different schools of psychological thinking located difficulties in specific emotional, cognitive and behavioural processes, and tended to take a developmental perspective in theorising how these difficulties may have come about. Mental ill-health was defined in terms of dysfunctional responses to current circumstances – perhaps misperceiving or misinterpreting current reality through depressive or delusional thinking patterns, or experiencing disturbances in feeling due to echoes of unresolved past experiences intruding into the present. Dysfunctional response patterns could also be viewed as defence mechanisms or coping strategies that may have been understandable in relation to specific circumstances that people may have faced.

Linking to broader psychological perspectives, a social causation approach to mental ill-health focused more on the sorts of external life experiences that may have triggered and reinforced such dysfunctional or damaging psychological responses (Tew, 2011). Émile Durkheim (1897), in his classic work on suicide, argued that social factors, especially isolation and loss of social bonds, were important in predicting and even causing suicide. Brown and Harris (1978) found that depressed women living in a London borough were more likely to have more young children at home, less part-time or full-time employment and fewer confidantes with whom they could discuss their worries than non-depressed women. More recently, research has shown how a range of social experiences can greatly increase the likelihood that people will experience forms of mental ill-health. These include:

- material and educational disadvantage (Dohrenwend, 2000; Harrison *et al.*, 2001; Wilkinson and Pickett, 2009);
- racism and other forms of social discrimination (Janssen *et al.*, 2003; Fearon *et al.*, 2006); and
- traumatic experiences, such as sexual abuse and being bullied in childhood (Read *et al.*, 2004; Bebbington *et al.*, 2004; Larkin and Morrison, 2006).

This increasing evidence base has led many people working in mental health to recognise the influence of social factors and the environment on developing mental ill-health (Tew, 2011). Similarly, there is strong evidence that social factors such as connectedness and social inclusion are important in determining people's chances of longer-term recovery (Tew *et al.*, 2012). Such a focus harks back to the moral treatment approaches of the early Enlightenment and suggests a need to focus on helping individuals find positive social roles, and addressing underlying social issues as part of any overall service package.

Over recent decades, there has been an attempt to reconcile biomedical and psychosocial approaches in order to produce a more integrated and holistic understanding of a person's mental ill-health. One approach has been the biopsychosocial (BPS) model. George Engel (1980) argued that, for psychiatry to generate a fully scientific and inclusive account of mental disorder, biomedical accounts

Box 1.3	Central tenets of psychosocial models

- Mental ill-health involves dysfunctional emotional, cognitive and behavioural processes (and the interrelationship between these).
- These may often be understood as responses to problematic life circumstances.
- Current difficulties may reflect beliefs, attitudes and coping mechanisms that may no longer be appropriate to current circumstances.
- Stressful personal relationships and wider societal factors, such as race, gender and social status, may increase likelihood of experiencing mental ill-health.
- Positive personal relationship and opportunities for social inclusion are crucial to prospects for longer-term recovery.

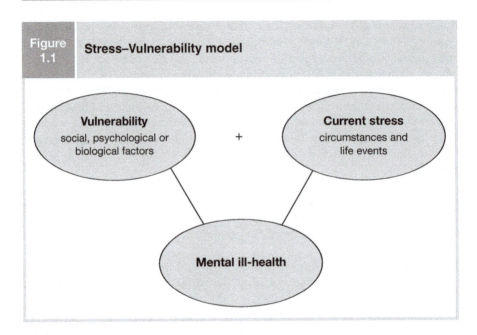

Figure 1.1   Stress–Vulnerability model

needed to be superseded by ones that incorporated ideas from general systems theory – so that psychological and social factors may be seen as interacting with biochemistry. Pilgrim (2002) argues that this BPS model does not object to diagnosis in principle, but it privileges the person and their longitudinal context over the medical categories applied to them – and that the model's inclusive approach creates the possibility of thinking about mental health problems in both scientific and humanistic terms. While the BPS model may appear to have achieved recognition in psychiatry, Pilgrim warns that its popularity may reflect service-level pragmatism and a form of mutual tolerance within increasingly multidisciplinary teams, rather than its acceptance as a stable theoretical orthodoxy. In practice, rather than the 'bio', the 'psycho' and the 'social' being seen as mutually interdetermining, the biological has tended to have been given priority, dictating the parameters of understanding and treatment (Tew, 2011: 24).

An alternative formulation is the Stress–Vulnerability model developed by Zubin and Spring (1977) – see Figure 1.1.

Although some have used this rather simplistically to suggest that vulnerability is biological and stress is psychosocial, it is more helpful to recognise that vulnerability may arise from social experiences (such as childhood trauma) as well as from genetic predisposition. A longitudinal study conducted in Finland with identical twins who were adopted separately into different families has shown that genetic factors alone had only a small effect on subsequent incidence of psychosis; difficult family relationships on their own had a rather greater impact, but the combination of the two greatly increased this possibility (Tienari et al., 2004).

More recently, it has been seen as important to include the development of resilience as well as vulnerability within the model: we know that the majority

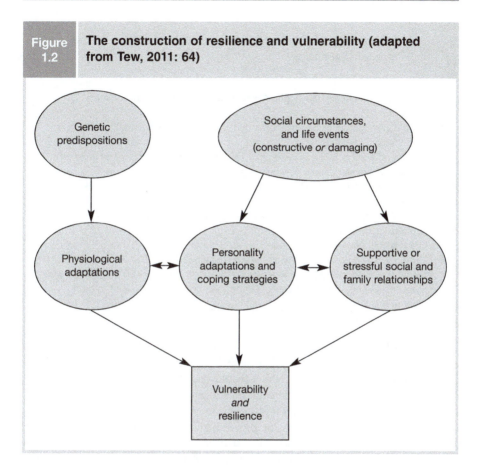

Figure 1.2 The construction of resilience and vulnerability (adapted from Tew, 2011: 64)

of people who have genetic predisposition do not go on to experience mental ill-health, and it does not seem likely that this is because they have lived entirely stress-free lives. Both vulnerability and resilience may result from the interaction between the physiological, the psychological and the social (Tew, 2011) – which suggests a slightly more complex model (see Figure 1.2).

The 'decade of the brain'

In the latter decades of the twentieth century, there was a shift within psychiatry from a more pluralistic understanding that was more inclusive of psychological, social and philosophical perspectives, to a more reductive biochemical explanatory framework in which mental distress was increasingly seen just as a set of symptoms caused by an underlying disease of the brain. This way of thinking became enshrined in (and has been reinforced by) systems of disease classification, such as the American Psychiatric Association's *Diagnostic and Statistical Manual* (DSM) which underwent a radical shift towards a more biological orientation in its third revision (DSM3) in 1980 (see Box 1.4).

> ### Box 1.4 The growth of the Diagnostic and Statistical Manual of Mental Disorders
>
> - In 1917, the American Psychiatric Association recognised 59 psychiatric disorders.
> - With the introduction of the *Diagnostic and Statistical Manual* (DSM) in 1952, this rose to 128.
> - The second edition, DSM-2 (1968), had 159 categories with more of an emphasis on describing dysfunctional psychological processes.
> - DSM-3 (1980) had 227 and the revised DSM-3R (1987) had 253 categories. It developed classification on the basis of different axes which, in practice, tended to marginalise psychosocial perspectives in favour of systems of symptom description related to medical diagnoses.
> - DSM-4 (2000) had 374 categories.
> - DSM-5 (2013) has a broadly similar number of categories as DSM-4, with the introduction of some new categories being balanced by the removal of certain other categories (such as the sub-types of schizophrenia) that were judged to be no longer of any value.

The 1990s have been described as the 'decade of the brain' in which there emerged a dominant expectation that medical research would be able to establish clear models of brain pathology which would then be able to explain, and then – it was hoped – to treat, the full range of experiences from which people were suffering. However, although DSM has continued to gather momentum in terms of codifying an increasing range of problematic human experiences as mental disorders, the science has so far failed to deliver the expected certainties – as two of the key figures in the development of DSM3 and DSM4 acknowledged (Spitzer and First, 2005: 1898):

> Little progress has been made toward understanding the *pathophysiological* processes and *aetiology* of mental disorders. If anything, the research has shown the situation is even more complex than initially imagined.

In particular, human genome research has not been able to point out any simple genetic difference that causes schizophrenia, and hypotheses about the role of chemicals such as dopamine and serotonin have also proved overly simplistic. As a result, the tide of opinion is turning with many across all mental health professions seeing mental ill-health as a more complex issue where the biological, the psychological and the social are all seen as potentially important, and as interacting with one another (Bracken *et al.*, 2012; Kinderman *et al.*, 2008; Tew, 2011). For example, brain imaging is now showing us that traumatic life experiences can affect the 'hard-wiring' of the brain, opening up the possibility of different paths of causation. Alongside this, there has been an increasing questioning of both the validity and utility of diagnoses such as schizophrenia (Boyle, 2002) – and an alliance between service user activists and sympathetic professionals has promoted a wider 'Campaign for the Abolition of the Schizophrenia Label' (Hammersley and McLaughlin, 2006).

Taking this position to its logical conclusion, Bentall (2003) has challenged the entire Kraepelinian foundation of psychiatric practice, suggesting that psychosis in particular should be seen as just part and parcel of human variation, rather than as an illness. He cites studies showing that up to 11–13 per cent of people have experienced hallucinations at some point in their lives (Tien, 1991) and the work of Marius Romme and Sandra Escher (1989) in the Netherlands, suggesting that many people hear voices, but have little difficulty coping with them and indeed have never sought psychiatric treatment for them. Bentall argues that the boundaries of madness are fluid and that many experiences that might be attributed, on DSM criteria, to a psychotic illness, are not necessarily pathological. His 'post-Kraepelinian' position is that:

> We should abandon psychiatric diagnoses altogether and instead try
> to explain and understand the actual experiences and behaviours of
> psychotic people … Once these complaints have been explained, there
> is no ghostly disease remaining that also requires an explanation.
> Complaints are all there is … an advantage of this approach is that it
> does not require us to draw a clear dividing line between madness and
> sanity. (2003: 141–2)

More subtly, there has emerged a tendency within some policy and practice contexts to use, instead of formal diagnostic categories, more descriptive terms such as psychosis – e.g. in defining the remit of early intervention services. This questioning and uncertainty has been reflected in an ongoing debate in the *British Journal of Psychiatry* with some feeling the need to reassert the primacy of the biological against a slide into more pluralistic models of understanding (Craddock *et al.*, 2008), while others have argued that such an approach has had its day and that it is time for psychiatry to embrace and work with alternative models of understanding (Bracken *et al.*, 2012; Priebe *et al.*, 2013).

Nevertheless, the legacy of the 'decade of the brain' may be seen to be influencing policy and practice. As will be discussed in Chapter 2, payment mechanisms within the NHS are requiring that people be slotted into 'PbR clusters' (Solomka, 2011) which give primacy to medical diagnosis, rather than any other measure of need, distress or complexity. Not only is the 'mental and emotional experience' side of the mind–body dualism potentially ignored within the institutional organisation of psychiatric services, it is also reflected in the separate services for people with physical *and* mental health problems. As Wade and Halligan (2004: 1398–9) suggest:

> Health commissioners, budgetary systems, health care professionals and the
> public all act as if there is some clear, inescapable separation between
> physical and mental health problems, ignoring evidence that the person's
> emotional state always affects their function and presentation of physical
> symptoms.

The impact of mental illness

Mental ill-health now touches most people's lives. At a global level, depression will be the second most common cause of 'disability', after ischaemic heart disease, by 2020 (WHO, 1999). The burden of psychosis is exceeded only by quadriplegia and dementia at a global level, when assessed by people's perception of disease burden (Ustun *et al.*, 1999). Mental and behavioural disorders affect more than 25 per cent of all people at some time during their lives, and are present in about 10 per cent of the population at any one time (WHO, 2001). Mental health problems account for 20 per cent of disability-adjusted life years (DALY) lost, compared to around 17 per cent and 15 per cent for cardiovascular disease and cancer respectively (Friedli and Parsonage, 2007).

Mental illness also contributes to individual as well as national poverty through lost production from people being unable to work, reduced productivity from people who are ill at work, lost production from absenteeism, and loss of the bread winner of a dependent family (see Chapter 3 for more detail). This cycle can sometimes be perpetuated to future generations through untreated illness in a parent leading to childhood educational failure, future unemployment and perhaps illness in adult life. The adverse economic consequences of more common (but still disabling) experiences such as depression have also been high-lighted by Lord Layard of the London School of Economics in his influential report (Layard *et al.*, 2006), which led him to make a powerful economic argument for putting more resources into therapies, particularly at primary care level, that would enable people to return to the workforce (Layard *et al.*, 2007)

Overall, data collated by the NHS Confederation Mental Health Network (2014) suggests that:

- There are nearly 1.6 million people in England in contact with specialist mental health services (of whom 105,000 or 6.3 per cent spent some time in hospital).
- 17.6 per cent of the English population aged 16 to 64 meet the criteria for at least one common mental health disorder.
- Following previous falls, suicide rates have risen to 1,333 deaths in 2011.
- Homicides by people with mental health problems have fallen, with 33 cases in England in 2010.
- Surveys suggest rising demand for services but real terms reductions in investment in a difficult financial environment – and the Care Quality Commission has expressed concerns about occupancy levels in mental health inpatient settings.
- In 2012/13 there were 50,000 detentions under the Mental Health Act (4 per cent greater than in 2011/12).

Despite significant increases in mental health expenditure during the early 2000s, many commentators would argue that the system as a whole was starting from a low base and that mental health has not experienced the same levels of investment as physical health services. More recently, there have also been significant concerns that mental health providers will be disproportionately hit by current financial pressures compared to general acute providers, with possible legal challenges threatened (see Lintern, 2014).

Key themes

Mental Health Policy and Practice has ten chapters, spanning the mental health system from professional, user and carer perspectives. An initial policy overview is followed by chapters on four specific service areas: primary care, community mental health, acute care and forensic mental health services. Chapters 7–9 address broader issues of user involvement, social inclusion, anti-discriminatory practice and carers' perspectives. The final chapter draws together key themes and suggests underlying reasons for the rhetoric–reality gap between policy and practice.

Traditionally, mental health services have tended to see themselves as different from the rest of health and social care because of the unique challenges they face. However, as we demonstrate throughout this book, mental health is also influenced by broader policy changes in health and social care and in social policy more generally. As a result, it is important for mental health students, workers and managers to understand how the issues and pressures they face fit into wider debates about welfare and service provision.

As you read through this book, you may notice recurring themes of a lack of real voice and choice for services users and carers, the rhetoric–reality gaps between policy prose and implementation in practice and the constant call by health and social care professionals and users and carers for a 'whole systems approach' to mental health. There are also a series of critical but uncomfortable issues that individuals and teams face around the culture of their organisation and the underlying attitudes and values of staff, managers and policy makers towards people with mental health problems. This book will, we hope, enable you to explore these issues, understand historical and current strengths and weaknesses of services and, above all, discover what we might be able to do to work towards more inclusive, integrated, user-focused services that make sense both to those providing and receiving them.

In Chapter 2, we provide an overview of mental health policy, which is key to understanding many aspects of the subsequent chapters. The chapter begins with a discussion of the meaning of the term 'policy' and influences on how policy is made, and concludes with some of the reasons why policies are not always implemented in practice. It also presents an overview of mental health policy, contextualised, from the 1970s onwards, through discussions of wider policy issues in generic health and social care. While there is not space within this book to discuss all the detailed differences in legislation and guidance across the four countries of the UK, more significant differences in policy directions will be highlighted. We suggest that although there is growing evidence that mental health has moved up the political agenda, chronic long-term underfunding means that many aspects of the mental health system were starting from a low baseline relative to services within the wider NHS. There is also a series of unresolved tensions particularly between a wider emphasis on patient choice, and mental health policy that, particularly in England, appears increasingly coercive and controlling.

Chapter 3 describes the complex world of primary care, which is perhaps the most rapidly changing part of the NHS. Primary care is a key partner in providing and increasingly commissioning good-quality mental health services, since most people with mental health issues, including serious mental illness, are seen and treated within this setting. After reviewing the evolution of primary care in the UK, we focus on the potential benefits offered by workforce developments such as the extended role of practice nurses, primary care graduate mental health workers (PCGMHWs) and GPs with a special clinical interest (GPwSI). We also explore recent developments improving access to psychological therapies for people with mental health problems, and conclude with a discussion of integrated models of working in primary care mental health.

Community mental health services are a complex and controversial area of practice that has received increasing attention in the last decade, within the context of wider deinstitutionalisation debates. Against this background, Chapter 4 explores the development of community mental health teams, the advent of more specialised functionalised teams and alternative ways of providing community-based services. We also discuss how the assessment and management of risk has often come to dominate practice at the expense of more therapeutic or recovery orientations – and ongoing issues as to how to coordinate care effectively.

Hospital services still play a key role in the UK health care system and consume a significant proportion of the overall health and social care budget. Despite this, the focus on community-based services has arguably led to a relative neglect of acute mental health services. In Chapter 5, we discuss trends in acute psychiatric care, highlighting concerns about pressures on acute beds, changes in admissions thresholds, the effects of high bed occupancy on standards of care and the poor quality of some service users' experiences of hospital services. We also discuss grounds for optimism, including national guidance to improve the physical environment of acute wards, and initiatives to develop a generalisable model of care that users experience as both safe and therapeutic, and where staff strengthen their skills and experience.

In Chapter 6 we focus on forensic mental health, exploring levels of unmet mental health needs in prisons and the potential number of people inappropriately placed in secure settings. To make sure we make best use of scarce resources and place people in the least restrictive settings possible, we need a broader spectrum of services to work together across organisational boundaries. We also discuss the 'mad vs bad' debate, and, in particular, stereotypes and misunderstandings about the alleged link between mental illness and crime/violence.

Until very recently, mental health service users were seen as passive recipients of care. However, over the past 20 years, users' views on service provision have become more accepted as a valuable part of health and social care. Chapter 7 charts the history of these changes, exploring the importance of user involvement in developing mental health services, barriers to user involvement and examples of positive practice. Tensions between notions of partnership and coercion of mental health service users, and evidence of professional ambivalence towards greater user involvement are also highlighted. We conclude that meaningful user involvement cannot be a one-off intervention or a discrete programme of work, but a much broader and more empowering way of working which affects every aspect of mental health provision.

Chapter 8 explores the many ways in which people with mental ill-health face stigma and exclusion from mainstream community life, and examples of how policy has sought to promote greater inclusion. Closely linked to this are issues of discrimination, both within society at large and within mental health services – and these are discussed in relation to different social groups (for example, the experience of women and of people from minority ethnic communities). Discrimination, like social exclusion, cannot be tackled simply by changing the way individuals behave. Instead, attempts to root out discrimination in mental health services need to be accompanied by similar efforts within wider society.

The family and friends of people who have mental health difficulties can often be marginalised by services – but it is they, rather than formal services, who provide the majority of support that people need while recovering and maintaining themselves in the community. It is also important to recognise that many people with mental health difficulties are themselves parents of dependent children and joined-up services that address the needs of both are crucial. In recent years, family members have increasingly been invited to take on the label of 'carer' which has become prominent in policy and practice discourses – which may or may not be helpful in reflecting the actuality of family relationships. This provides the focus for Chapter 9 which explores how the importance of informal carers has started to become recognised in policy and legislation – although not necessarily in ways that have effectively addressed the real needs, concerns and aspirations of family members and friends. Chapter 10 concludes the book.

Further resources

1. Key statistics can be found via the Health and Social Care Information Centre, including monthly bulletins and various other sources of routine data (www.hscic.gov.uk/mentalhealth)

2. Rogers, A. and Pilgrim, D. (2010) *A Sociology of Mental Health and Illness.* Buckingham: Open University Press.

    Classic text (now in its 4th edition) with a useful overview of perspectives on mental health and illness from both within and beyond sociology, including sections on labelling theory, critical theory and social constructivism.

3. Bentall, R. (2003) *Madness Explained: Psychosis and Human Nature.* London: Allen Lane.

    This is an interesting and deliberately provocative read that draws on a wide range of evidence from psychology, psychiatry, anthropology and the neurosciences, arguing that there is no discrete dividing line between mental health and illness. Bentall suggests that we can explain and understand many psychotic symptoms as part and parcel (or at least at the extreme end) of normal psychological processes.

4. Tew, J. (2011) *Social Approaches to Mental Distress*. Basingstoke: Palgrave Macmillan.

   Chapter 2 provides an overview of different ways of understanding mental distress with a particular emphasis on how these have been shaped by service users' and survivors' perspectives. Chapter 7 discusses models for understanding social causes and consequences of mental health difficulties.

5. Read, J. *et al.* (eds) (2004) *Models of Madness*. Hove: Brunner-Routledge.

   A challenging set of contributions from authors from different disciplines, providing critical examination of how we may understand and respond to mental distress.

6. Fawcett, B. and Karban, K. (2005) *Contemporary Mental Health: Theory, Policy and Practice*. Abingdon: Routledge.

   This provides an exploration of some of the key themes and tensions underlying current policy and the organisation of professional practice.

7. Reynolds, J. *et al.* (eds) (2009) *Mental Health Still Matters*. Basingstoke: Palgrave Macmillan.

   Interesting digest of readings from a wide range of material on mental health, much of which is authored by people with lived experience of mental health difficulties.

2 Mental Health Policy

In this chapter we discuss:

- Influences on how policy is made.
- Theoretical frameworks that help to understand key policy dilemmas and debates.
- A brief history of mental health policy within the broader context of generic NHS and social care policy.
- The influence of the modernisation agenda on mental health policy and practice.
- Recent developments in policy across the UK.
- The reasons why policies are not always implemented in practice.

In trying to unravel the complexities of mental health policy and practice, the most useful organising principle is probably a chronological (historical) perspective (Porter, 1987). Comparing mental health policy over time enables us to see how successive governments have built on or responded to previous policy and to the social, political and economic climate of the time. Up until the (re)establishment of devolved administrations across the four countries of the UK at the end of the twentieth century, much of this history is shared. However, in the twenty-first century we are now witnessing the unrolling of significantly different policy and legislative responses in each of the countries, reflecting different social, cultural, economic and political concerns.

Although we concentrate on mental health, we have also sought to contextualise more recent debates in mental health policy and practice through discussions of wider policy issues in generic health and social care. This approach enables us to see the origins of current policy and to appreciate that many current key debates have been rehearsed for decades. This, of itself, raises a number of interesting questions about the barriers and facilitators to implementation and the differences between policy rhetoric and the practical realities of delivering mental health services on the ground. The end result is, unsurprisingly, less a neat signposted pathway of incremental, evidence-based change than a messy trek with missed turns, sudden deviations from the highway and, at times, a sense of muddling through. Before setting out on the journey, however, it is worthwhile reflecting briefly on what we mean by the term 'policy' and on how policy is made. It is also important to have a grasp of some of the basic concepts that recur throughout this book to see how they help us understand why policy is formulated in certain ways and also why it sometimes fails to deliver anticipated outcomes.

What do we mean by 'policy' and how is it formed?

The concept of 'policy' is both highly contested and difficult to encapsulate. Ham (2009) suggests that the notion of policy is complex, involving a series of related decisions and a number of different people, many of whom are responsible only for policy making rather than subsequent implementation. In terms of mental health policy, Rogers and Pilgrim (2001: 226) suggest, 'The term mental health policy at the turn of the 21st century refers to legal arrangements, policy directives and service investments in relation to the aggregate picture which have accumulated over the past 100 years. It is partly about the control of behaviour, partly about promoting well-being, partly about ameliorating distress and partly about responding to dysfunction.' With such a broad remit, it is perhaps unsurprising that the mental health policy narrative is a complex and at times paradoxical story.

One of the consequences, Ham (2009) suggests, of the diverse interests in the policy community is that the history of the development of health and social care is characterised by long periods of incremental change and only occasional episodes of radical reform. Indeed, as we shall see, the move towards emptying asylums and providing care in the community is a story of slow, gradual change. Kingdon (1995) suggests that a 'step change' in policy is only likely to occur under two circumstances: a major event like war or an economic crisis that forces politicians to go beyond the accepted realms of possibilities (indeed, the NHS itself was established under such circumstances).

Sometimes policy has been made as a result of a bargain struck with key stakeholders. The concessions made to hospital doctors in terms of options for private practice and access to pay beds in NHS hospitals, for example, helped pave the way for the birth of the NHS in 1948. However, at other times, policy has been made and implemented despite opposition from the field. For example, the NHS and Community Care Act 1990, which introduced the controversial idea of the purchaser–provider split, was bitterly opposed by many in the medical profession. However, it was championed by a Conservative government sure of its majority and not afraid of taking on significant pressure groups.

Policy is also not always fully thought through at the time it becomes law. For example, a number of aspects of the NHS and Community Care Act 1990 were delayed in terms of implementation and modified and adapted as policy makers and practitioners realised that they needed to sort out how the new system was going to work, with the full Act not coming into force until 1993. The reform of the 1983 Mental Health Act in England and Wales which finally took place in the late 2000s was delayed through concerted and well-organised opposition from a coalition of professional and service user organisations – but was implemented anyway by a government that felt it had public (if not necessarily professional) opinion on its side. This was in contrast to a less divisive approach taken in Scotland and Northern Ireland, where the Mental Health (Care and Treatment) (Scotland) Act 2003 and the Mental Health (Amendment) (Northern Ireland) Order 2004 reflected much more of a consensus approach and resulted in earlier implementation.

From the discussion above, it is perhaps not surprising to learn that policy is not always evidence based. White Papers do not automatically carry annexes with detailed analysis of policy evaluations; ministerial speeches are not published with a list of references. However, since the mid 1990s, there has been a stated desire to move away from basing decisions primarily on expert opinion towards an approach which draws more explicitly on formal evidence of what works. At a national level, official health and social care research and development programmes are now in place, bodies such as the National Institute for Health and Care Excellence (NICE), and the Social Care Institute for Excellence (SCIE) have a remit to generate evidence of what works, and policy documents often stress the evidence base on which they draw. There have also been some (not always consistent) moves to collate and promote experiential evidence from service users and family members or informal carers – evidence that is effectively dismissed as worthless within the medical Cochrane hierarchy of evidence (www.cochrane.org/about-us/evidence-based-health-care), but which has been used by campaigning organisations such as Mind, and networks such as the Scottish Recovery Network, to influence policy development at a national level.

Many policy makers would probably argue that they are frequently faced with *excessive* rather than *insufficient* evidence about what works. The major difficulty is then to reconcile the interests of multiple partners and to ensure that policy reflects government pledges and financial flows. As Marmot (2004: 906) suggests:

> a simple prescription would be to review the scientific evidence of what would make a difference, formulate policies and implement them – evidence-based policy making. Unfortunately, this simple prescription, applied to real life, is simplistic. The relationship between science and policy is more complicated. Scientific findings do not fall on blank minds that get made up as a result. Science engages with busy minds that have strong views about how things are and ought to be.

It could, of course, be argued that basing policy only on research evidence might also be detrimental to health and social care. Research tends to focus on selected patient populations and so cannot tell clinicians what to do with specific individuals. There is also often an unacceptably long delay in publishing research findings, with a definite publication bias for studies that have positive findings (Higgitt and Fonagy, 2002). Within the research community, there are also debates over what we mean by 'evidence'. Often traditional research hierarchies favour more quantitative approaches such as systematic reviews and randomised controlled trials. However, small-scale qualitative work can provide a collectively powerful evidence base. For example, the collation of individual patient views (including 65,000 telephone calls, 124,000 website hits and 1374 emails) over the antidepressant medication Paroxetine in response to the television programme *Panorama* in 2001 helped to influence guidelines on depression issued by the National Institute for Health and Care Excellence (NICE, 2004a) and was a key factor in prompting subsequent calls for an investigation into the regulation of the pharmaceutical industry (Medawar *et al.*, 2002).

Frameworks for mental health policy

There are a number of models or frameworks that are helpful in making sense of the current policy environment in mental health. We highlight four frameworks that have been or are likely to be particularly influential.

Generic health service model

There has been an ongoing tension as to whether mental health fits easily within more generic approaches to health care. The relocation of psychiatric services from segregated asylums to wards in district general hospitals had great symbolic as well as practical significance in constructing the idea that mental ill-health was a health condition like any other. Viewed in this way, the primary focus of mental health services has been seen to be on the administration of medical and other forms of treatment by medically led multidisciplinary teams – with the appropriate form of treatment being determined primarily on the basis of a person's medical diagnosis.

However, not all mental health work fits neatly within a neat 'assessment–treatment–discharge' model which underpins much of general health care, as many people having more long-term, fluctuating and complex needs which potentially overlap between health and social care. Mental health does not fit neatly within either an acute care model or a 'management of long-term conditions' approach – many people do get better but not in a very straightforward or linear fashion. As will be discussed in more detail in later chapters, there has been a perceived need to develop 'bespoke' models for the organisation and delivery of mental health services that differ significantly from the mainstream of health service delivery.

Generic social care model

Primarily located within local authorities and the voluntary sector is a generic model of adult social care in which people are assessed in relation to definitions of need and risk. Need is understood in terms of the additional supports a person may require in order to be able to lead a life of acceptable quality. Risk is understood in a number of somewhat contradictory ways, including risk of harm to self, risk of harm to others, risk of exploitation or harm from others, and risk of the current situating deteriorating to a point where a more intensive input may be required, such as admission to residential care. Since the early 1990s, there has been a major shift in how an appropriate response to identified need or risk may be conceptualised. A 'social action' response with a social worker intervening to work with relevant people to resolve problems has increasingly been replaced by a 'provision of care services' response in which the social work task is simply to identify a package of social care services that can be purchased and deployed to address identified needs and risks.

As with generic health models, this approach has been found to have significant limitations when applied to the complex lives of many people with mental health difficulties. In particular, the 'provision of care services' model is only straightforward if people's needs or risks are immediately obvious and reasonably stable and predictable – as may be the case with frailty or physical impairment. Unfortunately, with their complexity and fluctuations, experiences of mental health difficulty do not easily lend themselves to a simple 'one-off assessment and review after six months' approach.

The social model of disability and the Independent Living movement

In the UK in the mid 1970s, the concept of disability began to be challenged by a number of different groups including the Union of Physically Impaired Against Segregation (UPIAS, 1976) and disability was recast in a socio-political light. Oliver (1983: 23) identified 'the social model of disability' in order to reflect the growing demand by disabled people and their allies for:

> nothing more fundamental than a switch away from focusing on the physical limitations of particular individuals to the way in which the physical and social environments impose limitations on certain groups or categories of people.

The social model of disability is based on the principle that disability is a denial of civil rights caused by exclusionary practices in all sectors of society. It recognises that people have impairments but argues that it is society which disables them. The social model has arguably provided the basis for a transformed approach to disability among disabled people, and informed the politics of the disability rights movement (Oliver, 1990, 1996). This has led to major changes in the UK and internationally in disability legislation, policy, practice and thinking including the passage of the Disability Discrimination Act (DDA) (1995), direct payments legislation (1996) and the establishment of the former Disability Rights Commission (2000).

At a societal level, this perspective has driven structural changes both in terms of making physical environments more accessible and creating the expectation that 'reasonable adjustments' should be made to a range of employment and other practices in order to address the often unthinking exclusion or discrimination faced by people with impairments – including those resulting from mental health difficulties. At an individual level, it has inspired the Independent Living movement through which people with impairments were given the financial and other resources to organise the support that they needed to be able to participate fully within mainstream social and economic life. From its origins in the Independent Living Fund, this has developed into more widespread models of direct payments and personal budgets by which people – perhaps with support from friends, family members or brokerage organisations – were able to organise their own personal assistance (see Chapter 4 for further discussion).

Initially, the social model of disability focused almost exclusively on physical impairment (Campbell and Oliver, 1996), which may perhaps reflect the relative invisibility of conditions that primarily affect the way someone thinks or feels. More recently, work around 'embodied irrationality', that is, the impact of having and living with a mental illness, has helped to focus thinking on aspects of mental illness as impairment and the ways in which impairment interacts with disability (Mulvany, 2000; Lester *et al.*, 2005). Beresford also argues that there are at least three key reasons why people with mental illness should recognise and indeed use the social model of disability:

> Survivors are now also among those experiencing the sticks and carrots of government welfare to work policy as disabled people. Thus *regardless of what survivors themselves may think*, they are frequently officially included as disabled. Secondly, there are significant overlaps between the two populations. Some survivors also have impairments, sometimes related to the damaging effects of the chemical and other treatments they have received, or to impoverishment ... Thirdly, disabled people and psychiatric system survivors are both subject to discrimination and oppression. While the forms these take may vary and restriction of rights is an explicit commitment of policy for psychiatric system survivors, the denial of their human and civil rights is a shared experience of disabled people and survivors. (2002: 169–70)

However, not all mental health service users have been comfortable with aligning their interests with the social model of disability (Spandler *et al.*, 2015). On a practical level, given the fluctuating nature of many mental health conditions, the prospect of managing a direct payment or a personal budget has often felt daunting and take-up has been low (Glendinning *et al.*, 2008; Webber *et al.*, 2014). On a more philosophical level, many people have been uncomfortable with defining their experience in terms of impairment and disability (Plumb, 1994). Nevertheless, with the anticipated roll-out of personal health budgets in mental health in England from 2015, we may see such approaches becoming more influential in policy and practice.

Despite the potential contribution of the wider disability and Independent Living movement, we would argue that current mental health policy and practice does not always reflect a rights-based approach in a consistent way. In England, at the same time as people were being offered the possibility of taking control over their social care support via personal budgets, their potential rights as citizens were being diminished through the reform of the Mental Health Act. Whereas, with very effective lobbying from Mind, the formulation of the 1983 Mental Health Act made a philosophical commitment to finding the 'least restrictive alternative' for people, its amendment in 2007 is underpinned by an implicit duty upon professionals to put possible concerns about public safety over the rights of people to exercise choice about their treatment and care. This is in contrast to the equivalent legislation in Scotland which explicitly foregrounds the principle that a person whose liberty is being curtailed should have a right to appropriate services, that their present and past wishes should be recognised, that they should participate in the design of their care and that there should be the minimum restriction on personal freedom (Grant, 2004). Similarly in Northern Ireland, the drafting of current Mental Capacity Bill (covering both capacity and compulsory intervention) has a strong rights focus with any potential intervention to be judged against the principles of autonomy, justice, benefit and least harm.

Recovery approaches

An influential approach that has emerged primarily from the mental health service user/survivor movement has been that of recovery (Deegan, 1988; Coleman, 1999). As with the social model of disability, this has involved a fundamental reframing (and claiming) of the meaning of a term which had previously been owned by professionals. Just as the meaning of 'disability' was refocused from individual impairment to disabling social practices and environments, so the meaning of recovery was shifted from a clinical focus on remission of symptoms to the idea of recovering a life worth living, irrespective of whether certain symptoms may remain (Anthony, 1993). At its heart is the notion of the person being enabled to reclaim control over both their life in general and, more specifically, over how their mental distress is managed.

In practice, both 'social' and 'clinical' aspects of recovery can be important – and are interrelated. Despite a therapeutic pessimism within services that had viewed serious mental illness as a chronic and ever-deteriorating condition, the evidence from longer-term longitudinal studies painted a rather more optimistic picture with around one-third of people achieving full recovery (both in terms of 'getting a life' and in terms of remission of symptoms) and another third achieving substantial improvement, albeit with some symptoms remaining (Harding and Zahniser, 1994).

Interestingly, at a population level, neither 'clinical' nor 'social' recovery rates in advanced countries show any time–series correlation with advances in clinical practice during the course of the twentieth century – such as the introduction of neuroleptic medication or shifts towards treatment in the community (Warner, 2004). Instead a correlation emerges with the state of the economy and rates of employment. This suggests that it may be the availability of social and economic opportunity that can be the single most important factor in enabling recovery. This potentially reverses the sequence of a more traditional health rehabilitation model: instead of the person waiting for treatment and care to make them sufficiently well so that they can resume mainstream social and economic participation, a recovery perspective suggests that it is 'getting a life' that may be the primary process and that remission of symptoms may, at least for some people, follow on from this. Interestingly, recent Europe-wide evaluations of a supported

Box 2.1   **Consensus definition of recovery**

Recovery is the process of regaining active control over one's life. This may involve discovering (or rediscovering) a positive sense of self; accepting and coping with the reality of any ongoing distress or disability; finding meaning in one's experiences; resolving personal, social or relationship issues that may contribute to one's mental health difficulties; taking on satisfying and meaningful social roles; and calling on formal and/or informal systems of support as needed ... For some people, recovery may mean exiting from mental health services either permanently or for much of the time. For others, it may mean continuing to receive ongoing forms of medical, personal or social support that enable them to get on with their lives.

Source: CSIP *et al.* (2007: 5)

mainstream employment model showed that this opportunity tended to lead, not just to improved social functioning overall, but also to a reduced level of symptoms (Burns *et al.*, 2009) – and this links to wider evidence that social factors can be very important in enabling recovery (Tew *et al.*, 2012).

However, recovery remains a contested concept. There is neither a universally accepted definition of recovery nor a single way to measure it (Pilgrim, 2008). Recently, there have been concerns emerging that the term has been appropriated by service providers as a form of intervention that could be 'done to' people, or as a way of legitimating closure of services – or simply as a way of re-badging existing services that did not actually facilitate people to take control over their own recovery journeys. Nevertheless, a consensus definition was reached between the DH Care Services Improvement Partnership (CSIP), the Royal College of Psychiatrists and SCIE in a joint position paper which asserts a person-centred vision of recovery (see Box 2.1).

Recovery from mental ill-health, according to mental health service users' writings, involves not only recovery from the symptoms themselves but also recovering from the stigma people experience and internalise, from the side effects of treatments and treatment settings, and from the negative effects of social exclusion such as unemployment and reduced social networks. Service users describe recovery as a personal journey of making sense of what has happened to them and of reconstructing a positive identity. It incorporates notions of hope for the future, of taking the least amount of medication necessary and of being involved in treatment planning in a partnership with professionals. It is not a linear process and setbacks can be part of the overall journey. Overall, a recovery approach suggests a shift from a primary focus on difficulties and deficits, to one on capabilities and potentials (Hopper, 2007) and on seeing recovery as a process that can be facilitated by mobilising different forms of social and personal capital (Tew, 2012).

Recovery was formally recognised in UK policy documents in 2001 when *The Journey to Recovery* (DH, 2001b) emphasised the need to replace hopelessness and pessimism in mental health services with a more positive and optimistic approach. It is also worth noting that, during the last decade, attempts to reduce barriers to recovery have extended beyond the realms of health and social care into, for example, the spheres of housing and particularly employment (see Chapter 8).

In practical terms, one of the more exciting developments has been the idea of 'Recovery Colleges'. In these, people are no longer located within an ethos dominated by the potentially debilitating 'expert knows best' power relations of clinical and social care, and instead have the opportunity to develop confidence and skills within the adult-learning educational ethos of a college environment (Perkins *et al.*, 2012). Where this is proving successful, service users are playing a large part in the running of Recovery Colleges and local education providers and employers are integral to providing the courses that are on offer. In this way, the College provides organic connections onward into mainstream employment, training and education opportunities, rather than providing a self-contained and inward-looking sanctuary against the vicissitudes of the outside world – which had been the effective modus operandi of many traditional day services.

However, despite such practical developments, the implementation of recovery thinking in mental health policy is still inconsistent and patchy – both at national and local levels. In England, as discussed above, the principles underpinning the 2007 Mental Health Act are antithetical to recovery – and this is probably having more impact on everyday practice and interactions with service users and family members that anything arising from a recovery strategy. In Scotland there is less contradiction at a national policy level and, in his ministerial foreword to the Scottish Mental Health Strategy 2012–15, Michael Matheson states that:

In Scotland we have had much success in promoting rights and recovery, addressing stigma and improving service outcomes. (Scottish Government, 2012: 1)

Initiatives across the UK, such as the Scottish Recovery Network and the Implementing Recovery through Organisational Change (ImROC) Project have been influential in promoting a recovery vision and evidence of what works in practice – and this has been supported by ambitious materials for use in professional education and practical models for organisational and cultural change. However, implementation of new ways of working has still been hampered by professional resistances to change (and giving up power) and an unfavourable funding climate which paradoxically has tended to funnel available funding into expensive 'core' NHS services with a poor track record of promoting recovery (such as inpatient units), and away from more innovatory services where investment might pay longer-term dividends in reducing the number of people who remain economically inactive and dependent on services.

A 'brief history' of mental health policy

Locking up the mad: the rise of the asylum

On the whole, throughout history and across civilisations, madness has usually been seen as a domestic responsibility, something that friends and families deal with (see Chapter 9 for a discussion of the role of carers). Indeed, it was not until the end of the Middle Ages that separation from society was used as a management strategy, with, for example, the religious house of St Mary of Bethlehem, known as Bethlem (Bedlam), set up to care for 'distracted' patients in London in 1377. Treatment was rudimentary, with patients chained to the wall in leg irons and whipped or ducked in water. From the early 1600s, visitors were allowed in to view the patients for a penny. A trip to Bedlam became a great treat for Londoners, with over 100,000 people a year paying to see the patients, who were placed in cages on the hospital's galleries.

The practice of private madhouses in England began in 1670, with some degree of licensing imposed a century later through the 1774 Madhouses Act. Some of these early private madhouses like Ticehurst House in Sussex allowed patients to bring their own personal servants and even to follow the hounds (Porter, 2002).

By 1800, there were approximately 5,000 people housed in a mixed economy of private asylums, far less salubrious state-run county asylums and workhouses. However, during the nineteenth century, the number of asylums and inmates increased dramatically. The underlying reasons for the rise in asylum care are complex (see Box 2.2). The 1845 Lunatics Act required the building of a network of publicly owned county asylums and formally established the Lunacy

Box 2.2	The rise of the asylum in Victorian England

- It has been suggested that the sheer force of human misery in an increasingly industrialised and urbanised nation pricked a new social conscience, sparking off philanthropic gestures including developing charitable institutions in which 'insanity might be healed by a gentle system of rewards and punishments, amusements, occupation and kind but firm discipline' (Murphy, 1991: 34) rather than leaving vulnerable mentally ill people open to exploitation in workhouses.
- Scull (1993: 3) suggests that the increase in institutionalisation was 'embedded in far more complex ways in broader transformations of the English political and social structure' as the asylum became a convenient dumping ground for a wide range of individuals who could not cope in the community and hence could not contribute to the political economy of early Victorian England.
- Pilgrim and Rogers (2010) suggest the change reflects the general move towards increased state intervention in social problems including the Poor Law Act of 1834, the Factory Acts of 1833 and 1844, the Mines Act of 1842 and the Public Health Act of 1848.

Commission, which inspected, licensed and reported (indeed performance managed) the progress of the new institutions. However, the new state asylums largely failed to live up to early expectations, particularly of the early philanthropists and proponents of moral therapy and non-restraint. For most people in Victorian England, as the number of inpatients increased, asylums became effectively warehouses for the unwanted.

To some extent, psychiatrists and policy makers were also victims of their own propaganda. The proclamation by Lord Ashley during debates around the 1845 Lunatics Act that asylum treatment would 'effect a cure in seventy cases out of every hundred' (Hansard 6.6, 1845, col. 193) was, to say the least, overly ambitious. Older people with dementia and people with general paralysis of the insane and epilepsy were increasingly admitted to asylums, yet were never realistically going to recover and leave. By 1890, Gibbons (1988: 161) describes a situation where 'there were 66 county and borough Asylums in England and Wales with an average 802 inmates and 86,067 officially certified cases of insanity – more than four times as many as 45 years earlier'. The 1890 Lunacy Act was also the first time that mental health legislation prioritised and protected the civil rights of individuals outside the asylum, rehearsing recent debates around the 2007 Mental Health Act.

The influence of the First World War

A major change in government policy and public attitudes occurred during and immediately after the First World War in response to the sheer number of soldiers experiencing 'shell-shock'. Until then, asylum doctors had emphasised the inherited vulnerability of mental illness and argued that a tainted gene pool accounted for most forms of madness, criminality, alcoholism, epilepsy, physical disability, prostitution and idiocy (Marshall, 1990) – a eugenic view that was common across Europe and North America at that time. However, during the First World War, between 4 and 7 per cent of volunteer soldiers were deemed to be suffering from shell-shock (now commonly known as post-traumatic stress disorder), including officers and gentlemen thought of as England's 'finest blood'. In some sense, this made the eugenic view of mental illness both illogical and, indeed, a form of near treason (Stone, 1985).

Prior to 1914, there had also been only a handful of British doctors using psychological methods of treatment, but by the end of the First World War this had changed dramatically. There was a relative boom in outpatient facilities in an attempt to deal with the thousands of ex-soldiers suffering from the effects of shell-shock, and an accompanying emphasis on using new psychological techniques (Coppock and Hopton, 2000).

The 1930 Mental Treatment Act gave full legislative support to the introduction of voluntary treatment and to local authorities spending money on outpatient facilities at a time when only 7 per cent of all admissions were voluntary (Leff, 1997). However there was no central money allocated to implement many of the changes in the Act, a recurring theme in the story of mental health and community care throughout the twentieth century.

The birth of the NHS

The 1911 National Insurance Act enabled working men to access free health care and was, in part, responsible for enabling debates on the benefits of a free NHS. However, it was William Beveridge's 1942 report on the development of a cradle-to-grave welfare state, followed by the success of the wartime Emergency Medical Service, that created a political climate where a huge step change in health and welfare policy could be both conceived and implemented. The NHS was born on 5 July 1948, after negotiations with the medical community that Aneurin Bevan, the Health Minister, rather euphemistically described as 'not ... altogether trouble free' (Bevan, 1948).

A central tenet of the new NHS was that it would be free at the point of use. The first page of the explanatory leaflet distributed to all homes at the outset of the new service proudly declared: 'It will provide you with all medical, dental and nursing care. Everyone – rich or poor, man, woman or child – can use it or any part of it. There are no charges except for a few special items. There are no insurance qualifications. But it is not a charity. You are all paying for it, mainly as tax payers, and it will relieve your money worries in time of illness' (cited in Webster, 2002: 24).

The NHS assumed responsibility for mental health which, up to that point, had been under the jurisdiction of the county councils and boroughs, a move that could potentially have led to equality of care between mental health and non-mental health services. However, by the 1950s, Mental Health Hospitals (the terminology introduced in the 1930 Mental Treatment Act) and Mental Deficiency Hospitals (for people with learning disabilities) were still overcrowded and underfunded. They contained 40 per cent of NHS inpatient beds but received only 20 per cent of the hospital budget (Goodwin, 1997). The average cost of treating a mental health inpatient was 3 pound 15 shillings and 11 pence in 1951 compared with 4 pound 13 shillings and 11 pence in 1959/60 (at 1950/1 prices). However, during the same period, the cost of inpatient maternity care rose from 6 pound 9 shillings and 5 pence to 16 pound 11 shillings and 3 pence. Goodwin suggests 'these figures clearly underline why the mental health services have earned the tag of a Cinderella service' (1990: 67). As we saw in Chapter 1, despite extra funding for services across the NHS in the last decade, mental health services still lag behind physical health services in terms of expenditure.

Community care policy imperatives

By the late 1950s, there had certainly been some progress towards community care as the number of outpatient clinic attendances increased from virtually none in 1930 to 144,000 in 1959. However, mental health was still dominated by a hospital-based approach. The need to move towards a more community-based system of care and treatment was again highlighted by the Royal Commission on Mental Illness and Mental Deficiency (1954–7) (the Percy Commission). The report suggested 'in relation to almost all forms of mental disorder, there is increasing medical emphasis on forms of treatment and training and social services which can

> | Box 2.3 | **The water tower speech** |
> | --- | --- |
>
> [I]n 15 years' time there may well be needed not more than half as many places in hospitals for mental illness as there are today. Expressed in numerical terms, this would represent a redundancy of no fewer than 75,000 hospital beds ... Now look and see what are the implications of these bold words. They imply nothing less than the elimination of by far the greater part of this country's mental hospitals as they exist today. This is a colossal undertaking, not so much in the new physical provision which it involves, as in the sheer inertia of mind and matter which it requires to overcome. There they stand, isolated, majestic, imperious, brooded over by the gigantic water tower and chimney combined, rising unmistakable and daunting out of the countryside – the asylums which our forefathers built with such immense solidity to express the notions of their day. Do not for a moment underestimate their powers of resistance to our assault.
>
> *Source*: Powell (1961)

be given without bringing patients into hospitals as inpatients or which make it possible to discharge them from hospital sooner than in the past' (Percy Commission, 1957: 207). It endorsed the development of a complex infrastructure of local authority community services such as hostels, day care, social work support and sheltered employment schemes that would support a policy of deinstitutionalisation and encourage greater use of treatments in a community setting. However, in a pattern repeated across the decades, the aspirations of the Percy Commission were never fully supported in legislation since the Mental Health Act of 1959 simply invited local authorities rather than required them to produce community care plans and no additional money was made available (Goodwin, 1990).

In 1961, Enoch Powell's now infamous 'water tower speech' once again heralded government intentions to shift the focus of mental health practice from the institution to the community (see Box 2.3 for a quotation from the speech). *A Hospital Plan for England and Wales* (1962) proposed the development of small-scale psychiatric units in District General Hospitals and envisaged that local authorities would provide a full range of domiciliary services to support patients in their own homes. However, despite the recognition of what needed to be done, financial pressures continued to undermine community care policy.

It is also interesting to note that, even at this stage, concerns were beginning to be expressed about the concept of community care and about the rhetoric–reality gap of an underfunded and understaffed community service. As Richard Titmuss, Professor of Social Administration at the London School of Economics, suggested:

We pontificate about the philosophy of community care; we may feel righteous because we have a civilised mental health act on the statute books; but unless we are prepared to examine it ... at the level of concrete reality, what we mean by community care is simply indulging in wishful thinking ... at present we are drifting into a situation in which, by shifting the emphasis from the institution to the community – a trend which, in principle and with qualifications, we all applaud – we are transferring the care of the mentally ill from trained staff to untrained or ill equipped staff or no staff at all. (1968: 106–7)

By 1974, there were 100,000 people in UK mental hospitals (60,000 fewer than in 1954), but very few extra services to support the people who had been discharged into the community, prompting notions of a 'careless community' (Harrison, 1973). Indeed, it is more than a little ironic that the push for deinstitutionalisation was in part a result of concerns about conditions experienced by long-term residents in the old mental hospitals yet, as Grove (1994: 433) claims 'it is clear that this group who were supposed to benefit most from the closure of the institutions have in many cases fared worse'. While subsequent research has highlighted the usually positive outcomes of discharging people from hospitals into the community, this was not the case for everyone (Leff, 1997; and see Chapters 4–5 of this book for further discussion).

Causes of deinstitutionalisation

There are a number of competing theories on the causes of deinstitutionalisation (see Box 2.4) – and it seems likely a complex mix of factors were at play.

Box 2.4	**Causes of deinstitutionalisation (Goodwin, 1997)**

1. *The development of new treatments*
   The development of anti-psychotic medication in the late 1950s is the most frequently cited factor for the shift to community-based services. However, there is little evidence to suggest a strong causal link since the coincidence of the introduction of psychotropic drugs and peaks of mental health inpatient populations are largely confined to the UK and the USA, not to other western countries.
2. *The development of social psychiatry*
   The association between the move towards community care and progressive social psychiatrists (that is, people interested in the effects of social conditions on behaviour and the relationship between psychiatric disorders and the social environment) is also inadequate since some professionals' livelihoods depended on the continued existence of the asylums.
3. *The emergence of anti-psychiatry and the civil rights movement*
   The views of the anti-psychiatrists (that is a group of psychiatrists who by and large felt that mental illness was a myth and a societal construct) and civil rights activists in the 1960s provided an academic impetus for arguing for greater equality and better provision of community health care for people with mental illness. However, the influence of these groups was relatively limited in policy circles.

4. *The poor conditions in the old asylums*
   By the late 1950s, many of the old asylums were overcrowded and increasingly dilapidated. However, this of itself was insufficient to provide a direct impetus for deinstitutionalisation.

5. *Increased community tolerance*
   In the 1950s, a number of policy statements suggested a substantial change in the public opinion so that people were more ready to tolerate mental illness in the community. However, the supporting evidence base for this is slim.

6. *Constitutional structures*
   Differences in constitutional structures between countries with similar onsets of deinstitutionalisation suggest that structures per se do not have a clear relationship with the development of community care.

7. *Funding systems*
   There is some evidence that insurance-based funding systems tended to hinder the development of community care. However, this is still only a relatively marginal influence concerned with the rate of policy change rather than its instigation or implementation.

8. *Fiscal pressure*
   Scull (1977) argues that the government increasingly struggled to contain the fiscal pressures of the welfare state and community care was seen as a cheaper option. However, further analysis suggests that adequate community care is no cheaper than inadequate hospital care.

9. *The changing nature of mental illness*
   Goodwin (1997: 111) suggests that 'the shift in the second half of the twentieth century from an institutional to a community based system of mental health service provision represents little more than the administrative façade for the more substantial aspects of this process: an increase in accessibility of treatment facilities in order to address the newly defined and expanded range of mental health problems'. This is supported by the rapid increase in the number of conditions, particularly more common mental health problems, classified as a mental illness throughout the twentieth century. Community care may therefore represent a policy response to the changing nature and expansion of mental health problems in the twentieth century.

Better services for the mentally ill?

In 1975, the White Paper entitled *Better Services for the Mentally Ill* explicitly championed community care (see Box 2.5). It also stated that 'joint planning of health and local authority services is essential' (p. 86) given that it is 'not easy to draw an exact line between the functions of day centres … [managed by local authority social services departments] … and those of day hospitals … [managed by the NHS]' (p. 34). However, by the mid 1970s, the Labour government, struggling with debt problems amplified by the oil crisis in 1973, approached the International Monetary Fund for a loan. A condition of the loan was that public spending had to be brought under control, precipitating a series of welfare cuts. As Webster points out (2002: 74):

The oil crisis precipitated an economic collapse throughout the western world. The economic growth rate which had been maintained since 1960 at an average of about 5% in the OECD [Organisation for Economic Co-operation and Development] area slumped to nothing. From 1975 onwards the entire OECD area shared the UK's experience of low growth, high inflation, high unemployment and an adverse balance of trade … gloomy voices declared that 1975 represented the death knell of the welfare state.

Box 2.5	**Better Services for the Mentally Ill**

Mental illness is … perhaps the major health problem of our time. It is also a major social problem … What we have to do is get to grips with shifting the emphasis to community care. The problems are many. Social services facilities have to be built up … Staff to run them have to be recruited and trained … Psychiatric services have to be developed locally, in general and community hospitals and in health centres. We have to recognise, moreover, that the pace at which community based care can be introduced depends not only on resources but on the pace of response of the community itself … Local services mean more day hospital treatment, more day care, more treatment and support in the home itself and less in-patient treatment … The policy can only be achieved if there is substantial capital investment in new facilities and if there is a significant shift in the balance of services between health and the local authority.

Source: Department of Health and Social Security (DHSS) (1975: 2–3)

Lack of funds to fully implement community care has been, as we have seen, a recurring theme throughout the history of mental health services but, set within this particular economic context, it is perhaps less surprising that few of the proposals and principles enshrined in *Better Services for the Mentally Ill* were implemented in practice.

The NHS: under new management?

When Margaret Thatcher became Prime Minister in 1979, the main focus of welfare policy was how to make it more businesslike in the face of increasing demands from an ageing population, rising patient expectations and advances in medical technology (Bloor and Maynard, 1994). The first defining NHS policy report associated with the Thatcher era was the *NHS Management Inquiry* (DHSS, 1983), produced by a team led by Roy Griffiths, who was then managing director of the Sainsbury's supermarket chain. The report identified the absence of a clearly defined general management function as the main weakness of the NHS and recommended that consensus management should be replaced by a system of general management at all levels (DHSS, 1983, paras 5 and 12):

The absence of this general management support means that there is no driving force seeking and accepting direct and personal responsibility for developing management plans, securing their implementation, and monitoring actual achievement. It means that the process of devolution of responsibility, including discharging responsibility to the units, is far too slow … If Florence Nightingale were carrying her lamps through the corridors of the NHS today, she would almost certainly be searching for the people in charge.

Part of the government's efficiency drive also included a programme of privatisation of state-owned enterprises, reductions in some forms of taxation and tighter controls over public spending. This tight fiscal background had a direct effect on the NHS. By 1988, the cumulative shortfall in hospital and community health service funding since 1981–2 amounted to £1.8 billion. For 1987–8 alone, expenditure was almost £400 million below the government's own estimated target funding level (King's Fund Institute, 1988).

In the face of a developing NHS funding crisis, highlighted by growing medical disquiet and perennial winter bed-shortage crises, the BMA called for additional resources to help meet the financial shortfall. The immediate government response included some initial extra funding and a ministerial review on the future of the NHS. There was little desire in the review for a major change in how the NHS was financed since experience from other countries suggested that the funding mechanism per se was not the key to running an efficient health service. The review instead focused on how resources could be used more efficiently through changes in how health services were delivered. A key proposal, based on the ideas of the US economist Alain Enthoven (1985), was that responsibility for purchasing care and providing services should be separated (the purchaser–provider split) to create the conditions for a competitive internal market within the NHS. In essence, services would be provided by hospitals and community units as self-governing trusts, and these services would be bought by health authorities and also by fund-holding practices (GP practices with a budget to purchase a limited range of services for their patients by negotiating contracts with NHS trusts). This meant, in effect, that providers would compete with each other to sell their services, creating a quasi-market, that would, in theory, encourage more cost-effective services and make the NHS more efficient.

At the same time, the pressures for reform of community care were also beginning to build up again, with growing criticism of a lack of joined-up working between health and social care (Audit Commission, 1986). In social services in particular, this was linked to concerns about the rapidly rising cost of care home placements for older people and a desire to bring this budget back under control (see Means et al., 2008, for an overview). There were also growing concerns about the essentially unpaid and significant contribution that informal, often family, carers were increasingly being expected to provide, harking back to the pre-Victorian, pre-asylum era of mental health care (see Chapter 9 for further discussion).

In 1988, the government commissioned Roy Griffiths (again) to review the funding and organisation of community care. His report *Community Care: An*

Agenda for Action (1988) reaffirmed criticisms of inadequate resources and the apparent abdication of responsibility by central government: 'community care, everyone's distant relative but no-body's baby' (Griffiths, 1988: iv). Griffiths recommended that in order to reduce the confusion between agencies, local authority social services department should be given the lead role in the provision of community care and suggested an increased role for the private and voluntary sectors. Many of these proposals were later enshrined in the White Paper *Caring for People* (DH, 1989a) and the NHS and Community Care Act (1990) (see below).

Within the NHS, ideas from the ministerial review and the 1988 Griffiths Report were drawn together in the White Paper *Working for Patients* (DH, 1989b). These proposals were described by Margaret Thatcher as 'the most far-reaching reform of the National Health Service in its forty year history' (foreword to *Working for Patients* (DH, 1989b)). The paper, however, provoked a storm of protest and opposition from the medical profession and others, and was further complicated by the difficult negotiations taking place with the BMA at the same time over a new contract for GPs. In spite of opposition, the NHS and Community Care Act became law in 1990 covering England, Wales and Scotland, with full implementation by 1993. Key changes included:

- Giving local authority social services departments lead responsibility for community care.
- The introduction of market principles into the provision of publicly funded health and welfare services, including purchasing from private and voluntary agencies. Further impetus for this policy also came when it was announced that 85 per cent of the funding for social services' new responsibilities would have to be spent in the independent sector. From the early 1990s onwards, this meant that social care practitioners gained considerable experience of working with a 'mixed economy of care' (that is, with the public, private and voluntary sector).
- Health authorities assuming responsibility for purchasing health care, with NHS trusts taking the responsibility for providing services. GP fundholders were to purchase care for their patients as well as provide primary health care to individuals and families.
- A requirement for local authorities to produce and publish community care plans.
- Recognition of the importance of carers' roles and their need for practical support (see Chapter 9).

However, a number of difficulties soon became apparent in terms of implementing the Act. Inefficient interagency collaboration (particularly where different parts of the system – NHS, social services and the voluntary/private sectors – had different ideologies and priorities), inadequate mechanisms for enabling the shift of finance from hospitals to community care and professional attachment to traditional working practices meant that problems soon developed. Partnership working was, in effect, part of government rhetoric rather than a practical reality (Bean and Mounser, 1993). In the specific context of mental health, the BMA (1992: 30) indicated that 'there is concern that most local authorities lack the skills and expertise to take on the responsibility for supporting mentally ill people in the community' (an accusation that some in local government would probably also have levelled at the medical profession).

More fundamentally, there appeared to be no awareness within the Department of Health that there was no join-up between the duties, structures and procedures set out in the NHS and Community Care Act and the simultane-ous introduction of the Care Programme Approach in England and Wales by government circular (DH, 1990a) in response to mounting concerns about the lack of coherent interagency working with people with mental illness who might potentially pose a danger to themselves or others. While the former focused on assessment in relation to a concept of *need*, the latter was concerned with the assessment of *risk*. The former proposed that the key professional role was the *care manager* who had a limited role in terms of assessing need and purchasing services in order to meet that need. The latter assumed a much more 'hands-on' role for the *key worker* (later renamed care coordinator) who would have an ongoing rela-tionship with the service user and make sure that all professionals and services were working together according to an agreed care plan. As Hannigan suggests, 'confusingly, both care management and CPA were introduced as mechanisms through which multidisciplinary and multi-agency continuity of care could be organised and delivered. In many areas the lack of integration between the two methods resulted in duplication of effort, excessive bureaucracy and construction of a barrier to effective joint working' (2003: 32).

In practice, most managers and practitioners in local authorities were so involved in bedding in new ways of working relating to the NHS and Community Care Act, that they were not even aware of their responsibilities under CPA. However, the lack of join-up only started to be acknowledged by the Department of Health in revised guidance in *Building Bridges* (DH, 1995) and, when this manifestly failed to resolve the splits and confusions, in a subsequent Social Services Inspectorate report entitled (with perhaps unconscious irony) *Still Building Bridges* (DH, 1999c).

However, not all the evidence on cooperation between sectors was as bleak, and there were examples throughout the 1990s of excellent dialogue between health and social services as a result of the community care reforms, especially where boundaries were coterminous (Means *et al.*, 2008). However, as we shall see, high-profile cases of poor joint working also led to significant shifts in community mental health policy and practice.

Modernisation of mental health services

The New Labour approach to mental health policy from 1997 reflected somewhat contradictory drivers. On the one hand, there was a mounting concern in relation to the supposed dangerousness of people with mental health difficulties, partly fuelled by the media, but also partly fuelled by government pronouncements and policies. This may be linked to certain high-profile homicides (see below) but has not been justified by the wider evidence (see Chapters 4 and 6). On the other, there was a genuine concern to improve the effectiveness of services and to take more seriously the voices of service users and carers. Part of this involved an increasing awareness of how issues such as discrimination, stigma and social exclusion can promote poor outcomes for people (see Chapter 8).

Running throughout, there was a relentless implementation of 'new public management' ideas in which professional autonomy became increasingly subjugated to top-down systems of performance management, including the use of narrow, quantitative targets (Simonet, 2013). While this may have had a positive impact on some elements of under-performance, and may have facilitated the implementation of (some) improved service models, many commentators have argued that, in many instances, its effect has been to disempower front-line staff, stifle initiative, create perverse incentives and encourage a limited vision of what service users or families may need – and a defensive 'we're just here to meet the targets' approach to practice.

During the New Labour governments of 1997–2010, a key focus was on the 'modernisation' of public services. Although difficult to define, this included (Cabinet Office, 1999):

- A focus on outcomes to enable working across organisational structures.
- The promotion of partnership between different areas of government and with the voluntary and private sectors.
- Greater use of evidence.
- Consultation with service users.
- The use of targets and performance monitoring to secure quality and continuous improvement.
- Additional investment to be conditional on improved results.
- A greater valuing of public services by developing skills and rewarding results.
- The development of information technology (IT) throughout government.

New Labour's first substantive NHS proposals were set out in the White Paper *The New NHS: Modern, Dependable* (1997a: 10) – with a stated commitment to a 'third way' of running the NHS:

> The Government is committed to building on what has worked but
> discarding what has failed. There will be no return to the old centralised
> command and control of the 1970s ... but nor will there be a continuation
> of the divisive internal market system of the 1990s ... Instead there will be
> a third way of running the NHS – a system based on partnership and
> driven by performance.

The concept of the 'third way' took on particular meaning at this time as it became associated not only with the politics of the Labour Party in the UK but also with the New Democrats led by Bill Clinton in the USA. At its centre was the idea of a new social contract based on the principle of 'no rights without responsibilities' (Giddens, 1998: 52). Third way politics also emphasised the need for active government intervention to respond to social exclusion with a transition from passive to active welfare policies.

There was a commitment to developing a stronger evidence base as to 'what works' in terms of health and social care interventions – with a view to funding only what could be shown to be cost-effective. In order to deliver this evidence base, two new institutions were established: NICE (initially the National Institute for Clinical Excellence and now the National Institute for Health and Care Excellence) and SCIE (the Social Care Institute for Excellence). These were charged with reviewing evidence for specific treatments or interventions and disseminating national guidelines on best practice – for example on treatment approaches for schizophrenia.

The New NHS also included an initial commitment to abolish the internal market in England, but retained the Conservatives' provider–purchaser split. The main change was that commissioning would be in the hands of Primary Care Groups (PCGs) – subsequently replaced by Primary Care Trusts (PCTs) and more recently by Clinical Commissioning Groups (CCGs) – and that competition would be replaced by collaboration and partnership between commissioners and providers. Although Northern Ireland retained a purchaser–provider split, both Scotland and Wales chose to revert to a unified service delivery structure in 2004 and 2009 respectively. In England, despite the initial displacement of the market for a more collaborative rhetoric, market mechanisms became ever more dominant, culminating in the rolling-out of a Payment by Results (PbR) framework across all sectors of the NHS including mental health (Solomka, 2011). For mental health, this has entailed allocating each person receiving NHS-funded care to a particular 'cluster' related to their diagnosis for which a specific payment tariff is developed. While in theory this aims to deliver a more equitable basis for funding approved treatments for specific mental health difficulties, the fact that mental health does not easily fit a generic health model means that this new funding mechanism may impose unhelpful distortions which may make it harder for people to receive the care and support that best fits their individual circumstances. Indeed, Chapter 1 was critical of the growing tendency to focus on biological definitions of mental distress during the so-called 'decade of the brain' – and PbR classifications could exacerbate this tendency.

In England, the mental health modernisation agenda was heralded in the White Paper *Modernising Mental Health Services: Safe, Sound and Supportive* (DH, 1998a) which was, in effect, the first comprehensive government statement about the future direction of mental health policy since *Better Services for the Mentally Ill* in 1975 and, unlike that White Paper, was underpinned by £700 million of new investment over three years. The following year, the *National Service Framework (NSF) for Mental Health for England* (DH, 1999a) set out a ten-year plan for the development and delivery of mental health services for adults of working age aimed at improving services in relation to seven standards – with a similar approach (although a different specification of standards), being rolled out in Wales in 2002 (see Box 2.6). In Scotland, a broader *Framework for Mental Health Services in Scotland* was laid out which provided a framework for service planning and identified a comprehensive set of 'Core Service Elements' – but did not choose a

Box 2.6	National Service Frameworks for Mental Health – England and Wales

England 1999–2009 (DH, 1998a)

The framework included seven standards in five areas of care:

Standard 1 – *Mental health promotion* – to ensure health and social services promote mental health and reduce discrimination and social exclusion associated with mental health problems

Standards 2 and 3 – *Primary care and access to services* – to deliver better primary mental health care, and to ensure consistent advice and help for people with mental health needs, including primary care services for individuals with severe mental illness

Standards 4 and 5 – *Effective services for people with severe mental illness* – to ensure that each person with severe mental illness receives the range of mental health services they need; that crises are anticipated or prevented where possible; to ensure prompt and effective help if a crisis does occur, and timely access to an appropriate and safe mental health place or hospital bed, as close to home as possible

Standard 6 – *Caring about carers* – to ensure health and social services assess the needs of carers who provide regular and substantial care for those with severe mental illness and provide care to meet their needs

Standard 7 – *Preventing suicide* – to ensure that health and social services play their full part in reducing the suicide rate by at least one-fifth by 2010

Wales 2002–12 (National Assembly for Wales, 2002)

The framework included eight standards:

Standard 1 – Social inclusion, health promotion and tackling stigma

Standard 2 – Service user and carer empowerment

Standard 3 – Promotion of opportunities for a normal pattern of daily life

Standard 4 – Providing equitable and accessible services

Standard 5 – Commissioning effective, comprehensive and responsive services

Standard 6 – Delivering effective, comprehensive and responsive services

Standard 7 – Effective client assessment and care pathways

Standard 8 – Ensuring a well-staffed, skilled and supported workforce

standards-based approach as a mechanism by which to drive improvement (Scottish Executive Health Department, 1997).

The NSF approach had a number of key strengths, including the fact that, for the first time, it set a common agenda for local agencies – although not necessarily providing the necessary shifts of financial resource by which to deliver each required area of improvement (Sainsbury Centre for Mental Health, 1999; Wanless, 2002). Both NSFs sought to be comprehensive in scope and focused on mental health promotion as well as improving services for those with more serious mental ill-health – with the English NSF also giving priority to improving the effectiveness of service responses at primary care level. They both stressed promoting access to the mainstream and social inclusion for people with mental illness, and started to recognise that taking this agenda forward would require concerted action across government, rather than just within the delivery of health services. In seeking to deliver more effective services for people with serious mental ill-health, the English emphasised a shift to services based on functionalised mental health teams (Assertive Outreach, Crisis Resolution and Early Intervention), putting greater organisational emphasis on services that could more effectively keep people out of hospital (see Chapter 4). In Wales, a key priority was re-provisioning in relation to a substantial number of old mental hospitals that were still in use – although there was some parallel development of functional teams as part of their new configuration of services.

It was recognised that implementation of the policies and standards would be challenging – and that successful delivery would not necessarily be achieved by edicts and exhortations from government, but by mobilising more organic coalitions of progressive clinicians, champions and stakeholders at local, regional and national levels who would be committed to pushing the modernisation agenda forward in their areas. Building on the locally successful partnerships model that had been developed in the West Midlands, the National Institute for Mental Health in England (NIMHE) was established with a regional structure to work collaboratively with local stakeholders (including service users and carers) to embed new thinking and new ways of working. However, as there was no compulsion on more recalcitrant NHS trusts or professional groups to engage with NIMHE, its influence on the ground was patchy. It was subsequently subsumed within the Care Services Improvement Partnership (CSIP) with a more general remit beyond mental health, before finally re-emerging in a much slimmed-down national grouping: the short-lived National Mental Health Development Unit (NMHDU). This became an early casualty of the new coalition government's desire to cut the number of 'quangos' with little thought as to whether or not these were working effectively as more inclusive organisations for stimulating and delivering service change.

In England, the impact of the NSF was probably greatest in relation to the implementation of a model of functionalised mental health teams which were intended to reduce demand for inpatient beds. To some degree, this objective was achieved with successive censuses of inpatients showing a decline in numbers (see Chapter 5 for further discussion). However, this may also be seen to have taken the spotlight off inpatient services themselves which were not given any developmental focus or standards to achieve. Perhaps as a consequence of this, the former Healthcare Commission (2008) found that 16 per cent of care records in inpatient care indicated that service users had not had a one to one session with nursing staff on any day during their first week in hospital.

Linked to the implementation of NSF and the modernisation agenda was a review of both the workforce itself and how well staff groups were being trained

Box 2.7   **The Ten Essential Shared Capabilities**

1. *Working in partnership*. Developing and maintaining constructive working relationships with service users, carers, families, colleagues, lay people and wider community networks. Working positively with any tensions created by conflict of interest or aspiration that may arise between the partners in care.
2. *Respecting diversity*. Working in partnership with service users, carers, families and colleagues to provide care and interventions that not only make a positive difference but also do so in ways that respect and value diversity including age, race, culture, disability, gender, spirituality and sexuality.
3. *Practising ethically*. Recognising the rights and aspirations of service users and their families, acknowledging power differentials and minimising them whenever possible. Providing treatment and care that is accountable to service users and carers within the boundaries prescribed by national (professional), legal and local codes of ethical practice.
4. *Challenging inequality*. Addressing the causes and consequences of stigma, discrimination, social inequality and exclusion on service users, carers and mental health services. Creating, developing or maintaining valued social roles for people in the communities they come from.
5. *Promoting recovery*. Working in partnership to provide care and treatment that enables service users and carers to tackle mental health problems with hope and optimism and to work towards a valued lifestyle within and beyond the limits of any mental health problem.
6. *Identifying people's needs and strengths*. Working in partnership to gather information to agree health and social care needs in the context of the preferred lifestyle and aspirations of service users, their families, carers and friends.
7. *Providing service user centred care*. Negotiating achievable and meaningful goals; primarily from the perspective of service users and their families. Influencing and seeking the means to achieve these goals and clarifying the responsibilities of the people who will provide any help that is needed, including systematically evaluating outcomes and achievements.
8. *Making a difference*. Facilitating access to and delivering the best quality, evidence-based, values-based health and social care interventions to meet the needs and aspirations of service users and their families and carers.
9. *Promoting safety and positive risk taking*. Empowering the person to decide the level of risk they are prepared to take with their health and safety. This includes working with the tension between promoting safety and positive risk taking, including assessing and dealing with possible risks for service users, carers, family members and the wider public.
10. *Personal development and learning*. Keeping up to date with changes in practice and participating in life-long learning, personal and professional development for one's self and colleagues through supervision, appraisal and reflective practice.

Source: DH (2004d)

to deliver 'new-style' mental health services. At one end of the spectrum, new roles were created and there was an expansion of professionally non-aligned roles including those of Primary Care Graduate Mental Health Workers (DH 2003b; and see Chapter 3 in this book) and Support, Time and Recovery (STaR) workers (DH 2003e). In order to provide a focus for the training of these new groups of workers, and potentially also the education and training of more established professional groups, the Ten Essential Shared Capabilities were introduced (DH, 2004d; see Box 2.7).

In addition, the Care Services Improvement Partnership, the Royal College of Psychiatrists and the DH (2005) developed joint guidance on the roles and responsibilities of consultant psychiatrists. *New Ways of Working* suggested that psychiatrists use their skills, knowledge and experience to the best effect by concentrating on service users with the most complex needs, acting as a consultant to multidisciplinary teams and promoting distributed responsibility and leadership across teams. This has required a significant culture change within mental health services and raised concerns around the ability of other disciplines to take on new roles given up by psychiatrists (Lelliott, 2008). Craddock *et al.* (2008: 8) go one step further, commenting that:

It is easy to understand how we have arrived at the model of distributed responsibility and leadership as a pragmatic, short term response to recent crises in staffing and morale in general psychiatry. However we should not assume that this pragmatic emergency solution is an ideal, or even a desirable state of affairs. Although distributed responsibility may make life easier for psychiatrists and appears to be the cheaper option, it does not follow that this is in the best interest of patients.

A survey by the Royal College of Psychiatrists found that 66 per cent of psychiatrists across all areas of England reported that the principles of *New Ways of Working* were being adopted and applied in their trusts (Kennedy, 2008), which suggests that, despite reservations from some quarters, implementation has been a relative success.

The costs of modernisation

By 2000, despite the plethora of policy reforms, a desire to stick within the previous administration's spending limits meant that 'Ministers were deluded by their own rhetoric into thinking that Labour's programme of modernisation possessed some kind of magic that permitted miracles to be wrought without the application of resources' (Webster, 2002: 215). In 1998, UK total health care expenditure was 6.8 per cent of gross domestic product (GDP) compared with an income-weighted average of 8.4 per cent in European Union countries. The UK's total health care spending per capita was then about 25–30 per cent lower than in Australia, France and the Netherlands, around 35 per cent lower than in Canada and Germany (OECD, 2001) and comparable to that of the Czech Republic,

Poland and South Korea. The OECD statistics show that the UK spent £863 per person on health in 1999, while Norway spent £1,484 on each person (Wanless, 2002).

Public disquiet over long waiting lists and variable treatment experiences, negative publicity and public criticism of the government's record on the NHS by respected experts put pressure on the government to consider changes in NHS funding. The prime minister announced that the government would, over a period of five years, increase the level of health spending to the European average (Tony Blair, interviewed by David Frost, BBC, 16 January 2000). The budget that year gave sufficient money to the NHS to allow it to grow in real terms by 6.1 per cent, nearly twice the historic average.

In July 2000, *The NHS Plan* (DH, 2000a) represented, in many senses, a relaunch of Labour's now more robustly funded NHS policy. New investment in staff and IT systems were announced, and three clinical priority areas were highlighted: cancer, coronary heart disease and mental health. From a mental health perspective, *The NHS Plan* promised an extra annual investment of over £300 million by 2003/4 to fast forward the NSF but was also, true to the principles of modernisation, fundamentally concerned with what had to be delivered in return for the money (see Box 2.8).

Unfortunately, despite pledges on primary and community care, there was relatively little emphasis on acute services (see Chapter 5) or mental health promotion. Indeed, it could be argued that the overall mental health emphasis was on compulsion and perhaps even re-institutionalisation, with funding being directed towards forensic beds, involuntary hospital admissions and places in supported housing to provide proactive care for people traditionally seen as difficult to engage in the community (Priebe *et al.*, 2005). *The NHS Plan* also relied heavily on a flourishing, well-trained and motivated workforce for implementation, which in terms of mental health, as in many other areas of the NHS, has not necessarily materialised.

Box 2.8	Mental health policy and The NHS Plan

- 1,000 new graduate mental health staff to work in primary care.
- An extra 500 community mental health team workers.
- 50 early intervention teams to provide treatment and support to young people with psychosis.
- 335 crisis resolution teams.
- An increase to 220 assertive outreach teams.
- Provision of women-only day services.
- 700 extra staff to work with carers.
- More suitable accommodation for up to 400 people currently in high-security hospitals.
- Better services for prisoners with mental illness.
- Additional placements and staff for people with severe personality disorders.

Although expenditure on the NHS increased dramatically throughout the 2000s, many would argue that mental health was starting from a particularly low base and that increases have been greater for physical health services. Parsonage (2009) has also confirmed earlier fears that there would be a 20 per cent shortfall in the funding level required to deliver the *NSF for Mental Health* in full. Perhaps more worryingly, McCrone *et al.* (2008) have projected needs and costs of mental health to 2026 and current service costs are estimated to increase by 45 per cent to £32.6 billion in 2026 (at 2007 prices). While some of this is due to increases in the number of people with dementia, it nevertheless highlights the continued need to keep mental health on the political agenda.

Over more recent years, following the impact of the financial crisis on the public finances across the UK, any development of mental health services has had to be within the context of a cap on overall NHS expenditure, so that increases in demand or costs of treatment in certain sectors could only be achieved through a programme of savings across the board – often resulting in a disproportionate and adverse impact on less 'glamorous' or influential sectors such as mental health. There is evidence of real terms reductions of investment in mental health services in England from 2011/12 onwards with particular pressure on non-inpatient services, such as early intervention, crisis resolution and assertive outreach, which had been prioritised in the NSF (NHS Confederation Mental Health Network, 2014). Over the same time period, particularly in England, much more substantial cuts in funding for local authorities contributed not just to a scaling down of funding for social care provision of around 20 per cent by 2014 (Community Care, 2014), but also to a substantial disengagement from any sense of responsibility for resourcing (let alone developing) mental health services – apart from some localised progress in relation to the provision of personal budgets (see below).

Post-modernisation: diversity in policy and strategy across the four countries

Prior to devolution, there was a tendency for innovations in mental health policy and practice to be pioneered in England with other administrations following suit to a greater or lesser extent. Whereas England had succeeded in closing all of the old generation of mental hospitals well before the turn of the century, other countries were still facing the challenges of re-provision. However, post-devolution, the new administrations had greater autonomy to develop their own policy responses and service innovations

Across all the four countries, there has been a recognition that, at a population level, reducing the incidence of mental health difficulties and improving prospects of recovery depended on factors beyond the immediate delivery of health and social care services – and hence any effective strategy to improve mental health would need to involve coherent and coordinated cross-governmental action. Interestingly, smaller geographical size has sometimes made it easier to bring about such change, particularly where this has involved wider collaborations across government – and Scotland, in particular, has taken over the initiative in terms of taking forward more strategic 'whole population' mental health agendas. Below we briefly discuss the overarching strategy documents that have been produced in each country and then look at how certain key themes have been played out across the four countries.

England

In reflecting on what the National Service Framework had – and had not – achieved, the Labour government and the mental health 'Tsar', Louis Appleby, took the view that further progress in terms of improving the nation's mental health could only be achieved by a cross-government strategy, *New Horizons* (DH, 2009c), which adopted a more holistic life-course view, and took seriously the evidence that addressing a range of social, economic and cultural factors determinants would be necessary if fewer people were to be disabled by the adverse impact of mental ill-health. Although based on an excellent analysis, it was not clear how this strategy was actually going to be delivered in practice – and how genuine would be the commitment of support from other government departments.

Following the creation of a Conservative–Liberal Democrat coalition in 2010, the NHS underwent a prolonged and disruptive period of uncertainty and structural change. Under the delayed and reworked 2012 Health and Social Care Act, Primary Care Trusts and Strategic Health Authorities were replaced with GP-led Clinical Commissioning Groups (CCGs) and the regionally based Area Teams of a new national commissioning Board (NHS England). Public health responsibilities were transferred to local government and new Health and Well-being Boards were created, chaired by the local authority, to oversee more integrated care at local level (see Edwards, 2013 for an overview of the impact of these changes; see also Bochel, 2011; Timmins, 2012). In spite of pledges before the 2010 election to avoid another reorganisation of the NHS, the 2012 changes were described by the then NHS chief executive as 'so large you can see them from space'.

While the extent of this reorganisation – together with the disbanding of the policy delivery unit, the National Mental Health Development Unit (NMHDU) – had a largely paralysing effect on the ability of the NHS to deliver any strategic development of mental health services, the underlying policy direction remained remarkably unchanged. Although *New Horizons* was axed, it was replaced by a new strategy *No Health without Mental Health* (HM Government, 2011) which maintained a focus on achieving better mental health outcomes and recognising the importance of good mental health to the economy. Subtitled, 'A Call to Action' and using the slogan 'Mental Health is Everyone's Business', it set out six key policy objectives that were agreed between government departments, local authorities and a range of other voluntary sector and stakeholder organisations (see Box 2.9). However, unlike the previous NSF, this document lacked any detailed framework or structure for implementation of the cross-government strategies that are identified as necessary for delivering these outcomes – with initial coordination and progress resting with two Cabinet Sub-Committees (Public

---

| Box 2.9 | **No Health without Mental Health** |

(i) **More people will have good mental health**
More people of all ages and backgrounds will have better well-being and good mental health. Fewer people will develop mental health problems – by starting well, developing well, working well, living well and ageing well.

(ii) **More people with mental health problems will recover**
More people who develop mental health problems will have a good quality of life – greater ability to manage their own lives, stronger social relationships, a greater sense of purpose, the skills they need for living and working, improved chances in education, better employment rates and a suitable and stable place to live.

(iii) **More people with mental health problems will have good physical health**
Fewer people with mental health problems will die prematurely, and more people with physical ill-health will have better mental health.

(iv) **More people will have a positive experience of care and support**
Care and support, wherever it takes place, should offer access to timely, evidence-based interventions and approaches that give people the greatest choice and control over their own lives, in the least restrictive environment, and should ensure that people's human rights are protected.

(v) **Fewer people will suffer avoidable harm**
People receiving care and support should have confidence that the services they use are of the highest quality and at least as safe as any other public service.

(vi) **Fewer people will experience stigma and discrimination**
Public understanding of mental health will improve and, as a result, negative attitudes and behaviours to people with mental health problems will decrease.

Source: HM Government (2011: 6)

Health and Social Justice) and overall oversight from a Ministerial Advisory group on Mental Health Strategy. As these bodies have tended to lack political weight and to be relatively marginal in much decision making within government departments, it is unclear (as with its predecessor *New Horizons*) what degree of impact this strategy is likely to have on the 'ground level' policies and practices that could impact on people's mental health.

Monitoring of progress is via a publicly available 'Mental Health Dashboard' (DH, 2013), which seeks to bring together published statistical indicators relating to each of these outcomes, including politically sensitive data such as that on income inequality, which are recognised as having a bearing upon mental health. However, despite its laudable aims, its reliance on existing data sets without commissioning any new data (e.g. on recovery rates) means that this tool is of limited value in assessing progress.

Perhaps as a recognition that the *No Health without Mental Health* strategy was not delivering effective change in a number of key areas, the Department of Health issued a further brief update of policy in 2014 entitled *Making Mental Health Services more Effective and Accessible* (see Box 2.10). This states the aspiration to put mental health on a par with physical health and 'to increase the impact of

---

Box 2.10	**Making Mental Health Services More Effective and Accessible – actions to prioritise mental health**

- Making better access to mental health services and shorter waiting times a priority for NHS England.
- Making reducing mental health problems a priority for Public Health England, the new national public health service.
- Making mental health part of the new national measure of well-being, so it's more likely to be taken into account when government creates policy.
- Providing £400 million between 2011 and 2015 to give more people access to psychological therapies – including adults with depression, and children and young people.
- Providing up to £16 million of funding over four years for Time to Change, the campaign against mental health stigma and discrimination.

Source: DH (2014)

---

mental health services by changing how we track success in mental health services, so that we measure the things that matter most to people using them' (DH, 2014: 2) – but does not give any indication as to how this will be done for the mainstream adult population.

What is missing from this policy update is any recognition of the emerging crisis within inpatient services with insufficient beds to meet demand (Buchanan 2013, 2014). This may be seen as resulting, depending on one's point of view, from excessive reductions in bed complements for acute psychiatry (Tyrer, 2011) or from disinvestment in the functionalised community services that were supposed to provide better alternatives to hospital admission (Johnson, 2011) – see Chapter 5.

Scotland

The starting point for the current Scottish policy journey was the passing of the Mental Health (Care and Treatment) (Scotland) Act in 2003. As discussed earlier, this had a much more collaborative and consensual tone than the equivalent legislation south of the border – and in particular took seriously the moral obligation on government to provide appropriate and high-quality health and social care services as a 'quid pro quo' for potentially depriving people of their liberty. Sandra Grant was commissioned to undertake 'a comprehensive assessment of existing mental health service provision' (Grant, 2004: 1) and her subsequent final report set out an ambitious agenda for change including both attitudes and organisational cultures within services, and specific areas of service improvement, such as locally available flexible and responsive 24-hour support services.

This was closely followed by a mental health strategy and delivery plan for Scotland, *Delivering for Mental Health* (Scottish Government, 2006), which set out 14 commitments across a range of initiatives to help improve services for people with mental health difficulties – adopting a more focused approach to delivery that was similar to that which had been used in the English and Welsh National

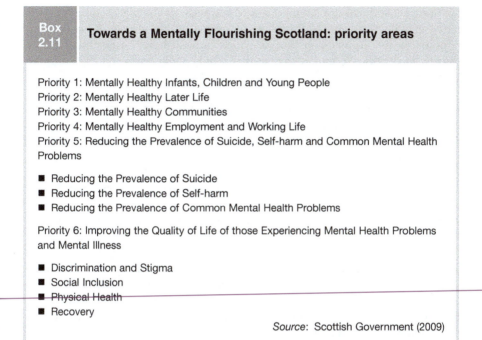

Box 2.11   Towards a Mentally Flourishing Scotland: priority areas

Priority 1: Mentally Healthy Infants, Children and Young People
Priority 2: Mentally Healthy Later Life
Priority 3: Mentally Healthy Communities
Priority 4: Mentally Healthy Employment and Working Life
Priority 5: Reducing the Prevalence of Suicide, Self-harm and Common Mental Health Problems

■ Reducing the Prevalence of Suicide
■ Reducing the Prevalence of Self-harm
■ Reducing the Prevalence of Common Mental Health Problems

Priority 6: Improving the Quality of Life of those Experiencing Mental Health Problems and Mental Illness

■ Discrimination and Stigma
■ Social Inclusion
■ Physical Health
■ Recovery

Source: Scottish Government (2009)

Service Frameworks. This was underpinned by three targets: halting the rise in anti-depressant prescribing; reducing the suicide rate; and reducing the number of hospital readmissions within one year.

Taking forward the wider mental health and well-being agenda, the Scottish Government published the ambitious strategy paper *Towards a Mentally Flourishing Scotland* (Scottish Government, 2009). This sets out a detailed action plan involving a range of government departments, local authorities and voluntary sector agencies. It set out six priority areas, each underpinned by a series of specific policy commitments (see Box 2.11).

Although the mechanisms for measuring the success of each initiative are not set out in the document, the Scottish government has supported the development and rolling out of the first well-being measurement scale to be tested and validated for the population as a whole in the UK – the Warwick–Edinburgh Mental Well-being Scale (WEMBWS) (Tennant *et al.*, 2007). This is now in routine use as an outcome indicator in relation to a broad range of initiatives – and this has been influential in introducing an explicit focus around well-being into many sectors and activities that are beyond the immediate remit of health and social care.

The most recent statement of mental health policy has come through the Scottish government's *Mental Health Strategy for Scotland 2012–15* (Scottish Government, 2012). It starts by celebrating achievement in relation to falling suicide rates and reduced hospital readmissions, which had been set as targets in the 2006 delivery plan – but interestingly there is no mention of the commitment to halt the increase in antidepressant prescribing. It also harks back to the Sandra

Grant report and makes a commitment to commission a similarly comprehensive ten-year follow-on review of the state of mental health services in Scotland. In response to the consultation process which informed the development of the strategy, it identifies seven key themes that should apply across the mental health work programme:

1. Working more effectively with families and carers.
2. Embedding more peer to peer work and support.
3. Increasing support for self-management and self help approaches.
4. Extending the anti-stigma agenda.
5. Focusing on the rights of those with mental illness.
6. Developing the outcomes approach to include personal, social and clinical outcomes.
7. Ensuring that we use new technology effectively as a mechanism for providing information and delivering evidence-based services.

Through this document, Scotland has signalled its own distinct policy direction – one that is giving increasing emphasis to service user rights, peer support and self-management, and a more social and inclusive perspective in which families come first rather than being an afterthought within the context of more traditional individually focused clinical services.

Wales

Unlike England or Scotland, the Welsh government chose to use legislation (and accompanying statutory guidance and training resources) as a primary vehicle for driving improvement in the delivery of core mental health services and improving coordination between the various parts of the health and social care sector that needed to be involved in this delivery. The Mental Health (Wales) Measure 2010 tidied up existing legislation and focused on the following areas:

- *Local primary care mental health support services* – to be delivered jointly by health boards and local authorities in partnership within or alongside GP practices.
- *Care coordination and care and treatment planning* – requiring more effective deployment of the Care Programme Approach by health and social care service providers (see Chapter 4).
- *Assessment of former users of secondary mental health services* – to enable those discharged to refer themselves back directly to secondary services if they started to become more unwell without the need to be re-referred by a GP or other gatekeeper.
- *Mental health advocacy* – to be made more generally available to both detained and informal in-patients

Source: Welsh Government (2010)

Having addressed what were seen as the key issues for core services, the next stage of policy development involved devising a broader cross-governmental

mental health and well-being strategy for Wales *Together for Mental Health* (Welsh Government, 2012) which mirrored many of the concerns which were addressed in the similar documents produced in Scotland and England. It envisages establishing a new 'partnership with the public', centred on improving information on mental health, increasing service user and carer involvement in decisions around their care and changing attitudes to mental health by tackling stigma and discrimination.

As with the previous National Service Framework, the strategy covers a ten-year period and is focused around six high-level outcomes:

1. The mental health and well-being of the whole population is improved.
2. The impact of mental health problems on individuals, families, carers, communities and the economy is better recognised and reduced.
3. Inequalities, stigma and discrimination suffered by people experiencing mental health problems and mental illness are reduced.
4. Individuals have a better experience of the support and treatment they receive and have an increased feeling of input and control over related decisions.
5. Access to, and the quality of, preventive measures, early intervention and treatment services are improved, and more people recover as a result.
6. The values, attitudes and skills of those treating or supporting individuals are improved.

The Strategy is supported by a delivery plan, overseen by a new national Mental Health Partnership Board, which sets out the actions the Welsh government and partner organisations will undertake in order to implement the Strategy. This may be seen to provide a somewhat tighter package to drive and monitor cross-governmental action than that which was put in place around the equivalent English strategy *No Health without Mental Health*. It will be interesting to see how effective this is in practice.

Northern Ireland

It is generally accepted that Northern Ireland started from a particularly low base, as historically (and perhaps particularly during the years of the troubles), mental health issues had 'been afforded a very low priority with facilities and resources [that were] woefully inadequate' (Heenan, 2009: 452). However, more recently, a more positive momentum has been established by the Northern Ireland executive.

What has perhaps been most distinctive about the devolved approach to policy development in Northern Ireland has been an integrated focus including both mental health and learning disability – and the development of such an integrated approach has been aided by the already existing organisational integration between health and social care services. Following a similar approach as that chosen in Scotland, the Department for Health, Social Services and Public Safety (DHSSPS) commissioned Professor David Bamford in 2002 to conduct a far-reaching review of mental health and learning disability law, policy and service provision. Out of this process came a strategic framework document (DHSSPS, 2005) and ten detailed reports with nearly 700 recommendations covering service areas (such as forensic and alcohol services) and specific issues (such as human rights and social inclusion).

Perhaps somewhat stunned by the very comprehensiveness of this reporting process – and the policy agenda that it set out – there was a significant gap before the Northern Ireland executive found itself ready to respond and determine how it was going to 'deliver the Bamford vision' (DHSSPS, 2009a). The potential to take this forward was also compromised, as in England, by the dislocation and distraction that resulted from a major organisational restructuring of health and social services trusts that followed on from Northern Ireland's *Review of Public Administration* which took effect from 2007. In the executive's two-year action plan, it recognised, as elsewhere across the UK, that delivery of improved mental health would involve broader cross-governmental action and 'a culture shift in our thinking' in order to bring about 'dignity, social inclusion and assurance of human rights for those with a mental health need or a learning disability' (DHSSPS, 2009: 2). For mental health, it promised a focus on:

- promoting positive health, well-being and early intervention;
- supporting people to lead independent lives;
- supporting families and carers;
- providing better services to meet people's needs; and
- providing structures and a legislative base for delivering the Bamford vision.

To take forward the last point, the executive initiated a policy consultation process to determine how best to embed the 'Bamford vision' in a new integrated legislative framework for mental health and learning disability (DHSSPS, 2009b) which would draw upon developments and best practice from across the UK, while foregrounding the key messages from Bamford's specific report on legislation (DHSSPS, 2007).

In 2011, the executive presented for consultation a comprehensive *Service Framework for Mental Health and Wellbeing* (DHSSPS, 2011) which proposes a standards-based approach along similar lines to the earlier National Service Frameworks in England and Wales. While attempting to embrace some wider issues that may impact on well-being at a population level, with specific standards around health improvement and mental health promotion, this remains a very clinically focused document, with little acknowledgement of the impact of wider social factors, and where the main focus is on specific standards relating to the treatment and care protocols for people with particular diagnoses.

Recovery, social inclusion and personal budgets

There is relatively little explicit reference to recovery in many of the strategy documents from across the UK that have been summarised above – although there are elements within many of these, for example in relation to promoting citizenship, social inclusion and empowerment, that are compatible with recovery-oriented practice. While *No Health without Mental Health* does use the language of recovery in objective (ii), this is expressed in such general terms that it does not translate into any clear programme for action either within mental health services or more widely. Similarly, recovery receives a mention in Priority 8 (Improving the Quality of Life of those Experiencing Mental Health Problems and Mental Illness) in *Towards a Mentally Flourishing Scotland* (Scottish Government, 2009) – see Box 2.11 – which hardly does justice to the Scottish government-sponsored work of the Scottish Recovery Network. Similarly, in Wales' *Together for Mental Health* strategy, recovery is mentioned, but is seen only as resulting from the delivery of mental health services – representing a very different conception of recovery from that articulated by the mental health service user movement (see Chapter 2).

Instead, a vision for recovery has been promoted in other documents that have been less central to the governmental policy discourse: *The Journey to Recovery: The Government's Vision for Mental Health Care* (DH, 2001b) and *A Common Purpose: Recovery in Future Mental Health Services* (CSIP et al., 2007) developed in conjunction with the Royal College of Psychiatrists and the Social Care Institute for Excellence (SCIE). This may be seen to reflect some ambivalence, both at a senior policy level and within services more generally, as to whether to move beyond rhetoric to introducing ways of working that genuinely situate services users as leaders or collaborators in relation to their own recovery journeys. In particular, both politicians and professionals may feel constrained by a more powerful discourse which requires them to be seen to be monitoring and controlling the behaviour of otherwise risky or dangerous individuals – as will be discussed later in this chapter.

There has been a concern with issues of discrimination and social exclusion and their impact on people with mental health difficulties, both within service provision and within wider society. This policy direction was initiated in Standard 1 of the NSF, and these themes were taken up in England in a series of policy papers addressing issues around race, gender, personality disorder and social exclusion more generally (see Chapter 8). More recently, *No Health without Mental Health* (England), the *Mental Health Strategy for Scotland* and *Together for Mental Health* (Wales) all situate mental health within wider social and life-course perspectives – recognising that treatment services only represent part of a much bigger picture.

However, apart from some nationally coordinated anti-stigma activity under initiatives such as *Time to Change* and *See Me Scotland*, the main government focus in practice has, rather predictably, been on getting people with mental health difficulties back into the workforce – both through some more positive Welfare to Work initiatives, but also with a major campaign to reassess people with mental health difficulties so that they are no longer entitled to receive disability-related state benefits. This emphasis on addressing social inclusion through work-related initiatives is potentially problematic for mental health service users who may not (yet) be able to sustain the pressures of full-time employment. For social inclusion to be meaningful, more attention should be paid to users' aspirations for education, relationships and other chosen routes to recovery (Spandler, 2007).

A major innovation in social care has been the introduction of personal budgets which have allowed services users or their nominees to have direct control over how they spend the overall budget that is given to them for their care (HM Government, 2007). The 'personalisation' agenda aims (at least in principle) to give greater choice and control to individual service users, viewing them more as citizens with a right to support than as passive recipients of traditional services (see Chapter 4 for greater detail). Although this has led to some exciting developments in community services, implementation in mental health has so far been a little tentative (Larsen *et al.*, 2013) – perhaps at least in part because of professional defensiveness around issues of risk and protection. Quite how the system seeks to balance individual choice and control with public protection seems a classic example of the tensions that can emerge within the policy process between rhetoric and reality. Nevertheless, while allowing for these caveats, there is still the potential for much greater impact when personal health budgets are due to become more widely available for mental health service users in England from April 2015.

Mental capacity

A key legal change with implications for mental health care and practice is the Mental Capacity Act (MCA) 2005 for England and Wales – with parallel provision in the Adults with Incapacity (Scotland) Act. This provides a legal framework for how to act and make decisions on behalf of people who lack capacity to make specific decisions for themselves (Department for Constitutional Affairs, 2007). It generally applies to people aged 16 or over, includes people with mental health problems and covers major decisions about health care and treatment. The Mental Capacity Act is underpinned by a set of five key principles:

1. A presumption of capacity – every adult has the right to make his or her own decisions and must be assumed to have capacity to do so unless it is proved otherwise.
2. The right for individuals to be supported to make their own decisions – people must be given all appropriate help before anyone concludes that they cannot make their own decisions.
3. That individuals must retain the right to make what might be seen as eccentric or unwise decisions.
4. Best interests – anything done for or on behalf of people without capacity must be in their best interests.
5. Least restrictive intervention – anything done for or on behalf of people without capacity should be the least restrictive of their basic rights and freedoms.

Particularly important for mental health service users is the positive presumption of capacity in relation to any specific type of decision. Just because someone is judged not to be capable of managing their financial affairs while they are experiencing an episode of mental distress, this does not automatically mean that they also lack capacity in making decisions with regard to medical treatment, or appropriate arrangements for looking after their children. Judgements of capacity should be made in relation to each sort of decision that a person may need to take. When well, people can make advance decisions to refuse treatment should they lose capacity in future. However, the Mental Health Act can overrule any advance decisions made about psychiatric treatment. Nevertheless, since November 2008, it has not been able to overrule an advance decision refusing ECT (except in an emergency). Since April 2009, the Mental Health Act has changed the MCA to address the 'Bournewood' problem: that is, to protect people who are detained in hospital but lack capacity to consent or refuse admission by introducing specific Deprivation of Liberty Safeguards and an accompanying Code of Practice.

The public safety agenda

Set against the mainly progressive thrust of much of the policy agenda discussed above is a countervailing tendency driven by an overriding concern about managing risk. The Ritchie report (1994) was a watershed in the recent history of mental health policy. It was the culmination of the inquiry into the killing of Jonathan Zito by Christopher Clunis at a London underground station in 1992 (before the full implementation of the Community Care Act). Although there were other high-profile cases of people with mental health problems harming themselves or others, this particular event helped to shift the emphasis from talking about greater care in the community to fear about the risk posed by a small number of people with mental health problems to the community. The Ritchie report did not, on the whole, blame individuals or suggest that the policy of community care should be reversed (and indeed noted that Christopher Clunis was in some sense a victim of the system since he had spent over five years moving between different sectors of the health, welfare and criminal justice system with no overall plan for his care). However, the report did state that 'the serious harm that may be inflicted by severely mentally ill people to themselves and others is a cost of care in the community which no society should tolerate' (para. 47, point 0.1). While Chapter 4 highlights the way in which the proportion of homicides committed by people with a mental health problem is not only very small but has also fallen, the intensity of the media coverage of Christopher Clunis and a small number of other cases in the 1990s (including the 1996 murders of Lin and Megan Russell by Michael Stone, diagnosed as having an untreatable personality disorder) have created considerable public unease and a series of government policies focused on notions of public safety.

In framing his introduction to the *Modernising Mental Health Services* White Paper (DH, 1998) Frank Dobson, the Health Secretary at the time, echoed the rhetoric of the Ritchie report, stating that:

Care in the community has failed because while it improved the treatment of many people who were mentally ill, it left far too many walking the streets, often at risk to themselves and a nuisance to others … Discharging people from institutions has brought benefits to some, but it has left many vulnerable patients trying to cope on their own … A small but significant minority have become a danger to the public as well as themselves … We are going to ensure that patients who might otherwise be a danger to themselves and others are no longer able to refuse to comply with the treatment they need.

Such statements heralded a series of papers and consultation documents on the revision of the 1983 Mental Health Act. A subsequent White Paper, *Reforming the Mental Health Act* (DH, 2001d, 2001e) attracted a great deal of attention, largely because of its overriding emphasis on risk and public safety (Grounds, 2001). An umbrella organisation, the Mental Health Alliance, consisting of over 60 mental health organisations was established in response to the Bill and was vociferous in its opposition. The Report of the Joint Scrutiny Committee of the House of Commons and the House of Lords was also highly critical (House of Commons and the House of Lords, 2005), prompting the government not to proceed with its planned Bill but instead to introduce amendments to the Mental Health Act 1983.

The new Mental Health Act 2007 for England and Wales finally came into force on 3 November 2008. Technically, the Act amends the Mental Health Act (1983) with a series of key changes (see Box 2.12). One of the most contentious aspects of the Act is the replacement of supervised aftercare powers with new supervised Community Treatment Orders (CTOs). Under this provision, patients compulsorily detained in hospital for treatment may, on discharge, be placed on a CTO which will require them to comply with certain conditions, such as attending outpatients. CTOs also enable individuals to have their treatment supervised and be recalled swiftly to hospital without the need for formal recertification to occur. They were intended to enable people with a chronic mental health problem to live safely in the community, increase opportunities for community inclusion and reduce the number of 'revolving door' admissions.

Initially, the government anticipated that they would be used for a very limited number of people who had a clear track record of non–compliance with treatment regimes leading to regular readmissions. It is interesting to note that while the earlier Supervised Discharge Orders were rarely used and were seen to be of limited effectiveness (Pinfold *et al.*, 2001), CTOs have been used much more widely than originally envisaged (Health and Social Care Information Centre, 2012) – and this has been despite initial opposition from all professional groups, including the Royal College of Psychiatrists, to their introduction. This is also in the face of emerging evidence that those subject to CTOs are just as likely to require readmission and do not experience any significant improvement in clinical or social functioning (Burns *et al.*, 2013).

Overall, it is difficult to see how the new Act fits with the agenda of partnership working, personalisation, access and patient choice. Instead, a more effective way of improving the safety of the public and the care of people with mental health problems is surely to devise mental health services that genuinely engage

Box 2.12	Key amendments in the 2007 Mental Health Act

- *Definition of mental disorder*: it changes the way the 1983 Act defined mental disorder, so that a single definition applies throughout the Act, and abolishes references to categories of disorder. The single category is 'any disorder or disability of the mind'. It now includes people with a personality disorder and autism.
- *Criteria for detention*: it introduces a new 'appropriate medical treatment' test which applies to all the longer-term powers of detention. As a result, it is not possible for patients to be compulsorily detained (or their detention continued) unless medical treatment which is appropriate to the patient's mental disorder and their circumstances is available to that patient.
- *Professional roles*: it broadens the groups of practitioners who can take on the functions previously performed by the approved social worker (ASW) and responsible medical officer (RMO). The approved social worker role is replaced by the approved mental health professional which is open not only to social workers but also to nurses whose field of practice is mental health or learning disability, occupational therapists and chartered psychologists. The responsible medical officer role is replaced by the responsible clinician role which is open to other senior appropriately trained professionals as well as doctors (NIMHE, 2008).
- *Nearest relative (NR)*: it gives to patients the right to make an application to displace their NR and enables county courts to displace an NR where there are reasonable grounds for doing so. The provisions for determining the NR will be amended to include civil partners among the list of relatives.
- *Supervised community treatment*: it introduces Community Treatment Orders (CTOs) for patients which mandate compulsory treatment of those thought unlikely or unwilling to comply voluntarily with a recommended treatment regime.
- *Mental Health Review Tribunal (MHRT)*: it introduces an order-making power to reduce the time before a case has to be referred to the MHRT by hospital managers. It also introduces a single tribunal for England.
- *Age-appropriate services*: it requires hospital managers to ensure that patients aged under 18 admitted to hospital for mental disorder are accommodated in an environment that is suitable for their age (subject to their needs).
- *Advocacy*: it places a duty on the appropriate national authority to make arrangements for help to be provided by independent mental health advocates.
- *Electro-convulsive therapy (ECT)*: it introduces new safeguards for patients (for example, an advance decision covering use cannot be overridden). However, ECT can still be used in emergencies where necessary to save life or prevent serious deterioration.

users, where users have information and are truly consulted and given control over aspects of their care (see Chapter 8). As Laurance suggests (2003: xxi):

> The most effective way to improve the safety of the public and the care of those who are mentally ill is to devise services that genuinely engage users and meet their desire for greater control so that they are encouraged to seek treatment and lead stable, risk-free lives. If instead, politicians pander

to public prejudice and adopt a heavy handed, coercive approach, they will drive people away from services.

Interestingly, the same polarisation of public opinion, stimulated by particular media constructions and aided and abetted by opportunist political responses, has not been so evident in Scotland. Instead, as has been discussed above, there has been no presumption that the public safety agenda must override any concern with the rights and choices of people with mental health difficulties – allowing a much more constructive and consensual approach to legislative reform and policy development.

Implementation

Despite increased policy focus and (until recently) funding, mental health services, like many other areas of health and social care, are still getting 'mixed reviews', particularly in terms of implementation. An interesting question, and one that could have been asked at almost any point in the last 150 years, is therefore why central policy imperatives are not consistently implemented on the ground. There appear to be at least five key issues:

1. Implementation is more likely to occur if different organisations have clear roles and responsibilities. However, in terms of mental health, there is significant overlap between different programmes and organisations. Suicide prevention, for example, featured not only as Standard 7 of the *NSF*, but specifically within the *National Confidential Inquiry into Suicide and Homicide, The NHS Plan, Adult Acute In-patient Care Provision* guidance and the *National Suicide Prevention Strategy* (DH, 1999a, 2000a, 2001a, 2002a, 2002b).
2. The culture of an organisation is important in implementing change. In a study exploring the relationship between organisational culture and performance in the NHS, Mannion *et al.* (2003) identified a range of cultural characteristics that appeared to be linked to positive organisational performance including:

   ■ strong leadership;
   ■ a culture of clear and explicit performance objectives;
   ■ clear lines of upward accountability;
   ■ a proactive approach to managing the local health community; and
   ■ a considerable emphasis on developing and harnessing staff potential.

Sadly there will be far too many practitioners reading this book who do not feel such factors are evident in their current workplace.

3. It is difficult to implement new working practices within a system that is in a constant state of change. For example, it is interesting that the shape and size of PCTs in England underwent major change twice in the early 2000s at precisely the point in their history when they required space to work on

implementing current policy initiatives, build relations with local health care communities and secure much-needed clinical engagement and improvements in service (Walshe *et al.*, 2004). This issue has been compounded by the large-scale structural reforms brought in by the 2012 Health and Social Care Act including the replacement of PCTs with Clinical Commissioning Groups.

4. There are also problems associated with a state of near hyper-active policy making. As Means *et al.* suggest, there is: 'the impression of a modernisation muddle in which managers and field level staff are struggling to keep pace with the demand for policy change and the ever increasing flood of directives, guidelines and indicators' (2008: 214). Successful implementation requires a break from new policy and time and space to understand and implement existing directives. Although the UK coalition government has promised to 'liberate' front-line staff, the reality feels even more hyper-active if anything.

5. Perhaps the key barrier to implementation is the age-old tension between central policy edicts and local flexibility, with implementation deficits due either to top-down or bottom-up problems (Hill and Hupe, 2002). In a seminal contribution, Pressman and Wildavsky (1973) argue that relatively small failures of cooperation between different organisations can easily multiply to create a major implementation deficit. Major policy change is especially likely to create this situation because of the complexity it both requires and engenders. As the government attempts to enforce change through a top-down approach, it is likely to provoke resistance from vested interests and also generate a mass of unintended consequences. In practice, national policy directives filter down through a range of different healthcare organisations before they can impact on services. All of these are semi-autonomous and can influence if and how central policy is implemented. In addition, social care is overseen by local authorities, and services are therefore accountable to locally elected representatives rather than nationally. Despite the apparent downward devolution of decision making powers to CCGs and mental health trusts, the modernisation agenda with its organisations, frameworks and widespread central quality controls, has exerted and continues to exert a powerful centralising influence within health and social care. This clash of top-down and bottom-up approaches creates tensions within the system and means that policies may not necessarily be implemented in practice.

Conclusion

Aneurin Bevan said: 'we ought to take a pride in the fact that despite our financial and economic anxieties, we are still able to do the most civilised thing in the world – put the welfare of the sick in front of every other consideration' (House of Commons, 1948). While this is a major achievement, there have been periods since when the NHS has slipped down the government's list of priorities and has been, at times, poorly managed and financially neglected. Since 2000, however, the NHS (and mental health) has become an increasing political priority for all major parties, and NHS finances have improved dramatically. More recently, there is evidence that the relative priority of mental health may be slipping back further within the current climate of austerity – and current services feel increasingly challenged. Above all, there is still a central paradox at the heart of mental health policy and practice. While there are legal structures that encourage partnership working, better acute and community mental health provision and policy directives that seem to be taking user involvement more seriously, compulsory mental health treatment in the community and ongoing social exclusion suggest an underlying culture of coercion. In a health and social care system that increasingly values patient and user choice, mental health presents a series of challenges to practitioners and users to shape mental health services in a way that truly reflects what users want, what the country is prepared to afford and what the workforce is able to deliver.

Further resources

1. Key textbooks on mental health policy include:

    Coppock, V. and Hopton, J. (2000) *Critical Perspectives on Mental Health*. London: Routledge.
    Explores the social, political and intellectual developments that have shaped mental health practice over the last four decades, using as a guiding framework the ideas of the anti-psychiatry, antiracism and radical feminism movements.
    Rogers, A. and Pilgrim, D. (2001) *Mental Health Policy in Britain* (2nd edn), Basingstoke: Palgrave.
    Key text, offering a critical analysis of mental health policy.
    Brooker, C. and Repper J. (eds) (2009) *Mental Health: From Policy to Practice*. Edinburgh: Elsevier.
    Edited book providing a series of critical overviews of the success/failures of the *National Service Framework for Mental Health*.
    Fawcett, B. and Karban, K. (2005) *Contemporary Mental Health: Theory, Policy and Practice*. Abingdon: Routledge.
    Useful analysis of the theoretical underpinnings of recent developments in mental health policy and how these influence practice.

2. Pilgrim, D. and Ramon, S. (2009) 'English mental health policy under New Labour', *Policy and Politics*, 37(2), 273–88.

    Critical account of the New Labour modernising agenda.

3. Laurance, J. (2003) *Pure Madness: How Fear Drives the Mental Health System*. London: Routledge.

    Powerful account of the state of mental health care in Britain, written by the health editor of the *Independent*.

4. For anyone interested in the history of madness, there is no better source than the unique and always fascinating Roy Porter (2002, 1999).

5. Means, R., Richards, S. and Smith, R. (2008) *Community Care: Policy and Practice* (4th edn), Basingstoke: Palgrave Macmillan.

   Detailed but accessible overview of the development of community care, placing key issues from this chapter in a broader context.

6. Gilburt, H. *et al.* (2014) *Service Transformation: Lessons from Mental Health*. London: King's Fund.

   Accessible review of the development of community care in mental health, with lessons for other parts of the health and social care system.

7. In terms of current services, the Joint Commissioning Panel for Mental Health (www.jcpmh.info) is a network of national organisations, co-chaired by the Royal Colleges of Psychiatrists and of General Practitioners, and produces accessible, practical guidance for commissioners of a range of mental health services. It was co-founded by Helen Lester, co-author of the first two editions of this book.

   Covering such a broad range of policy and practice issues, this book cannot provide a detailed summary of mental health law across the different jurisdictions of the UK. However, the following are excellent resources for those interested in exploring further:

   Barber, R., Brown, P. and Martin, D. (2012) *Mental Health Law in England and Wales* (2nd edn), London: Sage/Learning Matters.
   Maden, A. and Spencer-Lane, T. (2010) *Essential Mental Health Law*. London: Hammersmith Press.
   Patrick, H. (2006) *Mental Health, Incapacity and the Law in Scotland*. Edinburgh: Tottel.

3 Primary Care and Mental Health

In this chapter we discuss:

- The nature and potential of primary care.
- The history of primary care.
- Primary care and mental health.
- The role of the broader primary care team.
- Creating a new model of primary care mental health care.
- Barriers to partnership working.

The nature and potential of primary care

GPs, practice nurses, dentists, pharmacists and opticians form the primary care level of the NHS and, as such, are the 'front line' of the health service. On the whole, patients cannot consult a doctor in secondary care such as a hospital consultant or member of a community mental health team unless they are referred by a GP. This filtering process has led to GPs being described as the 'gate-keepers' of the NHS. The core group of staff working in a practice is known as the 'primary health care team'. The actual composition of any primary health care team differs between practices but the Royal College of General Practitioners (RCGP, 2002) has identified a core team as consisting of: GPs, practice nurses, district nurses, health visitors, practice managers and administrative staff. In some surgeries, midwives, physiotherapists, counsellors and community psychiatric nurses are also members of the team.

Primary care in the UK has a number of unique strengths. It offers rapid access for routine and crisis care in a low-stigma setting. It occupies an important space at the interface of users, families, communities and professional worlds and is able to address mental, physical and social aspects of care. It has, until very recently, also been able to guarantee a cradle-to-grave doctor–patient relationship, with informational, longitudinal and interpersonal continuity of care (Saultz, 2003). Primary care is also a place of great complexity. As Heath suggests (1999: 565): 'uncertainty, contradiction and complexity are the stuff of general practice and the measure of much of its fascination for us'. Each day, people arrive to see their GP or other members of the primary care team with coughs and colds and cancer and depression and have on average just ten minutes to explain their problems and negotiate a solution. This compares to 20–30 minutes in a hospital setting, where a referral letter has set the agenda and the doctor is an acknowledged specialist in that clinical area. Primary care is, by way of contrast, delivered by specialists in generalism (Willis, 1995), by people taking an interest in whatever is of interest to the patient. As a result, primary care has developed sophisticated ways of working with the uncertainty and complexity of its environment (Wilson and Holt, 2001). Decisions, for example, may be based more on intuition, experience and knowledge of the patient's previous history than slavish adherence to medical algorithms. GPs are also able, although not all are necessarily willing, to act not only as an individual's advocate within the wider system, but to combine this role with a wider social and political responsibility to speak out on behalf of the most needy and least heard within our society. As Tudor Hart suggests (1988: 332): 'if social factors influence the behaviour of disease on a community-wide scale, GPs and other primary care workers must concern themselves with them as a normal and central part of their work, not a fringe option to be added by some doctors and ignored by others'.

Primary care practitioners are also uniquely placed to understand both the general and the particular, an ability that Heath (1999) has termed the 'oscillating gaze'. Thus, when a practitioner focuses on the individual, they see the patient as a single human being (perhaps a tearful young woman with a new baby and sleep problems), and when they focus on the group, they see that young woman as part of a broader group (that is, as a person with possible postnatal depression):

> The categorisation of people devalues individual experience and can leave
> individuals feeling unrecognised and the reality of their symptoms unheard
> … the general practitioner while actively using the generalisation for
> biomedical science, has a constant responsibility to refocus on the
> individual, the detail of their experience and the meaning they attach to
> that experience. We cannot see the particular patient and the generalisation
> simultaneously. At a given instance we have to choose one way of seeing or
> the other. If we are to maximise our understanding, if we are not to
> become stranded and impotent at one pole of the dualism, we must learn
> to oscillate our gaze. (Heath, 1999: 652)

The history of primary care

During the last 20 years, primary care has become increasingly central to the development and delivery of health services, an emphasis that is a global phenomenon (Rogers and Pilgrim, 2003). The political and fiscal context of the 1980s are described in detail in Chapter 2, but, essentially, changes in terms of tighter public spending controls and the dominant political ideology focused on the importance of market forces led to a series of reviews of NHS funding mechanisms and organisation that culminated in the late 1980s, in the White Paper *Working for Patients* (DH, 1989b). This included radical ideas about the delivery of health services, creating competition through the separation of purchaser and provider responsibilities and the establishment of self-governing NHS trusts and GP fund-holding (where practices were given a budget to purchase a limited range of services for their patients by negotiating contracts with NHS trusts).

The election of New Labour in 1997 theoretically offered the prospect of quieter times for the NHS, although, as we have seen in Chapter 2, in fact the Blair and Brown governments developed policies for the modernisation of the NHS that were in many ways as radical as those contained in *Working for Patients*. Within months of coming into office, *The New NHS: Modern, Dependable* (DH, 1997a) announced the demise of GP fundholding and the internal market. Instead, it placed an emphasis on equity of access and provision and the need to ensure quality through clinical governance and accountability to local communities. However, *The New NHS* conceded that fundholding had demonstrated the value of GP commissioning of services, although it took a further seven years before this policy was developed more fully as 'practice-based commissioning' (DH, 2004b).

The major structural change introduced to deliver these policy goals was the formation of Primary Care Groups (PCGs), with the expectations that they would mature to Primary Care Trusts (PCTs) (that is, fully autonomous bodies commissioning a much broader range of services). In April 1999, 481 PCGs were established throughout England. Seventeen of these formed the first wave of PCTs a year later. When PCGs were formed, their board was constituted to have a majority of GPs. However, as PCGs developed into PCTs, the focus changed to one of stronger managerial leadership and greater accountability. The number of GPs on the PCT board was reduced and the post of chairman of the PCT board became an independent lay appointment. The professional voice was still influential through PCT professional executive committees, although their overall influence was reduced.

Shifting the Balance of Power (DH, 2001c) dramatically accelerated the time-frame for maturation from PCGs to PCTs and acknowledged them as the leading NHS organisation. In *Shifting the Balance of Power – The Next Steps* (DH, 2002c), PCTs were specifically given responsibility for commissioning all mental health services. The strength of PCTs was also increased by giving them complete control over the new personal medical services (PMS) schemes, an initiative developed under the 1997 Primary Care Act that encouraged new ways of working in primary care, particularly in deprived areas. The 303 PCTs controlled 80 per cent of the NHS budget (in effect becoming substitute health authorities for their geographical areas, but operating from primary care rather than acute care platforms).

Concentrating power at the PCT level exercised a domino effect on the rest of the system. Health authorities lost their main function, replaced by a smaller number of strategic health authorities, and the balance between the hospital and primary care has tipped further in favour of primary care. However, the rate and pace of change was almost certainly too great for some PCTs. Surveys suggested problems with management capacity and expertise in commissioning services including mental health (Sainsbury Centre for Mental Health, 2001a; Audit Commission, 2004). The experience of forerunners to PCT commissioning, such as the total purchasing pilots and GP commissioning schemes, also found difficulty in achieving effective involvement of grass-roots GPs, and noted the demands on lead GPs and the importance of good management in enabling improvements in services (Mays *et al.*, 1998; Regen *et al.*, 1999). Some PCTs also inherited debts from the old health authorities, making it more difficult to plan and provide new services. Primary care then went through yet another major structural reform in 2006, with the number of PCTs almost halved to 152. At the same time, the number of strategic health authorities was reduced from 28 to 10. One of the consequences of these changes was yet more instability at PCT level, with managers reapplying for their own jobs and inevitable loss of organisational memory.

From the mid 2000s, the advent of practice-based commissioning saw groups of GP practices given indicative commissioning budgets by their PCT (who continued to be legally responsible for money and its administration), accompanied by data about the cost and volume of services patients from their practice were using in the local NHS. In principle, this was designed to give GPs a greater incentive to deliver care closer to home, since a proportion of any money saved by preventing hospital admissions could be retained by practices. In practice, levels of GP engagement were patchy, the quality and timeliness of information provided to practices has varied and the degree of genuine behaviour change remains open to question (Lewis *et al.*, 2007).

Following the Health and Social Care Act 2012, PCTs have been abolished and replaced with new GP-led Clinical Commissioning Groups (CCGs). Similar in some respects to GP fundholding, CCGs are now responsible for some £60 billion of NHS funding and for commissioning the majority of local community, hospital and mental health services on behalf of local people (with some specialist services commissioned nationally by NHS England). While there have been several previous attempts to develop more primary care-led forms of commissioning over time, the abolition of local PCTs and regional strategic health authorities means that there is very little overall management of the system as a whole and that CCGs in general (and GPs in particular) are effectively the main players locally. Given that many GPs have little knowledge of or training around mental health issues (see below), this may make securing adequate funding for mental health services, improving the current quality of care and developing more recovery-oriented approaches difficult.

As the reforms come into force, there is a risk that mental health comes a long way down people's list of priorities. With so much change happening so quickly, there are large uncertainties – but also a series of unprecedented opportunities. Although primary care and mental health are often seen as separate parts of the system, the vast majority of people with mental health problems in this country are seen and supported primarily or even *only* within primary care (see below for further discussion). Physical and mental health problems also often coexist, and problems presented as physical can often have origins in terms of people's underlying mental health. With this in mind, the abolition of PCTs and the creation of CCGs are both a threat to current arrangements and a major chance to do something different. Although health and social care have often compartmentalised

physical and mental health, the advent of GP-led commissioning gives an opportunity to rethink this relationship and to learn lessons across this divide – learning from mental health providers/commissioners to help GPs in their new roles,
and learning from GPs about meeting patient needs locally and holistically. There
may also be scope for GPs to respond to mental health problems in the same way
as they do to patients with long-term physical conditions and to prioritise more
community-based approaches. If previous changes are anything to go by then it
may well be that little of this comes to pass, that mental health remains something
of a 'Cinderella service' and that recent reforms are soon unpicked by subsequent
organisational changes – but the advent of clinical commissioning nonetheless
provides a potential opportunity for more fundamental change (at least in some
localities).

Primary care and mental health

As far back as the 1960s, Michael Shepherd suggested 'the cardinal requirement
for improvement of mental health services … is not a large expansion of and
proliferation of psychiatric agencies, but rather a strengthening of the family
doctor in his/her therapeutic role' (1966: 176). The WHO echoed this belief in
1978 (WHO, 1978) stating that the primary medical care team was the corner-
stone of 'community psychiatry'. Throughout the next two decades, the emphasis both in international research and policy, was in documenting the extent of
morbidity of mental health problems in primary care and the quality of care
provided by primary care workers. A key theme was the need to increase the
recognition and treatment of depression in the community through, for example,
the development of guidelines for depression and numerous 'initiatives' on depression such as the Defeat Depression Campaign in the UK (Wright, 1995), the
DART programme (Depression Awareness, Recognition and Treatment) (Regier
et al., 1988) in the USA and the Beyond Blue project in Australia. More recently,
the focus has been on how to configure and deliver evidence-based mental health
care in the community and how to develop the interface between primary and
specialist care (WHO/WONCA, 2008).

According to the national Joint Commissioning Panel for Mental Health
(2012: 5):

In a group of 2,000 patients at any one time, an average general practice
will be treating:

■ 352 people with a common mental health problem;
■ 8 with psychosis;
■ 120 with alcohol dependency;
■ 60 with drug dependency;
■ 352 with a sub-threshold common mental health problem;
■ 120 with a sub-threshold psychosis;
■ 176 with a personality disorder;

- 125 (out of the 500 on an average GP practice list) with a long-term condition with a co-morbid mental illness; and
- 100 with medically unexplained symptoms not attributable to any other psychiatric problem (MUS).

This means about one in four of a full-time GPs' patients will need treatment for mental health problems in primary care.

Interestingly, there is relatively little published about the views of service users with mental health problems on primary care, although a number of features, particularly access and interpersonal and longitudinal continuity of care, appear to be particularly valued (Freeman *et al.*, 2002; see Box 3.1). Despite this, primary care has been frequently criticised for the standard of mental health care delivered (Docherty, 1997; Tiemans *et al.*, 1996). However, as described above, primary care is a complex environment – a messy swamp of experiences and interpretations that rarely conform to textbook definitions (Schon, 1983). Many GPs also have little formal training in mental health. One survey found that only one-third of GPs had had mental health training in the last five years, while 10 per cent expressed concerns about their training or skills needs in mental health (Mental Health After Care Association, 1999). Detection and diagnosis can also be affected by the way patients present their problems. Some people are reluctant to talk about their mental health symptoms and, even within the lower-stigma setting of primary care, are worried about the effects of divulging symptoms of mental illness.

More recently, the advent of General Practitioners with Special Interests (GPwSIs) offers an interesting opportunity. The RCGP defines GPwSIs as GPs with additional training and experience in a specific clinical area who take referrals for the assessment/treatment of patients that may otherwise have been referred directly to a secondary care consultant; or who provide an enhanced service for particular conditions or patient groups (RCGP, 2006). GPwSIs were originally heralded in *The NHS Plan* (DH, 2000a) which stated that by 2004 'up to 1,000 specialist GPs will be taking referrals from fellow GPs for conditions in specialties such as ophthalmology, orthopaedics, dermatology and ear nose and throat surgery. They will also be able to undertake diagnostic procedures such as endoscopy' (ch. 12, para.7). This was part of the broader government drive to keep care as close to home as possible, and the role could find a natural place within a system of clinical commissioning. Early on, initial evidence (in the context of dermatology) suggested that GPwSIs were more costly than hospital outpatient care, were more accessible, were preferred by patients and achieved similar clinical results (Coast *et al.*, 2005; Salisbury *et al.*, 2005). According to national guidance, GPwSIs in mental health should have a clinical role in 'providing assessment, advice, information and treatment on behalf of primary care colleagues for patients with common mental health problems … in most cases working alongside other mental health providers … and supporting the development of care pathways across the primary–secondary–community interface' (DH, 2003c: 2). Early on, less than 5 per cent of former PCTs were able to identify a GP with this role, although over 25 per cent stated they planned to do so (Pinnock *et al.*, 2005).

> **Box 3.1** **Service users' views of the value of primary care**
>
> - In Faulkner and Layzell's (2000) study, a user-administered semi-structured questionnaire with 76 mental health service users in six geographical areas across the UK emphasised that satisfaction is increased by longer consultations, and by a GP perceived as caring and who demonstrated respect for the patient's viewpoint. Access and continuity of care were also centrally important to service users.
> - Kai and Crosland's study (2001) involving in-depth interviews with 34 service users with enduring mental illness found that participants valued an empathetic and continuing therapeutic relationship with professionals in primary care.
> - Lester et al.'s study (2003) with 45 users with serious mental illness in Birmingham found that longitudinal and interpersonal continuity of care, relative ease of access and option of a home visit were valued features of primary care. This was often contrasted with the difficulty of seeing a constant stream of new faces in secondary care mental health services, with painful life stories told and retold for staff rather than patient benefit.
> - Gask et al.'s study of the quality of care for service users with depression (2003) found that the ability to offer structured care and proactive follow-up was important, since non-attendance may signal deterioration rather than recovery and the illness itself may preclude the assertiveness sometimes required to negotiate access.
> - Lester et al.'s focus group study of 45 patients with serious mental illness, 39 GPs and eight practice nurses (2005) found that where health professionals perceived serious mental illness as a lifelong condition, patients emphasised the importance of therapeutic optimism and hope for recovery in consultations.

From 2009, GPwSIs have to be accredited in line with competency frameworks developed by the DH, the RCGP and the Royal Pharmaceutical Society (see www.rcgp.org.uk/clinical-and-research/clinical-resources/gp-with-a-special-interest-gpwsi-accreditation.aspx).

The role of the broader primary care team

Although debates often focus on the role of GPs, the broader primary care team has a key role to play. To illustrate this, we explore the long-standing role of practice nurses, the advent of primary care mental health workers and the more recent focus on improving access to psychological therapies.

The role of practice nurses: the concept of a primary care team did not really become established until the 1970s and the number of directly employed primary care-based practice nurses remained very low until the mid 1980s. However, between 1982 and 1992, the numbers rose more than sixfold from 1,515 to 9,640 (NHS Executive, 1996), aided by incentives in the 1990 GP contract. By 1995 there were 18,000 practice nurses in England, equivalent to almost 10,000 full-time equivalent staff; by 2001 this had risen to 11,163 (RCGP, 2002) and in 2007 there were 14,554 full-time equivalent practice nurses in England (Information Centre, 2008b).

Mental health issues are a significant part of the workload of many practice nurses. Between 13 and 43 per cent of nurses feel that early identification of anxiety and depression is a routine part of their role (Thomas and Corney, 1993) and most spend more time responding to psychological problems than managing diabetes or asthma. Practice nurses also work with people with chronic physical illnesses who are often at particularly high risk of developing mental illness. Many practice nurses are also increasingly involved with people with serious mental illness (Kendrick et al., 1998). A national survey of practice nurse involvement in mental health interventions found that 51 per cent were administering depots (injections of anti-psychotic drugs) at least once a month, 33 per cent were involved in ensuring compliance with anti-psychotic medication and 30 per cent with monitoring side effects of medication. Up to 56 per cent of practice nurses were also involved in counselling people with depression (Gray et al., 1999).

While research over time has suggested that few practice nurses have had specific training in mental health issues and that many nurses feel they lack confidence in supporting people with mental health problems (Gray et al., 1999; Armstrong, 1997; Crosland and Kai, 1998), practice nurses nevertheless have considerable transferable experience (for example, in running specialist clinics for patients with chronic physical health problems that incorporate systematic assessment of symptoms, treatment effects and side effects, the use of protocols for modifying management and proactive follow-up of non-attendees). There is also an evidence base demonstrating the value and effectiveness of nurse-led interventions where nurses have been trained to manage mental health problems, particularly where this is part of a larger multifaceted programme (see Box 3.2).

The role of nurses in general and practice nurses in particular is currently undergoing a rapid re-evaluation and expansion. From being seen as the doctor's 'handmaiden', largely employed to undertake health promotion and prevention duties, practice nurses had opportunities, under the GMS contract, to become partners in a practice and to take on more advanced and specialised roles (DH, 2003a; NHS Confederation, 2003). They can extend their interests from the clinical to the business aspects involved in a practice and, with appropriate training, become sub- or specialist providers of services such as mental health. This advanced role mirrors the general direction of change within the wider NHS, with traditional professional hierarchies challenged by a changing workforce, greater emphasis on continuing professional development and a clinical governance agenda that values quality and performance as much as qualification.

The New Primary Care Mental Health Workforce: The NHS Plan (DH, 2000a) heralded the development of a number of new roles to help develop and deliver better-quality mental health services. A key component was the commitment that:

> One thousand new graduate primary care mental health workers, trained in brief therapy techniques of proven effectiveness, will be employed to help GPs manage and treat common mental health problems in all age groups, including children. (p. 119)

| Box 3.2 | **Evidence-based roles for practice nurses in primary care mental health** |

- *Problem solving*: practice nurses trained to deliver six sessions of problem solving in primary care for patients with depression showed significant improvements on patient depression rating scales at 12 weeks (Mynors-Wallis *et al.*, 2000).
- *Telehealth initiatives*: a randomised controlled trial involving practice nurse-based telephone follow-up for patients starting antidepressant medication was found to improve symptom resolution and increase user satisfaction with care (Hunkeler *et al.*, 2000).
- *Medication adherence*: a randomised controlled trial evaluating two different methods of improving adherence with antidepressant medication found that, for people with major depression, practice nurse counselling significantly improved adherence to medication from 50–66 per cent at 12 weeks with the expected clinical benefits (Peveler *et al.*, 1999).
- *Self-help treatments*: practice nurses may have a role to play facilitating skill acquisition for patient self-help for anxiety (Kupshik and Fisher, 1999).
- *Screening for co-morbidity*: psychological morbidity in patients with chronic physical illness is more prevalent than in the general population. Practice nurses often know these patients very well and are ideally placed to make mental health assessments and offer psychological support to their patients, for example, as part of asthma (Rimington *et al.*, 2001) and cardiovascular clinics (Sorohan *et al.*, 2002).
- *Practice nurse-led walk-in depression clinics*: a clinic in primary care was well received by patients and had good medication adherence rates and follow-up rates at four and six months (Symons *et al.*, 2002).
- *Collaborative care*: the Pathways Study (Katon *et al.*, 2004) in the USA targeted people with both diabetes and depression or dysthymia and evaluated a collaborative care model. This featured stepped treatment delivered by a specially trained nurse in collaboration with the primary care physician. The Pathways collaborative care model improved depression care and outcomes in patients with co-morbid major depression and/or dysthymia and diabetes.

Although the exact nature of their role may depend on their professional background, the content of their training and local needs, many primary care graduate mental health workers (PCGMHWs) focus on face-to-face client work, including provision of cognitive behavioural therapy (CBT), and on developing the infrastructure of primary mental health care. Some also have a liaison role with both the voluntary sector and secondary care mental health professionals (see Box 3.3). Research suggests that PCGMHWs are valued by patients, increase satisfaction with care and are cost neutral (England and Lester, 2007; Lester *et al.*, 2007). However, the lack of clarity about the different roles, and implied differing degrees of autonomy and job complexity, have raised concerns among some health professionals. Thus, Bower *et al.* (2004) found disagreement and ambiguity among some respondents around the relationship with the work undertaken by other mental health professionals such as counsellors, psychologists and nurses. Barriers to successful implementation have included the need to address variation

| Box 3.3 | Roles and responsibilities of primary care graduate mental health workers |

- *Client work*: brief evidence-based interventions such as anxiety management and CBT for people with common mental health problems. Information, assessment, screening and onward referral in partnership with the primary care team. Support for self-help, and mental health promotion.
- *Practice team work*: to provide support for audit, development of a mental illness register, routine measures of outcomes, and for integration of service users and carers into mental health service systems.
- *Work in the wider community*: liaising with primary care team members and statutory (housing, welfare and benefits) and non-statutory sector services (charitable and voluntary sector), as well as specialised services to provide effective services to patients including those with serious mental illness, who are managed in primary care.

in the level and quality of supervision and in payment and terms of service of workers (Fletcher *et al.*, 2008). These issues may help to explain why the five-year review of the NSF in 2004/5 found only 600 PCGMHWs in place (DH, 2004a) – albeit that an audit of higher education programmes offering the postgraduate certificate programme for this role identified 735 individuals entering training between January 2004 and August 2006 (Baguley *et al.*, 2006). The evidence to date, therefore, suggests that, if utilised and implemented effectively, PCGMHWs will be a useful adjunct to the primary care mental health team.

Improving Access to Psychological Therapies: in 2006, Lord Layard, a health economist at the London School of Economics, published an influential report on the costs of failing to treat anxiety and depression (Centre for Economic Performance's Mental Health Policy Group, 2006). The report stated that around 2.75 million people in England visit GP surgeries each year with mental health problems amenable to psychological therapies. Of these, around 4 per cent (11,000 people) receive non-directive counselling, 3 per cent (8,000) other 'psychotherapy' and only around 1 per cent (2,500) receive CBT. The Layard report recommended that the number of people referred for CBT each year should rise to around 800,000 in England. One of the central tenets of his argument was an economic one, based on the number of people unable to work due to mental health problems. Layard argued that: 'someone on Incapacity Benefit costs £750 a month in extra benefit and lost taxes. If the person works just a month more as a result of the treatment (which is £750), the treatment pays for itself' (Centre for Economic Performance's Mental Health Policy Group, 2006: 2). In response, the government announced funding for a new Improving Access to Psychological Therapies (IAPT) programme, with a commitment to train 3,600 new therapists to offer a limited number of sessions of psychological treatment to around 900,000 people and to enable GPs to offer people with anxiety and depression a range of different treatment options (see www.iapt.nhs.uk). There was a parallel expansion of computer-delivered CBT as part of the same programme (DH, 2007b). While positive for many people, there feels a certain naivety in expecting a short programme of CBT to significantly reduce the number of people receiving sickness benefits, and the fiscal reasoning behind funding for IAPT is perhaps at odds with the other main driver of promoting social inclusion through a return to work. More recently, there have been significant criticism of the coalition government's social security policy following high-profile examples of people with mental health problems apparently denied access to welfare benefits and put under undue pressure to return to work while still very unwell (see, for example, Gentleman, 2014).

Creating a new model of primary mental health care

Primary care, as we have seen, now employs a mental health workforce of its own and is in a position to commission and run services. All this has meant adjustments in the way in which primary care conceptualises itself and how other parts of the health and social care sector respond. This has provided a number of opportunities to re-examine how mental health services could be constructed and organised in primary care. There are currently four main working models of mental health care at the interface of primary/secondary care, all translocated from secondary care services (Gask *et al.*, 1997) (see Box 3.4). Although it could be argued that these models are part of a continuum that patients can access to meet varying needs at different stages in their illness, in practice, the variation in availability of locality-based resources means that primary care practitioners are often only able to access one or at best two of these models at a single point in time.

Box 3.4	Traditional models of mental health care at the primary–secondary interface

1. Community mental health teams that provide increased liaison and crisis intervention.
2. Shifted outpatient clinics where psychiatrists operate clinics within health centres.
3. Attached mental health workers, usually community psychiatric nurses (CPNs), designated to work with those with mental health problems in a primary care setting.
4. The consultation liaison model where primary care teams are provided with advice and skills from specialist mental health services.

Each of these models has particular strengths and weaknesses, yet none fully recognises primary care's central role in delivering good-quality mental health care. For example:

1. The creation of community mental health teams often brings about a major increase in the rate of new patients referred, but the new clientele consists largely of patients with common mental health problems who might otherwise

have been managed by their GP. There are also problems with non-attendance at community mental health team appointments (Killaspy *et al.*, 2000a) and the issue of 'inappropriate' referrals, where patients are seen on one occasion in secondary care and assessed as requiring a different type of response. Communication across the primary–secondary care interface can also be slow or incomplete, with missing information in referral letters and delayed clinic letters adversely affecting patient care (Killaspy *et al.*, 1999).

2. The shifted outpatient model attracts similar referrals and has similar signifi-cant non-attendance rates as traditional outpatient appointments in a hospital setting (Murray, 1998). It also appears that both the community mental health team and shifted outpatient models lead to little improvement in GP mental health skills (Warner *et al.*, 1993).

3. The impact of attached mental health professionals on referral patterns is still unclear. A Cochrane review of the effect of onsite mental health workers in primary care found that the effect on consultation rates is inconsistent (Bower and Sibbald, 2003). Referral to a mental health professional reduces the likeli-hood of a patient receiving a prescription for psychotropic drugs or being referred to specialist care, but the effects are restricted to patients directly under the care of the mental health professional. Roles and responsibilities are also unclear with consequently less efficient working patterns (Corney, 1999).

4. The same Cochrane review also concluded that consultation liaison interven-tions may cause short-term changes in psychotropic prescribing, but these are usually limited to patients under the direct care of the mental health worker.

The aspiration to achieve closer integration between primary care and community services should now enable the development of more integrated approaches to delivering primary mental health care. This direction of travel towards more integrated working reflects the growing emphasis on a partnership approach throughout health and social care. The extended role of practice nurses, the creation of GPwSIs, the advent of PCGMHWs and the creation of clinical commissioning all provide opportunities for developing a more integrated approach to primary care mental health. This is probably not a particular model of care, but rather a way of working that acknowledges the importance of creat-ing seamless patient pathways through the health system and which avoids the dichotomy of either physical or mental health when defining and treating a patient's problems. US work on collaborative care (Katon and Unutzer, 2006) builds on earlier work on the redesign of delivery systems for people with chronic health problems such as diabetes and has generated interest in developing more integrated approaches to delivering primary care mental health services. NICE (2009) guidelines for the care of depression have also highlighted the concept of 'stepped care' in service delivery, with differing levels of intensity of care from primary to specialist care provided seamlessly with decision making about 'step-ping up' or 'stepping down' according to severity, progress and patient choice. Models of integrated working based on collaborative care both in depression and for people with serious mental illness are also being trialled in the UK. To be sustainable, any integrated approach needs to be underpinned by opportunities for

Box 3.5	The benefits of integrated primary mental health care

- It can improve adherence to medication and satisfaction with care. A US initiative, involving collaborative management by the primary care physician and psychiatrist, improved adherence to antidepressant regimens in patients with persistent depression (Katon *et al.*, 1999).
- It is the best way of improving the skills of primary care providers in dealing with the psycho-social aspects of care, with training through teamwork and a significant transfer of expertise between team members (Mauksch and Leahy, 1993).
- Integrated approaches appear to break even or be cost saving in the longer term (Blount, 1998).

health professionals from different backgrounds to train and learn together. It depends on good communication across the interface, particularly around criteria for referral and discharge (NICE, 2003; WHO, 2004). Work, largely from the USA, suggests that a more integrated approach to care has a number of potential benefits (see Box 3.5).

Despite this, the emergence of a primary care agenda for the integration of mental health service delivery has sometimes been seen as more of a problem than an opportunity. Change, particularly if it impacts on professional roles and boundaries, can be perceived as threatening the power base of that individual or team and needs to be discussed in an open and non-confrontational way. The success of a more integrated approach to care will therefore depend on a number of factors (see Box 3.6).

Box 3.6	Factors affecting the success of integrated working

- New services are often championed by 'hero innovators' who are likely to move on and seek fresh challenges once a service is up and running (Georgiades and Phillimore, 1975). To be truly sustainable, new approaches to working need to be team owned, and not dependent on single individuals.
- Change in working practices requires a commitment from primary care health professionals and CCGs to the issue. Historically, however, there has been evidence to suggest that the *NSF for Mental Health* was marginalised in some PCT agendas, unable to compete on an equal footing with other clinical priorities (Rogers *et al.*, 2002).
- New ways of working rely on secondary mental health workers being comfortable and valued within a primary care working environment (Katon *et al.*, 1996; Peck and Greatley, 1999). Secondary care skills and knowledge in key areas such as triage, risk assessment and delivery of specific psychological therapies need to be acknowledged and valued when new integrated approaches to care are debated.

Conclusion

During the last 20 years, primary care has become increasingly central to the development and delivery of good-quality NHS care. Over time, a quiet primary care revolution has seen the end of the monopoly over provision of independently contracted GPs, changes to access and continuity, the implementation of an innovative pay for performance scheme and, latterly, a renewed interest in primary care-based commissioning. While mental health has always been a core part of primary care, this central role has only recently been recognised through policy imperatives around the new mental health workforce and opportunities to re-examine how mental health services could be constructed and organised in primary care (DH, 2004a). However, in the rush for the new, it is important to remember that a key strength of UK primary care is the open access, cradle-to-grave approach, where the patient is seen as part of a complex network of family, friends, work and social life. As David Widgery who was a socialist GP in the East End of London and political writer and activist, wrote prophetically in 1991 (p. 32):

> It is a process of decivilisation in which what doctors prided as a personal relationship between themselves and the patient, is now reshaped by the commodity process. Prevention for populations, service according to need, the family doctors' very idea of themselves as people who had time to grieve with their patients, to share the joy of childbirth, the crisis of illness and the time of day in the corner shop, are swept away.

Reflection exercises

1. The potential role of primary care (*exercise for all practitioners*)

If you had a mental health problem and could choose which setting in which to access care, would you prefer to receive support in primary care or in hospital-based services? What are the pros and cons of each setting, and would different people in different circumstances prefer different things?

If you were a GP working with someone with a serious mental health problem, what training and support would you need to feel confident and able to make a practical difference? What relationships might you need with other services/professionals and how easy might these be to establish?

Next time you visit your GP, consider how visible and prominent mental health issues are (for example, do the posters in the reception provide information on mental as well as physical health)?

2. The impact of clinical commissioning (*exercise for all readers*)

After reading this chapter and the policy chapter, talk to colleagues from a different professional background and consider:

- What impact have previous primary care-led commissioning reforms had on mental health services?
- Will it be different this time round and, if so, how?
- Carry out a SWOT (strengths, weaknesses, opportunities and threats) analysis of the current reforms – what can you do as an individual to build on the opportunities and overcome the threats/weaknesses?

Further resources

1. Key textbooks on primary care mental health include:

   - Armstrong, E. (2002) *The Guide to Mental Health for Nurses in Primary Care*. Abingdon: Radcliffe Medical Press.
   - Elder, A. and Holmes, J. (2002) *Mental Health in Primary Care*. Oxford: Oxford University Press.
   - Cohen, A. (2008) *Delivering Mental Health in Primary Care*. London: RCGP.
   - Gask, L. *et al.* (eds) (2009) *Primary Care Mental Health*. London: Royal College of Psychiatrists.

2. At an international level, helpful resources include WHO Europe (2008) *Policies and Practices for Mental Health in Europe: Meeting the Challenge* (www.euro.who.int/__data/assets/pdf_file/0006/96450/E91732.pdf) and WHO/WONCA (2008) *Integrating Mental Health into Primary Care: A Global Perspective* (www.who.int/mental_health/policy/services/mentalhealthintoprimarycare/en).

3. For up-to-date details on the mental health indicators included in the quality and outcomes framework, see: www.nice.org.uk/aboutnice/qof/indicators.jsp

4. For details of the competencies required of GPs with a special interest in mental health, see www.rcgp.org.uk/clinical-and-research/clinical- resources/~/media/E40AED508CAE41E8AD744532C4AAB1FB.ashx

5. For further information on Improving Access to Psychological Therapies (IAPT), see www.iapt.nhs.uk

Community Mental Health Services

The origins of community mental health care

At the beginning of the twenty-first century, most people in the UK, including those with serious mental illness, are now cared for in the community – either by primary care alone or more commonly by specialist mental health services. This follows a relatively rapid closure of hospital beds in the old Victorian asylums from the 1960s through to the 1990s, and continued declines in both the number of admissions and the duration of average hospital stays over subsequent years. There are multiple complex political and economic reasons underpinning the development of community care (see Chapter 2 for a detailed discussion) and the move towards our current community-based mental health care system has been slow and incremental.

The 1959 Mental Health Act made two key provisions that helped to establish community mental health services. First, it required outpatient follow-up for patients who had been detained (sectioned) and therefore, in some sense, began to recognise the importance of continuity of care. Second, the Act legislated for the involvement of local authority social workers (then known as Mental Welfare Officers) in the care of people with mental illness. Between 1962 and 1970, the *Hospital Plan* (Ministry of Health, 1962) proposed a 43.4 per cent reduction in asylum beds. However, this proved overambitious and the actual reduction was 14.8 per cent (Maynard and Tingle, 1975) – with no hospitals actually being closed during this period.

In response to this problem, the White Paper *Better Services for the Mentally Ill* in 1977 proposed what would be needed in terms of community provision in order to enable the full closure of the old asylums. It detailed the number of district general hospital inpatient beds, residential hostel beds, day centre places and other forms of provision that would be required per 100,000 population. It assumed a roughly equal commitment by the NHS and local authorities to providing the levels of care and support that were estimated to be needed, with the local authority social services department taking on the main responsibility for those requiring longer-term support and reintegration into mainstream community living. Government funding was made available to pilot this service model in the catchment areas of two old mental hospitals in Worcestershire in an experiment known as the Worcester Development Project (Turner and Roberts, 1992). This allowed for comprehensive services to be established in the community without having to wait for any capital to be released and revenue saved from the closure of the old hospitals. On the ground, progress was patchy, with the multidisciplinary teams in some areas moving quickly to relocate all their residents from the old institutions, while others were less committed to giving up old ways of working – leading to considerable delay in bringing about the final closure of the former asylums. Although GPs generally saw the new services as providing a better service for their patients, they also expressed concerns that they themselves were not properly trained for taking a greater role in mental health and that communication and responsiveness from social workers and community psychiatric nurses was not as good as it should have been (Bennett, 1989).

Unfortunately, as with many such policy innovations, insufficient funds were made available for the experiment to be properly evaluated – and so services were then developed across the country in a rather piecemeal fashion – without the benefit of learning what was actually needed, how much it would cost and how quickly the old hospitals could actually close. Whereas the Worcester Development Project had the benefit of bridging finance, so that community care services could be in place to receive those discharged from hospital, this was not generally available elsewhere. As a consequence, many people were discharged into lodgings or unsuitable accommodation with minimal support, arousing increasing public concern. Crucially, no mechanism was put in place for the funds which would ultimately be released in the NHS through hospital closures to be transferred over to local authorities to create an appropriate infrastructure of community-based facilities and social work and support staff. As it became clear that local authorities were not going to be able to provide the requisite support for people with long-term needs in the community, an alternative strategy became implemented within the NHS in which greater numbers of nurses were deployed as community psychiatric nurses (CPNs) and started to take over some of the community roles that had previously been undertaken by social workers. The number of CPNs thus increased from 717 in 1975 to 4351 in 1990 (White, 1990), and then to over 9,000 by the mid–late 2000s.

Partly as a consequence of poor planning and resourcing, the move towards community care was accompanied by concerns about the potential negative consequences of moving people out of long-stay wards into community accommodation. Perhaps the most influential and certainly the most detailed study of the outcomes of deinstitutionalisation was the Team for the Assessment of

The outcomes of the TAPS project

- Nearly 80 per cent of people were discharged to staffed houses and two-thirds were still living in their original residence at the end of the five years.
- 72 patients were considered to be too difficult to place in standard-staffed homes and were transferred to high-staffed facilities. However, 40 per cent of this group were subsequently transferred to standard community homes by the end of the five years.
- Re-provision did not increase death or suicide rates.
- Four patients were estimated as lost to follow-up because of homelessness, giving a 'vagrancy' rate of 0.6 per cent over the study period.
- There were 24 recorded criminal incidents committed by 18 patients.
- Psychiatric symptoms and social behaviour problems remained unchanged overall. The community homes were much less restrictive than the hospital wards with an average of 10 rather than 26 rules. Although social networks did not enlarge, patients increased the number of people they could confide in.
- Perhaps the biggest issue was that of readmission. The re-provision plans for the hospital closure included a reduction in beds in general hospitals which meant that, at times, there were no beds available for people in crisis. When admitted, many patients also found wards in general hospitals noisy, crowded and non-therapeutic.
- The overall readmission rate was 38 per cent. Of these, one-third of people remained in hospital for over one year, often because of a lack of rehabilitation services. These patients technically became long-stay patients once again.
- Overall, there was little difference between hospital and community costs. Coupled with the outcome findings, the economic evaluation suggests that community-based care is more cost-effective than long-stay hospital care.

Source: Summarised from Leff *et al.* (2000)

Psychiatric Services (TAPS) project. Established in May 1985 with the explicit purpose of evaluating the national policy of replacing psychiatric hospitals (in this case, Friern and Claybury hospitals in north London) with district-based services, the study followed up 630 people who had been inpatients for a period of five years, giving a comprehensive picture of life and care in the community (see Box 4.1).

As described here, the first wave of what was termed 'community care' often involved just the transfer of old long-stay patients from hospital to smaller-scale forms of institutionalised care outside – with little serious effort to integrate people back into mainstream community life. During the hospital closure phase, more attention was given to establishing psychiatric teams in new facilities in district general hospitals than to developing a coherent vision as to how to bring services to people in their own homes and neighbourhoods. While social workers were often better connected with local communities and with mainstream resources such as housing, education and employment support, local authorities were not given the additional resources to capitalise on this expertise. Instead the bulk of the work was taken on by CPNs whose training and experience had largely been in hospital settings. In some instances, good informal working relationships between social workers and CPNs resulted in a rapid sharing of expertise in both directions and effective models of collaborative working. However, this was not the general picture – and there was no accepted framework for joint leadership of community mental health services between the NHS and local authorities.

This lack of vision contrasted with what was happening over the same time period for people with learning disabilities who were also being moved out of long-term hospital care. Here many professionals across health and social services were inspired by a similar vision, grounded in the principles of normalisation, ordinary living and community presence (Wolfensberger, 1972). This resulted in a much clearer and coordinated focus on working with people to help them to take on valued social roles within communities, and also engaging with communities in order to break down barriers and open up opportunities. Although conceived somewhat separately, this approach of 'social role valorisation' nevertheless led to practice that was congruent with the spirit of the social model of disability (Race et al., 2005).

With hindsight, this period represents a missed opportunity for mental health services – where a lack of vision and appropriate funding mechanisms failed to deliver genuine social inclusion for people with mental health difficulties (see Chapter 8), storing up problems (including problems in public perceptions) which are still influencing current contexts of service delivery.

Coordinating community mental health services

Primarily developed in response to homicide enquiries that had criticised poor interagency working, the Care Programme Approach (CPA) has sought to provide a coherent structure by which to bring together the different services that may be involved in supporting someone with complex mental health needs in the community (DH, 1990a; 2008b). As discussed in Chapter 2, its early implementation was hampered by confusion created by the Department of Health which introduced this at the same time as the NHS and Community Care Act (DH, 1990b) with the civil service teams responsible for the respective pieces of guidance and legislation being apparently unaware of each others' activities. It was only after two attempts to revise the guidance – Building Bridges (1995) and Effective Care Coordination in Mental Health Services – Modernising the CPA (DH, 1999b) – that a more workable framework emerged which started to reconcile a requirement for care coordination across health and social care with the different language and approach of care management. This heralded the integration of CPA with care management to form a single approach, anchored through the role of the care coordinator with a remit across health and social services and the ability to arrange the purchase of social care services as appropriate.

CPA owes its origins to models of intensive 'case management', which were developed in the USA for people with complex mental health needs and which have been influential in the models of working used in Assertive Outreach (Onyett, 1998). This usually involves a combination of 'carrot' and 'stick' approaches to encourage compliance with treatment, but also focuses on the importance of the case manager making a close personal relationship with the service user. The role of the case manager is to make sure that the other professionals and agencies involved in a person's care, from psychiatry to housing and employment services, are working in a coordinated fashion towards achieving the outcomes set out in an overall care plan. However, although such an approach may appear attractive, a Cochrane review (Marshall *et al.*, 1998) found no evidence that case management improves outcomes on any social or clinical variable other than ensuring that more people remain in contact with psychiatric services – with, on average, one extra person remaining in contact for every 15 people who receive case management.

As rolled out in the UK context, earlier iterations of CPA tended to lack any clear outcome focus and tended instead just to require ongoing monitoring and regular reviews with a primary emphasis on assessing and managing risk (see below). As there was no inbuilt exit mechanism from CPA for service users, it tended to reinforce an assumption of ongoing 'chronicity' with no sense of working towards progress or recovery. Such concerns only started to be addressed with the issuing of the third set of guidance, *Refocusing the Care Programme Approach*, which explicitly states that 'assessments and care plans should routinely include arrangements for setting out, measuring and reviewing outcomes' (DH, 2008b: 20). Although the language of recovery is not explicitly used, the guidance states that:

> Services should consider at every formal review whether the support provided by (new) CPA continues to be needed. As a service user's needs change ... moving towards self-directed support will be the natural progression and the need for intensive care co-ordination will end. (p. 15)

What has been the impact of CPA?

Research has shown that:

- Service users prefer integrated health and social care services (Carpenter *et al.*, 2004) and both service users and carers feel more involved in the planning of care when they are included in the CPA process (Carpenter and Sbaraini, 1997). However, a patient survey conducted by the former Healthcare Commission found that only 50 per cent of patients had had a review in the previous year and only a similar percentage had been offered a copy of their care plan (Healthcare Commission, 2004).
- Many service users have experienced CPA as being a professionally driven rather than a collaborative process (Rose, 2001). Some CPA reviews, particularly in the early days of CPA, tended to be organised like ward rounds with service users and carers being ushered into a room full of professionals, some of whom they hardly knew, who proceeded to take decisions about them, rather than genuinely involving them in developing a care plan that reflected their needs and preferences. However, other research showed that there were

significantly higher user satisfaction ratings where a more user-centred, 'strengths-based' approach to CPA was employed (Carpenter and Sbaraini, 1997) and the majority of service users have reported that they felt able to express their views at CPA meetings (Healthcare Commission, 2004).

■ GPs were ill informed about CPA and reported very little opportunity to contribute to the process (Carpenter and Sbaraini, 1997). However, there has also been a widespread perception among specialist mental health practitioners that GPs were unwilling to participate in CPA meetings – perhaps reflecting a lack of interest among some GPs in mental health, but also reflecting the problem that such meetings were often convened at times and in places which did not easily fit in with the pattern of a GP's working day.

CPA refocused

The 2008 guidance, *Refocusing the Care Programme Approach*, takes CPA back much closer to the original case management model. Instead of a two-tier system aiming to include all specialist mental health work, it is now clearly targeted at those with complex needs and requiring multi-agency input, and who are seen to be at higher risk. Complexity is understood not just in terms of a person's diagnosis, but also in terms of their social situation: for example, whether they have parenting or other caring responsibilities or whether they are in unsettled accommodation. Crucially, it provides a hitherto missing vision of what high-quality care in the community should actually look like – with an explicit commitment to person centredness, social inclusion and recovery (see Box 4.2). What is less clear is the degree to which this vision has actually been implemented in terms of policies and practices on the ground.

Box 4.2	Values and principles of the refocused Care Programme Approach

■ The approach to individuals' care and support puts them at the centre and promotes social inclusion and recovery. It is respectful – building confidence in individuals with an understanding of their strengths, goals and aspirations as well as their needs and difficulties. It recognises the individual as a person first and patient/service user second.

■ Care assessment and planning views a person 'in the round' seeing and supporting them in their individual diverse roles and the needs they have, including: family; parenting; relationships; housing; employment; leisure; education; creativity; spirituality; self-management and self-nurture; with the aim of optimising mental and physical health and well-being.

■ Self-care is promoted and supported wherever possible. Action is taken to encourage independence and self-determination to help people maintain control over their own support and care.

■ Carers form a vital part of the support required to aid a person's recovery. Their own needs should also be recognised and supported.

- Services should be organised and delivered in ways that promote and coordinate helpful and purposeful mental health practice based on fulfilling therapeutic relationships and partnerships between the people involved. These relationships involve shared listening, communicating, understanding, clarification and organisation of diverse opinion to deliver valued, appropriate, equitable and coordinated care. The quality of the relationship between the service user and the care coordinator is one of the most important determinants of success.
- Care planning is underpinned by long-term engagement, requiring trust, team work and commitment. It is the daily work of mental health services and supporting partner agencies, not just the planned occasions where people meet for reviews.

Source: DH (2008b: 7)

Mental health and risk

There has been a common public misconception, often reinforced by the media, that mental health is equated with dangerousness. A good example is the 'not in my back yard' approach, whereby many people recognise the need to move away from institutional forms of care, but resist attempts to locate new community services near to where they live (see Chapter 5). More recently, there has also been an enormous public outcry about the presence in the community of people with personality disorders, who have typically been portrayed as 'fiends' and 'perverts' (Markham, 2000: 28). That such fears are not always well founded on fact and an accurate assessment of risk is demonstrated by events in South Wales, where a children's doctor was hounded out of her home because neighbours confused 'paediatrician' with 'paedophile' (Hall, 2001).

At its most extreme, a key image is of the 'axe-wielding maniac' waiting on street corners to attack unsuspecting passers-by (see Box 4.3 for a quote which illustrates this issue). Research suggests that two-thirds of all British press and television coverage of mental health includes a link with violence, while around 40 per cent of daily tabloids and nearly half of the Sunday tabloids contained derogatory references like 'nutter' and 'loony' (ODPM, 2004: 26). In the most part, such media stereotypes have been fuelled by a small number of very high-profile and brutal murders (for example of Jonathan Zito or Megan and Lin Russell). While these are human tragedies, they are clearly not representative (as evidenced by the substantial media coverage which they received) – albeit that they do raise important questions about the nature and management of risk.

Despite public concerns, there is substantial evidence to suggest that the association between violence and mental health is weak, and that the implementation of care in the community (however inadequately this has been resourced) has not resulted in any increased threat to public safety:

1. Very few people with mental health problems commit homicides – and the proportion of overall homicides committed by people with serious mental health difficulties has actually tended to decline in both the UK and internationally during the period in which there was a transition to community care

> ## Box 4.3   Violence, mental health and the media
>
> Violence is firmly linked to mental illness in media coverage ... Different specific 'panics' have emerged in different countries, states and cities, often attaching the fear of madness to other potent concerns of the moment: violence in the workplace – almost none of which is in fact perpetrated by people with mental health problems – an American panic fuelled by one heavily publicised case of a 'crazed' Post Office employee who turned a gun on colleagues; infanticide – a Chicago panic, stemming from the killing of a child by a woman with mental health problems, which exacerbated concerns about the safety of public agencies' decision making; and random street violence, a British panic, fuelled by the emblematic, but highly atypical, British case of Christopher Clunis, a man with mental health problems who killed a total stranger in a London Underground station.
>
> In different localities, 'stories' emerge and succeed each other in varying patterns, not in line with actual trends in crime or other social phenomena but according to subtler cultural shifts. Some countries have a stronger record in including positive 'stories': in Italy, the push for 'democratic psychiatry' enabled users to appear somewhat heroic, of interest for their successes in getting out of institutions rather than for more 'demonic' qualities (Ramon, 1996). British and American experiences are not, however, unique, and globalisation of the media is likely to make 'stories' increasingly international, as framed by more influential nations. This could mean a spread of moral panics – rather as movie watchers internationally are influenced by American films, which make frequent links between madness and violence.
>
> *Source*: Wahl, 1995, in Sayce (2000: 7)

(Taylor and Gunn, 1999; Simpson *et al.*, 2004). In the UK, only around 5 per cent of those responsible for homicides have a diagnosis of schizophrenia (Shaw *et al.*, 2006). In 2010, 33 cases of homicide by mental health patients were reported – with figures the lowest since current data collection processes began in 1997 (NHS Confederation, 2014).

2. Most homicides carried out by people with mental health problems are committed against family members or people they already know. According to the National Confidential Inquiry into Suicide and Homicide (2006; and see DH, 2001a) – so-called 'stranger homicides' (where the perpetrator and victim do not know each other) are very rare and the risk to the public is not increasing.

3. While mental health is a factor in a small number of deaths, other factors such as substance abuse and a previous history of violence may be much more significant (Swanson *et al.*, 1990; Steadman *et al.*, 1998; Walsh *et al.*, 2002; Walsh and Fahy, 2002; National Confidential Inquiry into Suicide and Homicide, 2006).

4. There is no significant correlation between any psychiatric diagnosis and the likelihood of committing assault (Monahan, 1993; Hiday, 2006). However, there can be links between certain very specific types of experience and an

increased possibility of violence – for example when people have 'command hallucinations' (hearing internal voices that may goad them on to commit acts of harm against self or others).

Despite popular (and governmental) misconceptions, research has demonstrated that, using the best available tools, professionals working in the community cannot predict risk with an accuracy that is of any practical use. Where a group was identified as being at high risk, 80 per cent did not go on to commit any acts of violence – resulting in an unhelpfully large proportion of 'false positives'. Conversely, around one-third of reported incidents of violence were committed by those identified as being at low risk (Shergill and Szmukler, 1998). A key finding from a range of mental health enquiries has been that many violent incidents committed by people with mental health problems have been hard to predict. In the case of homicides of strangers by people with mental health problems, international research suggests that such events are so rare (especially in people receiving treatment) that attempts to reduce homicides by trying to predict which patient might commit one are 'inevitably futile' (Nielssen *et al.*, 2011: 6). This leads to the unequivocal conclusion that:

> The stark reality is that however good our tools for risk assessment become ... professionals will not be able to make a significant impact on public safety. (Petch, 2001: 203)

Indeed, an overall analysis of findings from homicide enquiries suggests that an investment in improving overall service quality and accessibility, rather than in devoting professional time to formal risk management procedures, is more likely to prevent potentially avoidable deaths (Munro and Rumgay, 2000). Nevertheless, as we shall see, practices of risk assessment, safeguarding and risk management have come to dominate community mental health practice.

Risk assessment and positive risk taking

By the time that community mental health teams were starting to take shape in the late 1980s and early 1990s, a 'moral panic' about the supposed risk posed by people with mental illness was beginning to dominate the professional agenda (Holloway, 1996) to the detriment of a more considered focus on treatment and recovery. This was further reinforced by a very small number of high profile homicides (see Chapter 2) which led to the introduction of the CPA, Supervised Discharge Orders and, more recently, Community Treatment Orders, and which was exemplified by the health secretary's assertion in the introduction to the *Modernising Mental Health Services* White Paper that: 'Care in the community has failed' (DH, 1998).

Particularly in the early 1990s, a plethora or risk assessment tools and pro formas were developed in order to enable practitioners to make supposedly objective and systematic assessments of risk which could then be used to predict and prevent potential incidents of harm to self or others. However, as we have seen, research has shown that such 'tick-box' actuarial approaches were actually of little if any practical value (Tew, 2011). Nevertheless, these were then often used as the template for local CPA documentation and had a pervasive influence on professional practice – although more experienced practitioners tended to continue using more sophisticated and often intuitive approaches, using their close relationship with and knowledge of the service user to spot when their condition might be deteriorating and potentially posing concerns (Dixon, 2005).

More recently, we have seen a shift within policy discourses towards 'positive risk taking' (Stickley and Felton, 2006), recognising that some degree of informed risk taking is part of normal life and that people cannot be enabled to move towards recovery if they are overprotected (and potentially over-medicated). This approach is embedded in the Ten Essential Shared Capabilities for all mental health workers (DH, 2004d) and has been particularly influential in the training of professionally non-aligned support workers (see Chapter 2).

Safeguarding

Despite media constructions of people with mental health difficulties as posing a pervasive threat to 'normal' citizens, the reality is more frequently the reverse: they are more likely to be the victims rather than the perpetrators of crime (Jewesbury, 1998; McCabe and Ford, 2001; ODPM, 2004; Sayce, 1997, 1999), and they may also be subject to forms of abuse from financial to sexual which may never reach the criminal justice system because they are seen as 'unreliable witnesses'. Unlike in Scotland where the safeguarding and protection of adults is now governed by legislation (Scottish Government, 2007), practice in England has emerged without any legislative mandate or scrutiny. Following on from the *Valuing People* White Paper (DH, 2001h), there has simply been a statement of government policy on adult safeguarding (DH, 2011) which is enforced on local authorities through somewhat opaque systems of performance management and inspection regimes.

While the intention is to promote sharing of information and joined-up strategy between agencies (primarily local authorities, the NHS and the police), what has emerged is a new set of bureaucratic practices governing investigation and interagency decision making that are completely separate from CPA and which are tending to take away already limited specialist mental health social worker resources from important longer term roles such as care coordination. There are concerns as to the effectiveness of this activity given that the courses of action post-investigation are severely limited by the legal context. Even if concerns are found, there is no legal framework, such as that of the 1989 Children Act, by which to intervene if necessary – for example, by being able to move a vulnerable person to a place of safety. Instead, all that is possible is recourse to criminal law (if sufficient evidence is there to support a prosecution) or civil law (for example taking out an injunction against someone who is seen to be acting abusively). Neither of these approaches may be very suitable in the field of mental health as they can put an inappropriate onus on the person with a mental health difficulty to give evidence in court – potentially against friends or family members – which may not be feasible given their vulnerable mental state.

Compulsion and coercion in the community

It has long been thought important to have some statutory powers to regulate the lives and ensure the safety of a minority of people with serious mental health difficulties living in the community who were unwilling or unable to comply with professional advice. The 1983 Mental Health Act introduced provision for guardianship with gave the local authority the potential power to state where a person should reside and where they should attend for medical or other forms of care or treatment – although it stopped short of enforcing treatment itself. This power was little used in practice as there were no effective sanctions to enforce compliance – other than the longer-term threat that, if their condition worsened significantly as a result of their non-compliance, they might be compulsorily readmitted to hospital. Much more common has been the use (and abuse) of Section 17 leave, by which a person still technically detained under Section 3 of the Mental Health Act was allowed home for periods of trial leave – but could be recalled back to hospital at any time if there were concerns, without having to institute any further reassessment under the Act.

In response to continued political concern in relation to those seen as causing serious risk to self or others, the English government introduced new powers, called Supervised Discharge Orders (SDOs) (DH, 1996b). These provided for similar powers as under guardianship, with the additional power that a person could be forcibly 'conveyed' to a place of treatment, although they could not be compelled to accept any treatment once there. These powers could be applied for by the psychiatrist rather than by the local authority. Perhaps due to the perceived difficulty in applying for these powers, they were not greatly used – even though, when they were used, they were generally seen as being effective in increasing compliance with medication (Franklin et al., 2000).

Community Treatment Orders

Although there was no convincing evidence to show that a combination of already existing powers (SDOs/Section 17 leave) were insufficient to deal with 'at risk' people who were refusing treatment, the Labour government nevertheless saw the introduction of Community Treatment Orders (CTOs) as the central plank of their reform of the Mental Health Act in England and Wales – the measure that would address the perceived failure of care in the community to ensure public safety. This policy direction was in the face of international evidence from countries that had introduced such measures which demonstrated no consistent positive effect on key outcomes such as hospital readmission, length of hospital stay or medication adherence (Churchill et al., 2007). Concerns were also raised that CTOs would almost inevitably increase the overall use of compulsion (Lawton-Smith et al., 2008), potentially and that compulsory treatment would frequently be imposed on people who had capacity – thereby infringing legitimate patient autonomy and encouraging professional paternalism (Okai et al., 2007).

Unlike the SDOs that they have replaced, CTOs have been used much more widely than anticipated, and people are being required to stay on these orders for much longer (DH, 2006a; Health and Social Care Information Centre, 2012). This is despite concerted opposition prior to their introduction from all professional groups, including the Royal College of Psychiatrists. The key to this trend would seem to be in the detailed drafting of the legislation which both makes it easy for a patient coming up for discharge to be put on a CTO and leaves a clear audit trail back to the psychiatrist if anything should go wrong with someone who is discharged and subsequently causes harm to self or others. Consequently, when decisions are made and subsequently reviewed, the principle of the 'least restrictive alternative' which was fundamental to the original drafting of the Mental Health Act in 1983, no longer seems to hold sway – and there is no automatic right of access to independent advocacy.

In practice, CTOs cannot be used to treat people forcibly in the community except in an emergency. However, they can be used to secure immediate recall to hospital at any point where a person may refuse treatment. In this way, the coercion may be seen to be more implicit that explicit, but can nevertheless have a pervasive influence on the ethos of community care. No longer is it the duty of professionals to find a way of joining with people in their worlds and negotiating an alliance to support inclusion and recovery. Instead, professionals can demand compliance on their terms and ride roughshod over the idiosyncratic ideas and preferences of service users – ideas and preferences which actually may be crucial in service users' particular journeys towards recovery.

Although psychiatrists and other mental health professionals seem persuaded to make use of CTOs, the first large-scale randomised study of their effectiveness has shown that CTOs are no better than Section 17 leave at keeping people out of hospital. Nor are there any other benefits in terms of treatment compliance leading to any reduction in the severity of people's symptoms, or any improvement in their social functioning in the community (Burns *et al.*, 2013). All that they have achieved is to increase the duration of initial compulsory outpatient treatment from a median of eight days for those managed via Section 17 leave to a median of 183 days for those on CTOs – a very substantial infringement of individual liberties for no measurable benefit. According to the lead researcher on this trial:

> We were all a bit stunned by the result, but it was very clear data and we got a crystal clear result. So I've had to change my mind. I think sadly – because I've supported them for 20-odd years – the evidence is staring us in the face that CTOs don't work. (Burns, quoted in NHS Choices, 2013)

What will be interesting is whether, in terms of evidence-based policy making, findings such as these will lead to new approaches – or whether this is an issue where appeasing the media and public perceptions will be allowed to override what seem to be clear and indisputable research findings.

Models for organising mental health services in the community

Community Mental Health Teams (CMHTs)

As ad hoc local arrangements became formalised, multidisciplinary CMHTs began to be established across the country throughout the 1980s. CMHTs usually consisted of CPNs, psychiatrists, occupational therapists and psychologists with some form of integration with social services. A generic catchment area CMHT became available to over 80 per cent of the population by the early 1990s (Johnson and Thornicroft, 1993). CMHTs were tasked with assessing and treating any adult patient referred to them, and supporting and advising local GPs. In fact, by 1993, CPNs were taking over 40 per cent of their referrals from primary care professionals (White, 1993). Potentially being asked to do all things for all people, CMHTs were faced with some contradictory pressures and dilemmas in how to prioritise their work. These included:

- *Serious mental illness vs common mental health difficulties*: major tension, almost from the inception of CMHTs, arose from their location in the 'middle ground' between primary care and hospital-based services, resulting in conflicting pressures from GPs to take on work with people with short-term, more common mental health problems rather than to provide longer-term support to those with serious and more enduring mental illness (Sayce *et al.*, 1991). Although relatively disappointing effectiveness and cost-effectiveness outcomes in studies of CMHTs in the late 1980s (Gournay and Brooking, 1994, 1995; Patmore and Weaver, 1991) helped convince policy makers that CMHTs should focus on people with serious mental health problems, this issue has never been properly resolved – with staff left in a difficult position, torn between the different needs of service users, employers and policy imperatives (Secker *et al.*, 2000).
- *Risk assessment and coercion vs therapeutic intervention and enablement of recovery*: as discussed above, the excessive policy focus on risk led, not just to defensive and risk averse practice, but to the diversion of considerable staff time into the completion of risk assessment pro formas and related activities which were of very limited value in predicting actual incidents of violence. While, in some instances, this may have alerted practitioners to issues of which they might otherwise have been unaware (such as suicidal ideation), more often it could serve as a distraction which took them away from focusing on the issues that may have been of most importance to the person in terms of managing their mental ill-health or promoting their recovery – issues that may have more relevance to the longer-term successful reduction in risk. Perhaps, even more damaging was the way that a bureaucratised approach to risk had an adverse impact on the relationships that staff were able to make with service users: instead of entering into a therapeutic alliance with service users and seeking to enable their recovery, they appeared only to be interested in checking up on people and treating them as potentially dangerous 'others'.

The evidence base on the effectiveness of CMHTs is largely descriptive and relatively difficult to interpret because of variations in team structures and functions. As Burns (2004: 49–50) suggests:

> They evolved by word of mouth as clinicians tried to find ways of dealing with a changing health care system and rising expectations within fixed resources. As a result there have been many blind alleys along the way and enormous local variation in how they are managed, staffed and function …
> A consequence of this is that the 'feel' of CMHTs can vary enormously even if their core activities are fairly uniform.

However, the evidence suggests that, at least in comparison with traditional psychiatric units, CMHTs provide better-quality care at both two and four years after referral (Gater et al., 1997). Generic CMHT management also appears more effective than standard non-team hospital-oriented care for people with serious mental illness, particularly in terms of accepting treatment and also in possibly reducing hospital admissions (Malone et al., 2000).

CMHTs have also been criticised for having overambitious aims, and a tendency to neglect people with the most challenging health and social care needs (Patmore and Weaver, 1991). Their role in providing assessment and management of people with a range of needs and in integrating the health-led CPA with social services-led care management has meant that community mental health managers have had a difficult brokering role (Onyett et al., 1997). Despite these controversies, CMHTs have flourished during the last 20 years, becoming the backbone of mental health services. Numbers have increased from 81 in 1987 (Sayce et al., 1991) to 826 in 2006 (Centre for Public Mental Health, 2006) and their core roles have since been defined by the DH (see Box 4.4).

There are, inevitably, a number of challenges for CMHTs in the coming years. The advent of clinical commissioning groups may, once again, put pressure on them to develop services for people with more common mental health problems at the expense of their broader roles. The increasing policy focus on social inclusion, citizenship and rights will also add pressures both in terms of workload and resources to teams that have seen a net loss in nursing and social work staff since the advent of functionalised teams (Goldberg, 2008).

Box 4.4	The roles and responsibilities of CMHTs

1. Giving advice on the management of mental health problems by other professionals – in particular, advice to primary care and a triage function enabling appropriate referral.
2. Providing treatment and care for those with a time-limited disorder who can benefit from specialist interventions.
3. Providing treatment and care for those with more complex and enduring needs.

Source: DH (2002d)

The advent of functionalised teams

Particularly since the publication of the *NSF for Mental Health* (NSF) (DH, 1999a), community mental health debates have increasingly centred on the need for more specialised community-based mental health teams such as assertive outreach, crisis resolution/home treatment and early intervention teams – based on service models developed in North America (Stein and Test, 1980) and Australia (Hoult, 1986). This approach was reinforced by a number of team-specific Policy Implementation Guides (DH, 1999a, 2000a, 2001g). *The NHS Plan*, for example, heralded the creation of 220 assertive outreach teams, 335 crisis resolution teams and 50 early intervention teams by 2004, with the *Mental Health Policy Implementation Guidance* describing the more detailed team structure and functions.

This guidance stated that 'Community Mental Health Teams ... should provide the core round which newer service elements are developed' (DH, 2002d: 3). Although the guidance was not prescriptive about the relationships between CMHTs and new functionalised teams, it suggested that 'mutually agreed and documented responsibilities, liaison procedures and in particular transfer procedures need to be in place when crisis resolution, home treatment teams, assertive outreach teams and early intervention teams are being established' (2002d: 17). CMHTs were therefore seen as the central hub of mental health care, liaising with the more specialised teams as well as with primary care.

Assertive outreach

Assertive outreach teams (AOTs) are the best developed, described and most evidence based of the functionalised teams. They were first established in the late 1970s in Madison, Wisconsin, as the Program for Assertive Community Treatment (PACT) (Stein and Test, 1980). This was essentially a form of intensive case management, with patients with serious mental illness who seemed likely to need an admission allocated either to intensive case management and given intensive help with social functioning and clinical care, or to standard treatment. A service evaluation found that patients in the PACT group were less likely to require inpatient admission, had improved clinical and social functioning and were more satisfied with their care. The service was also judged to be cost-effective (see Box 4.5). Despite this, the funding for the original PACT ran out after 14 months and the significant gains were lost almost as quickly as they were established, indirectly confirming the effectiveness of the programme. The programme was also replicated by a group in Australia (Hoult, 1986) with similar positive outcomes.

A Cochrane review of assertive community treatment (ACT) for people with severe mental disorders (Marshall and Lockwood, 1998) found that, compared to standard community care, patients receiving ACT were more likely to remain in contact with services, less likely to be admitted to hospital, spent less time in hospital and had better clinical and social outcomes in terms of accommodation, employment and satisfaction. The review also concluded that, when

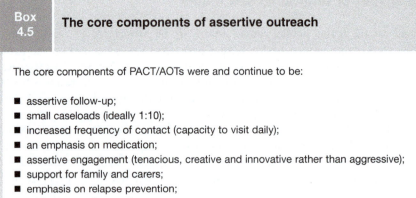

Box 4.5   **The core components of assertive outreach**

The core components of PACT/AOTs were and continue to be:

- assertive follow-up;
- small caseloads (ideally 1:10);
- increased frequency of contact (capacity to visit daily);
- an emphasis on medication;
- assertive engagement (tenacious, creative and innovative rather than aggressive);
- support for family and carers;
- emphasis on relapse prevention;
- crisis intervention; and
- availability 12 hours a day, seven days a week.

targeted on high users of inpatient care, ACT can substantially reduce the costs of hospital care.

The *Mental Health Policy Implementation Guidance* suggests that AOTs are most appropriate for people with:

- severe and persistent mental disorder associated with a high level of disability;
- a history of high use of inpatient or intensive home-based care;
- difficulty in maintaining lasting and consenting contact with services; and
- multiple complex needs including self-harm, homelessness and substance misuse.

This group has been estimated to be about 15,000 people at any one time in the UK (Sainsbury Centre for Mental Health, 1998a).

Although the AOT model has been well described, there were initially a number of uncertainties over how best to apply the core principles. A report from the Sainsbury Centre for Mental Health (Chisholm and Ford, 2004: vi) suggested that:

> Setting up AO teams means changing not merely structures and processes but cultures and attitudes within mental health services. Such a paradigm shift takes time and resources – it cannot be achieved overnight. It relies on an acceptance of the need for changes, good project management and a shared understanding of how services will be improved.

There are also potential tensions between fidelity to the AO model and individualised care/local flexibilities, and between assertive treatment and individual patient civil rights. As Burns (2004: 101) suggests, 'assertive outreach teams … need to maintain a broad psychosocial approach to their patients while not losing sight of the central importance of evidence based medical practice. In short, their research based and prescribed approach is both their greatest strength and their Achilles' heel.'

Despite these concerns, considerable progress has been achieved in establishing new teams. By March 2004, 263 AO teams were in place (*The NHS Plan* target was 220) and the number of staff recorded as either designated AO staff, or working within an AO team increased from 1,742 in 2003 to 2,762 in 2007 (CSIP, 2008). There are also high levels of satisfaction with services and good service user engagement, although research remains equivocal in terms of some hard outcomes such as number of days spent in hospital (Killaspy *et al.*, 2006). Interestingly, however, a systematic review of randomised controlled trials that compared the impact on the use of inpatient services of various forms of intensive case management (including assertive community treatment) with standard community mental health care found that the way in which the team organised its approach to the work and whether it was implemented in an area with high use of inpatient services accounted for the differences in findings (Burns *et al.*, 2007). Burns suggests that similarities in the organisation of the team between CMHTs and AO teams could explain the lack of efficacy in the UK, and concluded that case managers should work as teams rather than as individuals when caring for people with a severe mental illness. Killaspy (2007) has also suggested that the evidence base now highlights the critical success factors for AO as a team-based approach, extended hours and a high proportion of home- or community-based visits.

Crisis resolution and home treatment teams

Although the terms are often used interchangeably, crisis resolution and home treatment have distinct origins and emphases. Essentially, both approaches offer an alternative to inpatient care for people experiencing an acute mental health crisis. The crisis resolution approach has been in existence in the USA and Australia since the 1980s and owes its origins in the UK to the pioneering Barnet Intensive Crisis Intervention Service which was set up by psychiatrists and social workers in 1974. This takes a whole systems approach which seeks to understand and resolve the contextual triggers for an episode of acute mental ill-health, and to mobilise effective family and community support, as well as offering medical treatment (Sainsbury Centre, 2001b). The model 'is based on the assumption that social factors are of central importance in understanding and managing … crises' (Johnson and Needle, 2008: 6). Responded to in this way, acute psychotic episodes may often abate within a period of a few weeks so that a hospital admission can be avoided. In contrast, home treatment is a distinct model and is more limited in its scope, essentially focusing on the delivery at home of the same sort of medical treatment and care that a person would have received as an inpatient through an intensive short-term programme of home visits available 24 hours a day (Dean and Gadd, 1990).

As originally specified, crisis resolution was to be the model for functionalised teams (Sainsbury Centre, 2001b). However, in subsequent guidance and performance monitoring, the two models became conflated (DH, 2001k; McGlynn, 2006) and practice has tended to revert towards a more individualised home treatment approach, which may be more straightforward to manage but may be less successful in keeping people out of hospital. Unfortunately, as there has been no systematic differentiation and evaluation of the two models in practice – in terms of results achieved – it has been hard to make the case for implementing a more radical vision of crisis resolution in UK mental health services.

Overall, the evidence suggests that crisis resolution/home treatment (CR/HT) services may achieve reduced admissions and bed use (Glover *et al.*, 2006), better service retention and equal clinical outcomes to inpatient care (Johnson *et al.*, 2005). They are also generally preferred by patients and relatives (Minghella *et al.*, 1998; Smythe and Hoult, 2000) but may be less applicable in rural areas.

The *Mental Health Policy Implementation Guidance* (DH, 2001g) states that CR/HT should be targeted at adults (16–65 years old) with severe mental illness (schizophrenia, manic depressive disorders, severe depressive disorder) with an acute psychiatric crisis of such severity that, without the involvement of the CR/HT team, hospitalisation would be required (see Box 4.6).

Teams are meant to cover approximately 150,000 people and have a caseload of 20 to 30 service users shared between a multidisciplinary team of around 14 people. The intensity of the service means that there is continuity of care – although delivered on a team basis rather than by an individual practitioner. Although the guidance suggests patients should stay in contact with the team for three to four weeks, in practice it appears this may be as long as three to six months (Burns, 2004).

The National Audit Office (2007) reported that by 2007 there were 343 crisis resolution and home treatment teams across England (target 335) delivering over 95,000 episodes of care (target 100,000). They reported that the introduction of CR/HT reduced pressure on beds and, in some cases, speeded up discharge from hospital. They also reported favourable user and carer views, including the value of having this as an alternative to being admitted. However, they also reported a wide variety of development of CR/HTs nationally, with large differences in

Box 4.6	Core components of crisis resolution/home treatment teams

A CR/HT team should be able to:

- Act as a gatekeeper to mental health services, rapidly assess individuals with acute mental health problems and refer them to the most appropriate services.
- For individuals with acute severe mental health problems, for whom home treatment would be appropriate, provide immediate multidisciplinary community-based treatment 24 hours a day, seven days a week.
- Remain involved with the person until the crisis has resolved and the service user is linked into ongoing care.
- Have an assertive approach to engagement.
- If hospitalisation is necessary, be actively involved in discharge planning and provide intensive care at home to enable early discharge.
- Provide a time-limited intervention.

Source: DH (2001g: 11–12)

spending and on staffing levels between teams. They also estimated that full use of CR/HT services in appropriate cases costs approximately £600 less per crisis episode than one in which CR/HT is not available. Gatekeeping by CR/HT services (being involved in all decisions of whether or not to admit a person to inpatient psychiatric care) is crucial to the success of services and indeed the ability to deliver effective and efficient returns to a local health economy. DH guidance (2006b) defined full gatekeeping as encompassing all requests for admission, including pending Mental Health Act assessments and assertive outreach. The National Audit Office, however, found that there was a significant way to go nationally for CR/HTs to be fully gatekeeping. In a review of experiences of supporting CR/HTs, McGlynn (2007) also identified a number of problems including teams' lack of understanding of the role and their unrealistic expectations of other teams, rigid exclusion criteria and a lack of flexibility for those trying to access the system. The challenges now appear to be the need to isolate the key ingredients for success in CR/HTs, and then to implement teams in a way that makes sense within the wider local service context.

Early intervention services

Early intervention (EI) services have been a feature of health care in Australia, Scandinavia and the USA for over a decade. They have, however, only relatively recently become part of the landscape of UK mental health care. The policy imperative for EIS for young people with first-episode psychosis has been driven by user and carer dissatisfaction with existing poor-quality services (Rethink, 2003a), health professional concerns about the state of services and a growing evidence base that links long duration of untreated psychosis (DUP) with poorer long-term prognosis (Norman and Malla, 2001). Evidence has also emerged that the early phase following the onset of a first psychotic illness could be conceived of as a 'critical period', influencing the long-term course of the illness. Providing timely and effective interventions at this stage might therefore alter the subsequent course of the illness and have a disproportionate impact relative to later interventions (Birchwood et al., 1998).

Evidence also suggests that patients' needs during the early phases of the illness differ from those of individuals with longer-standing illness and therefore require different treatment options (Norman and Townsend, 1999). Young people have to deal with the initial personal trauma of psychosis in addition to the normal anxieties associated with young adulthood and have high hopes of returning to a normal level of functioning. Engagement, or the formation of a 'therapeutic alliance', is therefore crucial and can be fostered by developing youth-sensitive services in as flexible a way as possible.

Most of the EI evidence initially concentrated on justifying the need to provide services at an earlier stage in the illness. However the more recent evidence has focused on the effectiveness of EI itself. Data from the Lambeth Early Onset trial revealed statistically significant differences in terms of relapse and rehospitalisation for young people in contact with EI compared to standard care (Craig et al., 2004). Early results from OPUS, a large randomised clinical trial of integrated treatment versus standard treatment for patients with first-episode psychosis, suggested that integrated treatment improves clinical outcomes and adherence to treatment (Peterson *et al.*, 2005). Lester *et al.* (2009) evaluated established and emerging EI services across the West Midlands and found high levels of service engagement at 12 months and of service user and carer satisfaction. Economic modelling suggests that over 12 months the EI pathway for each individual is £5,000 cheaper than standard care; over three years, the saving is £14,500 (CSIP, 2008). McCrone *et al.* (2008) suggest that the potential annual savings from expanding EI could be in the region of £13–65 million for people with schizophrenia and £8–31 million for people with a bipolar disorder by 2026 because of a reduced need for services at a later stage.

The *Mental Health Policy Implementation Guidance* (DH, 2001g) states that EI should be targeted at people aged between 14 and 35 with a first presentation of psychotic symptoms during the first three years of psychotic illness (see Box 4.7). *The NHS Plan* originally suggested that there should be 50 EI teams across England and a national client total of 22,500 by December 2006. These targets were, however, missed. A mapping exercise jointly conducted by NIMHE and Rethink (Pinfold *et al.*, 2007) found that funding difficulties were a barrier to development for at least half of the EIS contacted, exacerbated by new and inexperienced service commissioners in PCTs. The DH therefore launched a recovery plan in 2006 to reconfirm EI as a key government priority and get EI implementation back on track (Selbie, 2006). This appeared to have a positive effect, with EI staffing increasing from 206 in 2003 to 1,136 in 2007 (591 per cent) with a further increase in staff between 2006 and 2007 of 25 per cent. It was also encouraging that the mental health tsar went on record saying that 'I now believe that early intervention will be the most important and far reaching reform of the NSF era. Crisis resolution has had the most immediate effect but I think

Box 4.7	Key features of EI

EI services should be able to:

■ Reduce the stigma associated with psychosis and improve professional/lay awareness of symptoms of psychosis and the need for early assessment.
■ Reduce the length of time young people are undiagnosed and untreated.
■ Develop meaningful engagement, provide evidence-based intervention and prioritise recovery during the early phase of illness.
■ Increase stability in the lives of service users, facilitate development and provide opportunities for personal fulfilment.
■ Provide user-centred services (a seamless service available for those from 14 to 35 that effectively integrates child, adolescent and adult mental health services and works in partnership with primary care, education, social services and youth services).
■ Ensure that care is transferred thoughtfully and effectively at the end of treatment.

Source: Summarised from DH (2001g: 46–7)

early intervention will have the greatest effect on people's lives' (Appleby, 2008). Despite this, there remain a number of challenges, including around entry points from Child and Adolescent Mental Health Services. As EI matures and more young people exit 'gold standard' services, discharge policies into usual care within a primary care setting also need to be carefully considered.

The future of functionalised teams

Over time, the added value of functionalised teams has been questioned, with some suggesting that positive research findings may reflect the commitment and charisma of the 'hero innovators' of new models rather than the inherent value of a functionalised approach (Burns, 2004). Service users have complained about being passed between teams for different stages of their care – and hence having to start again with a different team of professionals who do not know them as a person. The interface between different teams can also cause wider organisational problems when service users do not quite fit existing criteria. Faced with budget cuts, some mental health trusts have sought to merge functionalised teams in order to make savings in management costs. Other trusts have responded to the policy of Payment by Results (PbR) by reorganising services on the basis of PbR clusters – somewhat arbitrary categories based on clinical diagnosis which attract the same payment tariff even though people within these clusters may have very divergent needs in terms of treatment and support. Such service configurations may create even more unhelpful boundary issues where people do not fit consistently within one diagnostic group.

Alternative crisis services

As Chapter 5 suggests, users frequently report negative inpatient experiences. Hospital beds are also a relatively scarce and expensive form of service provision. Government policies that emphasise patient choice should, in theory, have led to a concerted exploration and evaluation of alternative models of crisis provision for those for whom staying at home, and receiving a crisis resolution or home treatment service, is not a viable option. For a significant proportion of these, a full residential option may not be needed and evidence suggests that up to 40 per cent of people in need of hospital admission could be treated successfully in a day hospital setting with few differences in clinical or social outcomes (Creed et al., 1990) and that the costs associated with day hospital care are less than inpatient care (Creed et al., 1997; Marshall et al., 2001). Day hospital treatment for voluntary psychiatric patients in an inner-city area also appears more effective in terms of reducing psychopathology in the short term (Priebe et al., 2005). However, unlike other areas of health provision such as surgery, there have been no significant moves to reorient provision in the light of these findings.

Where a short-term residential option is needed, an alternative model of provision, much favoured by many service users, is that of a small informal crisis house

Box 4.8	Key differences between crisis houses and inpatient care

- Higher staff to resident ratio, but most paid staff and volunteers are professionally unqualified and often with lived experience of surviving crisis themselves.
- Therapeutic and homely environment – less stigmatising and stressful for the individual and their family and friends.
- Individualised and holistic support planning – not just focus on medical treatment.
- Personal space and privacy combined with communal living area – own room and sometimes the option for parents to bring in young children with them.
- Open front door policy – for residents, friends and family.
- Support to maintain daily living skills – residents supported to prepare their own meals and do their own laundry wherever possible.
- Close communication with, and support for, the family and friends of those in crisis.
- Maintaining connection with, and signposting to, mainstream community activities and services to facilitate social inclusion and recovery.

Source: Adapted from Gofal Cymru (2008: 5)

in which much of the support may be given by people with their own experience of surviving mental health crisis (see Box 4.8). An evaluation of three such houses by the Sainsbury Centre for Mental Health (2002a) found that all of those interviewed felt the service met all their needs, and that it was more cost-effective than inpatient care. Users particularly valued support from recovery guides with similar experiences and the non-judgemental atmosphere of the house. It should, however, be noted that such initiatives are often fragile in terms of funding streams and at least one of the examples studied, Anam Cara in Birmingham, is no longer providing this service.

One particularly successful model has been that of Drayton Park Women's Crisis House and Resource Centre in London (Killaspy *et al.*, 2000b) which has been able to provide a much safer and more therapeutic environment for women that the potentially sexually threatening and abusive environments that can characterise many current inpatient services (see Chapter 8). Although still very few in number, crisis houses are being established across the UK (Scottish Development Centre for Mental Health, 2004; Gofal Cymru, 2008) but, perhaps because they challenge the institutional power base of psychiatry within hospital-based services, funding and roll-out of such services has been very sporadic and piecemeal – and the great majority of service users in crisis are not able to be offered alternatives in terms of where they may be able to go and what sort of service they might receive.

Personal budgets and direct payments

A further hopeful development is the expansion of direct payments and personal budgets. Under the Community Care (Direct Payments) Act 1996, social services departments can make cash payments to a range of different adult user groups in lieu of directly provided social services (and in some children's services). Research suggests that direct payments give recipients greater choice and control, are more cost-effective than directly provided services and lead to greater user satisfaction, a more creative use of resources, greater continuity of care and fewer unmet needs (Glasby and Littlechild, 2009). Since April 2003, it has been a legal duty for councils to make direct payments to individuals who are eligible and wish to receive a direct payment, and take-up has risen significantly. In 2007, the government launched a wider strategy of 'personalisation' in adult social care (HM Government, 2007) which introduced the idea that service users could be allocated a personal budget in relation to their social care (and potentially other) needs. At their most simple, personal budgets involve being clear with the person from the outset how much money is available to spend on their needs and allowing them a greater say in how this money is spent. Beyond this, options for how the money is controlled can vary from the full amount being taken as a direct payment right the way through to the person's keyworker managing the money on their behalf (but with the person still determining how the money should be spent). Unlike direct payments, personal budgets can also be used to purchase public services (as well as private and voluntary services), and this spectrum of control could be especially relevant for some mental health service users. In order to see how this could work in practice, personal budgets were piloted across a number of sites (DH, 2006c). In general, it was found that this was both a cost-effective approach and one that was valued by service users and their families because it gave them more choice and control (Glendinning et al., 2008). Indeed, such has been the early success of personal budgets that successive governments have taken them up with enthusiasm, rolling them out across the whole of adult social care and extending their application into health care.

However, progress in relation to take-up of direct payments and personal budgets by people with mental health difficulties has not been consistent across England. In 2003, only five local authorities had ten or more direct payment recipients with mental health problems (and 57 per cent had no recipients with mental health problems at all) (Spandler and Vick, 2004). Similarly, the use of personal budgets to meet mental health needs was lower in comparison with other groups in the personal budget pilot sites, although, when they were used, outcomes were seen as positive (Glendinning et al., 2008). This is somewhat in contrast to experience in the USA where take-up of self-directed support has been much higher in mental health and this has resulted in a significant diversion of resources towards whatever service users may find most useful in reducing their need to access crisis services (Alakeson, 2007; see also Alakeson, 2014 for an introductory guide). Various barriers to greater uptake of personal budgets in mental health have been suggested (see Box 4.9).

Nevertheless, despite relatively low take-up overall, some areas have promoted substantial and successful use of personal budgets in mental health, and this has been seen as a particularly effective way of increasing choice and control, of allowing people to make desired changes in their lives and of connecting people more fully to their communities (see Glasby and Littlechild, 2009; Poll et al., 2006;

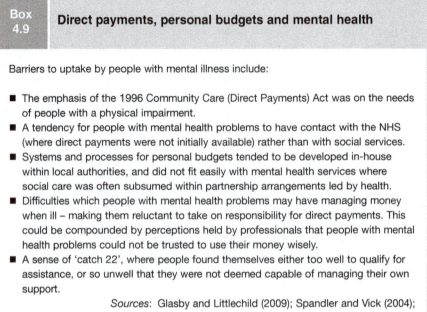

Barriers to uptake by people with mental illness include:

- The emphasis of the 1996 Community Care (Direct Payments) Act was on the needs of people with a physical impairment.
- A tendency for people with mental health problems to have contact with the NHS (where direct payments were not initially available) rather than with social services.
- Systems and processes for personal budgets tended to be developed in-house within local authorities, and did not fit easily with mental health services where social care was often subsumed within partnership arrangements led by health.
- Difficulties which people with mental health problems may have managing money when ill – making them reluctant to take on responsibility for direct payments. This could be compounded by perceptions held by professionals that people with mental health problems could not be trusted to use their money wisely.
- A sense of 'catch 22', where people found themselves either too well to qualify for assistance, or so unwell that they were not deemed capable of managing their own support.

Sources: Glasby and Littlechild (2009); Spandler and Vick (2004); Larsen *et al.* (2013)

Hatton *et al.*, 2008; Webber *et al.*, 2014). Success factors have included effective engagement between health and social care systems, clear vision and local leadership, ownership by all key stakeholders (including front-line practitioners) and a focus on using personal budgets to achieve positive outcomes, rather than just provide ongoing support (Larsen *et al.*, 2013).

Following the Darzi review in 2007, personal budgets have been piloted in relation to people with a range of long-term conditions, including mental health. While these ways of working are likely to prove very counter-cultural in some areas of the NHS, they have the potential to link well with concepts such as recovery, user-led crisis services, advance directives and developing alternatives to acute care – and access to some sort of crisis and/or recovery budget could be a powerful new approach to more genuinely rebalancing the current system. Broadly speaking, the subsequent national evaluation was positive (see Box 4.10), with personal health budgets being found to be cost-effective for people with mental health problems, and it is anticipated that they will be made more generally available to people with mental health difficulties from April 2015.

> **Box 4.10**   **Findings from the personal health budget evaluation**
>
> ■ The majority of budget-holders and carers reported positive impacts on their health and well-being.
> ■ High-value personal health budgets were most cost-effective, suggesting that personal health budgets should be initially targeted at people with greater need, to act as a substitute for conventional service delivery.
> ■ Most interviewees appreciated the increased choice, control and flexibility of the personal health budget, although some thought the benefits were curtailed by restrictions on what the budget could be used for.
> ■ More positive outcomes were seen where sites chose to be explicit in informing patients about the budget amount; provided a degree of flexibility as to what services could be purchased; and provided greater choice as to how the budget could be managed. Some negative impacts were found for sites using configurations with less flexibility and choice than other sites.
>
> *Source*: Forder *et al.* (2012)

Conclusion

Community mental health care has developed in a piecemeal fashion, influenced by a range of factors including economic constraints, difficulties in partnership working between health and social care and public concerns over safety. The closure of asylums and the development of community teams 'have occurred unevenly across the country ... in no instance however has a psychiatric hospital simply withered away because all its functions were replaced by a network of community services' (Leff, 1997: 189). At times, the development of community services has been overshadowed by a 'moral panic' around public safety. However, there is considerable evidence that current approaches to risk management and safeguarding, and the large-scale increase in the use of coercion using Community Treatment Orders, are at best ineffective and at worst constitute a major diversion of activity away from the building of long-term therapeutic relationships that may both enable recovery and, by maintaining positive engagement, minimise any threat to public safety.

A range of generic and more specialised community-based mental health teams have been developed across the UK. While the development of function-alised teams was seen, particularly in England, as the best model for improving services, the continued development of acceptable, appropriate, accessible and effective user-centred services is complex and may not necessarily follow this model over the next decade. We will need to continue to test the evidence base for both CMHTs and functionalised teams and ensure the 'black box' element of what works best, for whom and in which context, is better understood.

Looking forward, greater involvement of GPs in commissioning and the advent of personal budgets may lead to significant changes in the emphasis and ethos of community mental health services. There will be pressure further to reduce reliance on inpatient beds by greater investment in preventive activity focused on well-being, and the provision of a better range of alternatives in terms of crisis care and crisis resolution than are currently provided by home treatment teams. However, any developments will be taking place in a climate of financial austerity, which is currently having an impact on most severely on local author-ity social care and other community services, but which is also requiring cost savings across the NHS. It may well be the need to save money that will be the biggest driver of change and, while this may just be reflected in a diminution of already overstretched services, it may also lead to new and creative approaches in which services users and family members become more actively involved as co-producers of more effective and person-centred services (see Needham and Carr, 2009).

Reflection exercises

1. Working practices between teams (*exercise for practitioners*)

Think about the ways in which you communicate with the other mental health teams, primary care services and social care in your area.

■ Are patient pathways between sectors well coordinated? If not, why not and what can you do to improve the situation?

Consider the entry points for your service:

■ Does your team have a gatekeeping role, or are all referrals accepted from other mental health teams and/or primary care? Discuss the strengths and weaknesses of both ways of working.

Now consider the exit points from your service:

■ Try to map the patient pathways of a number of clients who have been discharged and then re-referred to your service during the last 24 months. Think about the reason behind the re-referral – was this something that could have been avoided through better communication or discharge planning?

2. What would a good community mental health service look like? (*exercise for all readers*)

Current services have evolved over time and may not make the most effective use of limited resources. If you were to design a community mental health service from scratch – and design this around the needs and aspirations of service users, rather than the ways that professionals have traditionally organised themselves – what would it look like?

- What would be the roles and ways of working of professionals?
- How would services be accessed? Where would they be based?
- How would you balance the safety of service users, family members and the wider public against enabling service users to make their own choices and pursue their own aspirations?

3. The implications of direct payments and personal budgets (*exercise for all readers*)

Some people are passionate about the potential of direct payments and personal budgets to increase choice and control for people using services. After reading the literature and/or talking to people receiving direct payments/personal budgets, make a list of the key success factors that might be needed and the main barriers that exist in mental health services. If someone you were working with wanted to find out more about this way of working, would you know where to signpost them, and how comfortable would you feel supporting them to explore these concepts?

Further resources

1. Thornicroft, G. *et al.* (eds) (2011) *Oxford Textbook of Community Mental Health.* Oxford: Oxford University Press.

   Comprehensive and authoritative overview of the field, with contributions from leading figures representing a range of disciplinary perspectives on research, policy and practice.

2. Burns, T. (2004) *Community Mental Health Teams: A Guide to Current Practices.* Oxford: Oxford University Press.

   Personal view of the current state and future challenges facing the generic CMHT with the newer functionalised teams written by Professor Tom Burns (who has a long and distinguished career as both a researcher and consultant psychiatrist).

3. Hannigan, B. and Coffey, M. (eds) (2003) *The Handbook of Community Mental Health Nursing.* London: Routledge.

   Comprehensive edited collection providing an easy-to-read resource for practising community mental health nurses. It includes chapters that contextualise the area, as well as thought-provoking contributions on a broad range of issues, including ethics and the law.

4. Tew, J. (2011) *Social Approaches to Mental Distress*. Basingstoke: Palgrave Macmillan.

   Chapters 8–11 provide an overview of practice models in relation to early intervention, crisis resolution, recovery, risk and assessment in community settings.

5. For a more detailed understanding of the policy and practice of functionalised teams, see:

   Birchwood, M. *et al.* (eds) (2002) *Early Intervention in Psychosis*. Chichester: Wiley.
   Johnson, S. *et al.* (eds) (2008) *Crisis Resolution and Home Treatment in Mental Health*. Cambridge: Cambridge University Press.

6. For information on the latest developments and resources in relation to personalisation, see the Think Local Act Personal website www.thinklocalactpersonal.org.uk

5 Acute Mental Health Services

In this chapter we discuss:

- Pressures in inpatient services.
- The hospital stay.
- Hospital discharge.
- Grounds for optimism.

Despite their apparent popularity with the public and the media, hospitals can be ambiguous places. If you are suddenly or seriously ill, then having immediate access to skilled professionals trained in managing your condition can be, quite literally, a matter of life and death. For people who have become ill over a longer period of time, finally realising that someone is going to take care of you and (it is hoped) make you better can also be a major relief – prompting feelings of extreme gratitude. However, some people probably do not want to end up in hospital in the first place, and for them the same process can be much more distressing and intimidating. Often, they can feel scared, unsure what is happening and desperate to do anything they can to get home. Nationally, there have been debates about the availability of single-sex wards, the nature of the built environment, the quality of hospital food and the cleanliness of wards – all of which can vary significantly and have a significant impact on health and well-being. As people get better, moreover, they can become increasingly frustrated by the institutional nature of many ward routines. For those with ongoing needs, there have also been long-standing debates about how best to organise follow-up support, so that people do not stay in hospital too long, are not discharged too soon and are not sent home before appropriate community support is in place.

In a similar way, the role of hospital services within the broader NHS can also be ambiguous. While hospitals have a key role to play, they are only part of the overall network of services needed to respond to the nation's ill-health. Because they provide such specialist and intensive services, hospitals also tend to be very expensive and resource-intensive places. Although this is appropriate when people have very serious needs, the way in which the NHS has evolved over time has tended to mean that a number of services continue to be based within hospitals when arguably they could be better provided in community-based settings. As part of the 'care closer to home' agenda, therefore, the government has sought to encourage a shift away from some hospital-based services, and the role of hospitals seems to be changing. With advances in medical technology, it is possible that future hospitals may move away from the traditional 'district general' model to a situation in which health care is provided much more locally for some conditions and in much larger, regional centres of excellence for other conditions. While hospitals will still be a crucial part of the spectrum of care, they will be working alongside more specialist community services and are likely to be working more flexibly, rather than as standalone services. As a result, a range of current policies are designed to keep people living more independently in the community, reduce emergency hospital admissions, ensure swift and effective discharge for people once they are medically fit to leave and concentrate specialist services in larger units. For all these reasons, hospitals can often seem like part of the solution or part of the problem – depending on your point of view – and the ongoing reform of hospital services remains controversial.

If hospital services arouse contradictory feelings within the wider NHS, then this is even more the case in mental health. Because of the nature of people's conditions and previous contact with services, it is particularly important that we are clear about the proper role of hospital care within the broader spectrum of support available and that we make this a positive experience. As the Sainsbury Centre for Mental Health (1998b: 9) observes:

> If and when people with severe mental health problems can no longer
> manage to live in the community … they, their relatives, and society
> expect care to be available in a therapeutic and humane place. In practice,
> this means admission to an acute psychiatric ward and inevitably losing
> some degree of freedom and privacy. Most people suffering from a severe
> mental illness will have been in hospital at some stage in their lives. A
> considerable proportion will have been admitted against their will under
> the Mental Health Act because they were judged to be a danger to
> themselves or others. At the point of admission people become patients,
> and will be in a severe state of crisis, both personally and mentally.
> Imagine being transported to a frightening unknown place, possibly in an
> ambulance or police car, while suffering from deep despair or confusion.
> It is unlikely that at any point in their life anyone could feel more
> vulnerable, and would be more in need of high quality and sensitive care.

Pressures in inpatient services

Traditionally, mental health services have been dominated by institutions, with many people placed in long-stay hospitals or asylums. As discussed in Chapter 4, this emphasis on institutional care was replaced in the second half of the twentieth century with a recognition of the need to care for more people in the community, either in their own homes or in community-based settings which are as homely as possible. As a result, the number of hospital beds for people with mental health problems has fallen considerably (both in the UK and internationally). In 1954, there were 154,000 residents in UK mental hospitals. By 1982, this figure had fallen to 100,000 and, by 1998, to 40,000. This number has continued to decline, with the number of beds in NHS mental health settings falling to 27,914 in 2006–7, a drop of 23.7 per cent from 1997–8 (NHS Confederation, 2009: 5).

However, this does not necessarily mean that the number of hospital admissions has been decreasing. On the contrary, the number of admissions increased from 155,000 in 1964 (347 per 100,000 population) to 192,000 in 1984 (409 per 100,000 population) and 224,000 in 1993–4 (462 per 100,000 population) (Payne, 1999: 247). More recently there have been indications of a new process of 'reinstitutional-isation' (see Chapters 2 and 6) with an increase in formal admissions under the Mental Health Act and an increase in certain types of bed (for example, the number of NHS medium-secure beds increased from 1750 to 2060 between 1998–9 and 2002–3 – an increase of 18 per cent; see CSIP, 2008; NHS Confederation, 2009). However, the overall trend for many years has seen the number of hospital beds falling at the same time as admissions have been increasing. As is also the case for other user groups, this has been achieved by a reduction in the length of hospital stay, and by changes in community services to work with people with increasingly high-level needs. In older people's services, this is often described in terms of people being discharged from hospital 'quicker and sicker' (Neill and Williams, 1992: 17), with community services having to support a growing number of people who would previously have been cared for in an acute setting. Such changes also require a shift in the thinking from inpatient services, so that they see themselves as part of a broader spectrum of care rather than as a stand-alone service.

Hardly surprisingly, this puts extra pressure on hospital services (to treat and discharge people as quickly as possible) and on community services (to support people with increasingly significant and complex needs). This not only means that community services have a heavier caseload, but that those people who are admit-ted to hospital are likely to have particularly severe needs and that the whole serv-ice becomes increasingly intensive in its focus. This has a number of implications which are discussed in further detail throughout the remainder of this chapter. As Quirk and Lelliott (2001: 1567) observe:

The emergent picture is that:

- The reduction in bed numbers has created a 'concentrating' effect whereby the threshold for admission has increased.
- High bed occupancy rates mean that quality of care is compromised. Some people have to be admitted to distant hospitals with subsequent loss of conti-nuity; nurses spend most of their time managing crises rather than giving care.
- Because of the concentrating effect, wards are disturbed places where 'violence breeds violence'.
- Unavailability of beds compromises the quality of community care which requires easy access to beds for short-term management of crises or for respite.

Interestingly, however, the statistics do not tell the full story. As Payne (1999: 248) explains, some of this increase in psychiatric admissions is actually the same people being admitted and readmitted to hospital:

The pattern for many patients, however, is one of admission to psychiatric hospital and discharge which is then followed by subsequent readmission at a later date. If one compares figures for first admissions ... with figures for total admissions it is clear that the vast majority of the increase in psychiatric admissions ... is accounted for by the readmission of those who have already been treated as in–patients and discharged from hospital – the phenomenon of the so–called 'revolving door'.

Although the concept of the 'revolving door' admission is discussed in more detail below, it is significant to note that these trends within mental health can also be seen in services for other user groups. As an example, the Audit Commission (1997, 2000a) describes a 'vicious circle' in services for older people in which the number of hospital admissions is rising, lengths of hospital stays are declining, opportunities for rehabilitation are reduced, there is an increased use of expensive residential/nursing home care and less money for preventive services, thereby leading to more hospital admissions.

Hardly surprisingly, one of the main results of the decline in the number of psychiatric beds and rising demand has been a significant increase in pressure on hospital services. In response, the tendency has been for mental health services to seek to treat more people with fewer resources by increasing bed occupancy rates (more people seen per bed). This can be done using a variety of tactics, all of which are 'unsatisfactory' (Quirk and Lelliott, 2001, p.1566; see also Box 5.1). Despite this, the answer may not necessarily lie in expanding hospital services – and a fascinating debate by Tyrer (2011) and Johnson (2011) in the *British Medical Journal* summarises these debates very succinctly (see Box 5.2).

Box 5.1	**Dealing with pressures in acute care**

Tactics for managing rising acute pressures include (summarised from Quirk and Lelliott, 2001):

- Transferring patients to hospitals outside the local area (a practice traditionally known as extra-contractual referrals (ECRs), sometimes referred to as 'out of area transfers' or 'individual patient placements').
- Maintaining waiting lists, with people needing inpatient care waiting in settings such as general medical wards, community settings, prison or police cells.
- Sending some patients home on short-term leave (sometimes prematurely and often at short notice) in order to free up beds for others.

As a result of this, the bed occupancy rate (when all those in the above categories are added in) can frequently exceed 100 per cent – clearly, the implications of such pressure on beds can be extremely serious:

- Quality of care can be compromised by admitting patients to hospitals at a long distance from their homes, discharging or sending people on leave early and not admitting other patients.
- The use of ECRs is not only unpopular with service users, but is also very costly, diverts money away from community services and disrupts continuity of care.
- Sending people out on leave can also create significant administrative difficulties as patients can sometimes return at any time, making it difficult to use temporarily vacant beds for other people requiring admission.

Box 5.2	**Have bed closures gone too far?**

Peter Tyrer (2011) – Yes:

I have been a community psychiatrist for the past 45 years. However, I am now rueing the success of the community psychiatric movement in the UK, where the inane chant of 'community good, hospital bad' has taken over every part of national policy... The difficult question to answer is, at what point does a further reduction in beds lead to harm and substandard care? I believe this point was reached some years ago and that the NHS needs at least 30,000 beds for good psychiatric care:

- We have run out of successful initiatives to reduce bed use further
- Risk of preventing admissions is getting too great
- We have demonised inpatient care by neglecting its function
- Discontinuity of care has been enhanced

Sonia Johnson (2011) – No:

Increasing psychiatric bed provision would ... be both profligate and pointless. Let us instead dedicate the limited resources we have to improving the quality of existing inpatient services... and to implementing as fully as we can the knowledge we already have about how reliance on inpatient services may be reduced:

- Our bed numbers are not especially low [compared to other systems]
- Community care is not toxic... Most people with serious mental illnesses live peaceful lives in the community most of the time, many achieving reasonable subjective well-being despite considerable adversities
- High quality long-term support in the community is the priority [the main function of wards is now containment of immediate risk – and this is not a good environment for tackling broader issues such as low rates of employment, poor health, substance misuse and social isolation/stigma]
- [There is still] potential to reduce bed use [through exploring further alternatives to hospital beds].

The hospital stay

Once in hospital, some people will receive high-quality services that meet their needs. Despite this, many accounts of inpatient care suggest that some service users have very poor experiences of hospital services, with few people having 'anything good to say about acute hospital care' (Royal College of Psychiatrists, 2002b). In 2000, a national survey carried out by Mind revealed a series of extremely worrying findings (see Box 5.3), which painted 'a grim picture of life on many psychiatric wards – a depressing environment, unsafe, dirty, with illegal drugs easily available, minimal contact with staff, not enough to do and not enough access to food, drink, bathing facilities, interpreters if needed, telephones and fresh air' (Baker, 2000: 31). Unfortunately, many of these findings are mirrored in other studies, suggesting that they may not be unique to the Mind survey (see Boxes 5.4–5.5).

Box 5.3   Mind national survey

In 2000, the mental health charity Mind published the results of a national survey of 343 people with experience of hospital services:

- More than half (56 per cent) of patients said that the ward was an untherapeutic environment.
- Just under half (45 per cent) said that ward conditions had a negative effect on their mental health.
- Just under half (45 per cent) said they found the atmosphere on wards 'depressing' and bleak.
- Almost one-third (30 per cent) of patients said that they found the atmosphere on wards unsafe and frightening.
- Just under a third (30 per cent) said illegal drugs were being used on the wards. Two-thirds of these patients (66 per cent) said that drugs were easily available to patients.
- Almost two-thirds (64 per cent) of patients who needed an interpreter did not get one.
- More than half (57 per cent) said they didn't have enough contact with staff. Only 35 per cent said they did.
- The vast majority (82 per cent) of patients who said they didn't have enough contact with staff said that they spent 15 minutes or fewer with staff each day.
- Almost one in six (16 per cent) of patients said they had experienced sexual harassment on the ward. 72 per cent of those patients who complained said that no action was taken to prevent it happening again.
- Almost two-thirds (60 per cent) of patients had problems getting a restful night's sleep.
- Just under half (45 per cent) of patients said they didn't have enough access to food, and 31 per cent said they didn't have enough access to drinks.
- One-quarter (26 per cent) of patients said the toilets weren't clean.

Source: Summarised from Baker (2000: 6)

Box 5.4	Acute concerns – the views of social work students

In Merseyside, social work students observing local psychiatric wards highlighted the following:

- *Institutional aimlessness*: patients are often bored, do little other than watch TV and are regularly moved around by cleaning staff. Ward routines have become ends in themselves and the physical atmosphere is debilitating. The limited activities on offer are seen as being very patronising. but users take part to try to demonstrate that their mental health has improved and secure an early discharge.
- *Poor staff-patient relationships*: most staff time is spent on administration tasks, talking to each other in the office and watching patients rather than engaging with them.
- *Narrow approaches to mental health:* staff see patients as being 'ill' and pay little attention to users' social backgrounds. As a result, the presenting problem is often seen as the issue to be addressed with no consideration of the factors that may have caused this problem in the first place. There is an almost total reliance on psychiatric drugs as the solution to mental health problems.
- *Indifference to civil and human rights:* staff tend to treat all patients the same way irrespective of whether or not they have been admitted as compulsory patients. Some people have little knowledge of the law and have had no training at all in this area. Ward routines are very rigid and some are unnecessarily stressful (such as denying people drinks outside set times even though dry mouths are a common side effect of medication or the oppressive nature of ward rounds, with patients unable to contribute due to the large number of professionals that come to see them).

Source: Walton (2000)

Box 5.5	Ongoing concerns about acute care

In 2004, Mind conducted a second national survey as part of its 'Ward Watch' campaign. Based on 335 responses from people with recent or current experience of mental health inpatient services, the survey found that:

- 23 per cent have been accommodated in mixed sex wards (two years after a government target to eliminate mixed-sex wards). 31 per cent did not have access to single-sex bathroom facilities.
- 27 per cent said they rarely felt safe in hospital.
- 51 per cent reported being physically or verbally abused, with 20 per cent reporting physical assault.
- 18 per cent reported sexual harassment, 7 per cent reported being subject to harassment due to their race and 10 per cent reported harassment due to their sexuality.

- 53 per cent thought the hospital surroundings had not helped their recovery. 31 per cent thought it had made their health worse.
- Only 20 per cent felt they were treated with respect and dignity by staff, while 17 per cent said they were never treated with dignity and respect by staff.

Source: Mind (2004: 3)

Service users commented that:

- 'I had to spend the first night on a fold-up bed in the male wing because there were no beds on the female dormitory.'
- 'I was too scared to sleep.'
- 'I was disgusted by the way I was treated by my consultant. I felt bullied and threatened. I was a voluntary patient but when I decided to leave the hospital I was threatened with being sectioned.'
- 'A staff member said "cheer up, at least you're not black or gay".'
- 'They did absolutely nothing when I was sexually molested and didn't even write it down.'
- 'The complete absence of any meaningful daily activity led my condition to worsen.'
- 'There was little therapy apart from smoking and television.'
- 'The ward was dirty and unkempt. Carpets were badly stained and burnt. Furniture was damaged. My room smelt of urine. Doors were locked, even though it was an open ward. The whole environment gave out a clear message that you were not worth caring about and did not deserve to be looked after.'
- 'The staff did not encourage patients to participate in the few therapeutic activities that were available. They often overreacted to situations, which made them worse. Making sure that patients were given access to fresh air and exercise was not considered a priority.'
- 'The staff were go, go, go all day. They were pushed by management to breaking point.'
- 'The whole ward should be demolished and started again. It is unsafe. Drugs are being bought and sold in the ward. Staff do not seem interested in their jobs. Patients are left to wander around with nothing to do (it is a long day). The place smells like an old ashtray. Service users all feel demoralised and get little help from staff.'

Source: Mind (2004: 6–19)

Also in 2004, the Sainsbury Centre for Mental Health carried out a survey of acute mental health inpatient wards in England:

- The national average vacancy rate for qualified nurses on acute wards was 13 per cent.
- The national average sickness rate among ward staff was 6.8 per cent.
- The national average use of bank and agency staff per week per ward was 152 hours (equal to more than four full-time staff).
- 26 per cent of wards had lost staff to community teams in the past year.
- 12 per cent of ward managers had no administrative support.
- 48 per cent wards did not have a lead consultant and 13 per cent had no ward manager or nurse above grade F.
- 18 per cent of ward managers reported they did not have access to a Psychiatric Intensive Care Unit (PICU).

- Communication with community teams was felt to be poor during patient admissions by 16 per cent ward managers.
- Cognitive behavioural therapy was available on fewer than 20 per cent of wards.
- Three-quarters of managers believed their wards offered a good environment for mental health care, while 86 per cent said their wards were safe places to be.
- 55 per cent of wards had a cultural sensitivity policy, but in a quarter of wards no staff had had cultural sensitivity training.

Source: Sainsbury Centre for Mental Health (2004: 2)

In 2005, the former Healthcare Commission (2005) published results of a national audit of violent incidents in mental health and learning disability wards and units. Key factors felt to be contributing to violent incidents included: unsafe environments, inadequate staffing, overcrowding, substance abuse, high levels of boredom, and limitations in staff training in the prevention and management of violence. In 2008, the same body (Healthcare Commission, 2008) reviewed the quality and safety of care provided by all 69 NHS trusts providing mental health acute inpatient care. Despite many positives, no trust scored 'excellent' on all four of the key criteria (acute care pathway, whole person care, involvement of service users and carers, and safety), 39 per cent were scored weak on involving users and carers and around one in nine trusts were scored weak on whole person care and safety. Although progress had been made in some areas, the audit identified four key priority areas:

1. Putting a greater focus on the individual and care that is personalised.
2. Ensuring the safety of service users, staff and visitors.
3. Providing appropriate and safe interventions.
4. Increasing the effectiveness of the acute care pathway.

While many of the negative aspects of the hospital stay relate to the trends and pressures in acute care described above, Quirk *et al.*'s (2006) study of three acute psychiatric wards in London makes a fascinating contribution to this debate through the notion of a 'permeable institution'. While mental health hospitals are often seen as closed environments, Quirk *et al.* demonstrate how much interaction there is with the outside world – including turnover of patients (with increasingly short stays and high turnover), patients' links to families and friends, other professionals visiting the ward, etc. Although this is positive in so far as it reduces the danger of institutionalisation, it can also cause risks, with unwanted people coming onto the ward (for example, a former patient returning to threaten staff, drug dealing, etc). As a result, staff face a series of legal, ethical and practical dilemmas, including (Quirk *et al.*, 2006: 2116):

- How to respect the freedom of movement of informal patients while detaining those held involuntarily under mental health legislation.
- How to provide acceptable accommodation for people with a prolonged stay as well as acute care for people in a crisis.

- How to prevent informal patients from engaging in criminal or antisocial activity.
- How to help people maintain positive links to the outside world while also preventing the intrusion of damaging or antisocial influences.

In response to all these issues, a number of commentators have suggested that this may, in part, be the result of a tendency to focus on the development of community-based services, effectively turning something of a blind eye to conditions in acute care. Thus, Higgins *et al.* (1999: 52) have argued that:

> In recent years, political and managerial attention has focused predominantly on the consequences of the failure of National Health Service community services to provide effective care to people with severe mental illness in the United Kingdom ... However, what happens inside hospitals has received less scrutiny. Not since the reports and inquiries of the 1960s and early 1970s into the poor standards of nursing care provided in some long-stay psychiatric hospitals has hospital care been under the spotlight.

As the Sainsbury Centre for Mental Health (1998b: 11) concludes:

> There is scant evidence about the effectiveness and quality of care of acute wards in dealing with people with psychiatric problems. Relatively little is known about exactly who are the people who stay on acute psychiatric wards and what happens to them while they are there. There is a sense that hospital care is a black box, with people entering and leaving, and we have high but vague expectations about what happens in between. The issue about quality and effectiveness of care is crucial, however, not least because acute inpatient treatment is the most intensive and expensive form of mental healthcare – but also because patients on acute wards have to sacrifice both privacy and freedom during their stay. Moreover, they are unpopular with many of these patients. It is crucial, therefore, that hospital stays are used to best advantage, treating the patients who need and benefit most from this regime and for the shortest necessary time.

Leaving hospital

Although hospital discharge can be problematic for other user groups such as older people, it is also a central concern in acute psychiatric inpatient services. In 1999, a DH-funded study of acute psychiatric nursing care found that the pressure on beds meant that patients were discharged from hospital before they had sufficiently recovered and were often quickly readmitted after their community services broke down (Higgins *et al.*, 1999). At the same time, research by the Sainsbury Centre for Mental Health (1998b) indicated that discharge arrangements were often dealt with in an ad hoc way during ward rounds, with only one-third of patients receiving a formal or separate meeting to plan for leaving hospital. Most patients had very little notice of their discharge and had little involvement in discussions about their futures. Involvement from carers and community staff was also limited. These are fairly common themes in the literature, with an overall sense that current inpatient care may not be enough or the best way of preparing people for discharge or trying to resolve longer-term issues. As one woman being discharged from hospital said in a study of service users' experiences (Nolan *et al.*, 2011: 363):

> They have no idea what my situation is like at home, the endless boredom, lack of social contact, it's intolerable at times. I am told I should be coping, but the reality is I need more help to change my life than is available here. I can see no way of breaking this pattern. (female, 38, with 2 previous admissions)

Although some patients may be discharged from hospital prematurely, others may remain in hospital much longer than they need to because of a lack of community services. In 1999, a review of alternatives to acute psychiatric beds found that between 20 and 60 per cent of patients could be better placed (although the latter figure was produced by a study outside the UK) (Bartlett *et al.*, 1999). The following year, a systematic review of the appropriateness of acute bed usage found that between 24 and 58 per cent of days of care were not considered appropriate (McDonagh *et al.*, 2000). In both studies, key factors included a lack of housing, a lack of community services (such as group homes), a lack of rehabilitation services and, in a small number of cases, the need for higher levels of care. Similar findings have also been produced by a range of other commentators, suggesting that a substantial number of people would be able to leave hospital if community alternatives were more readily available (see Table 5.1).

Table 5.1	Delayed hospital discharges	
Study	**Rate of delayed discharge**	**Causes/possible alternatives**
Fulop *et al.* (1992)	37 per cent	Lack of accommodation and long-stay hospital care
Lelliott and Wing (1994)	61 per cent	Lack of continuing care provision, rehabilitation, supported group homes or low-staffed hostels
Fulop *et al.* (1996)	23 per cent	Professional support in the patient's home, housing/more appropriate housing, group homes, rehabilitation

Study	Rate of delayed discharge	Causes/possible alternatives
Koffman *et al.* (1996)	24 per cent	Residential and/or nursing home care, total dependency psychiatric care, community services (such as day care or home care), housing
Connolly and Ritchie (1997)	54 per cent in 1994 46 per cent in 1995	Some patients with stays of three months or more could have been discharged to other NHS services (for people with complex needs), supported accommodation or mainstream housing
Beck *et al.* (1997)	42 per cent	Of patients with stays of at least 60 days, some could have been discharged to alternatives such as a non-acute low-level observation inpatient facility, the patient's own home, a group home, day hospitals and support by a CPN
Minghella and Ford (1997)	10 per cent	Problems finding suitable accommodation (including forensic care)
Shepherd *et al.* (1997)	27 per cent	Lack of supported housing/ rehabilitation services, secure accommodation and specialist services
Sainsbury Centre for Mental Health (1998b)	19 per cent (after one week)	Lack of accommodation, home-based support and rehabilitation, and patients requiring higher levels of supervision
Bartlett *et al.* (1999)	Systematic review	A spectrum of provision is required, including support at home as well as residential care staffed by specialist nurses
McDonagh *et al.* (2000)	Systematic review	Delayed discharge could be reduced by services such as more appropriate housing/housing plus support, group homes, rehabilitation and services with higher levels of supervision
Paton *et al.* (2004)	46 per cent	Insufficient specialist resources for placement or return home, lack of money to finance placements, no alternative to acute ward and users and carers refusing placements/ refusing to pay for care

Study	Rate of delayed discharge	Causes/possible alternatives
Lewis and Glasby (2006)	Average of 7 per cent beds (or 1,691 bed days) lost per trust	Lack of funding, awaiting residential/nursing home, awaiting further NHS care, awaiting assessment, awaiting domiciliary package and/or patient/family exercising choice
Tyrer *et al.* (2006)	39 per cent	Not explored in detail

Source: Adapted/updated from Glasby and Lester (2004)

Grounds for optimism?

To date, much of the research and commentary in this area has raised serious concerns about the quality of inpatient care. While these remain significant issues, it is important to emphasise that there have been a number of national initiatives to improve acute care. At a local level, there is also a range of activities under way to tackle some of the problems identified in this chapter, and these should not be overlooked. As Quirk and Lelliott (2001: 1571) observe:

> [Research to date has] generated much useful information about what happens on acute psychiatric wards ... However, such accounts are limited by the fact that they tend to present an unremittingly bleak picture of life on the wards – something that is unlikely to be the case for all the patients all of the time and across all wards.

One example is the Sainsbury Centre for Mental Health's Acute Solutions project (2006a), which sought to build on previous negative research findings by working in depth with four case study sites to find ways of improving acute mental health care. Their summary of *The Search For Acute Solutions* helpfully describes the approach taken, the results produced and the lessons learned, seeking to demonstrate what can be achieved in the current system by enabling staff and service users to make changes at ward level. At a national level, there has been additional guidance, extra investment and a series of policy and practice developments (see Box 5.6). Even more important has been an explicit acknowledgement that problems exist within acute care, that inpatient services have not received the same emphasis as community services in the past and that this needs to change (Rooney, 2002: 3):

> Too often acute inpatient services are not working to everyone's satisfaction. A range of reports and surveys and the reported experience of service users and staff have clearly and consistently demonstrated a high level of criticism and dissatisfaction with current provision ... It is clear

that the physical, psychological and therapeutic environment of care must all be attended to.

Despite these grounds for optimism, a number of doubts remain about what the future holds for acute inpatient care. In particular, the persistent and long-standing nature of many of the issues outlined above suggests that the problems associated with acute inpatient mental health services are extremely complicated and entrenched. As an example, Box 5.7 compares findings from the hospital scandals of the 1960s and 1970s with a 2003 Commission for Health Improvement report on mental health services, providing a stark reminder of the relatively low base from which acute care is starting and a traditional lack of progress in hospital services. While this 2003 report pre-dates many more recent changes, the fact that so many of the key issues have remained so difficult to tackle over many years suggests that an even bigger shift in thinking may be required in future if current changes are to be truly effective.

Box 5.6	**Positive developments in acute care**

Star Wards is a national project run by the charity Bright to work with mental health trusts to improve mental health inpatients' daily experiences and treatment outcomes. It currently has over 400 wards as members (see www.starwards.org). The former NHS Institute sought to support work to improve the effectiveness, safety and reliability of mental health wards through its *Productive Mental Health Ward: Releasing Time to Care* initiative (see www.institute.nhs.uk). National and regional work has been undertaken in order to improve ways in which inpatient services are reviewed, improve workforce development, promote good practice, to improve the sexual safety of mental health service users, to improve the management of violence and to promote race equality (see CSIP/National Mental Health Partnership/DH, 2006).

Some wards have been introducing changes to working practices based on concepts of recovery and on techniques such as Wellness Recovery Action Planning (WRAP – see www.mentalhealthrecovery.com).

The Royal College of Psychiatrists has developed AIMS (a standards-based accreditation service to improve the quality of care in psychiatric wards – see www.rcpsych.ac.uk/clinicalservicestandards/centreforqualityimprovement.aspx). There has also been much greater recognition of the needs of young people in adult mental health inpatient services, with this issue highlighted nationally by the Children's Commissioner for England (11 Million, 2007) and through new standards developed by the Royal College of Psychiatrists (2009).

Box 5.7	Long-standing problems in acute care

Inquiries into the hospital scandals of the 1960s and 1970s identify a range of contributing factors, including:

- The isolated nature of some acute services (including not only geographical isolation, but also staff being left in charge of large numbers of people and lack of visits by medical staff).
- Closed, institutional settings and a tendency to suppress complaints.
- A corruption of care (focusing on the maintenance of order and routine rather than on providing care).
- Failures of leadership.
- Staff shortages and inadequate training.

Source: Martin (1984)

The former Commission for Health Improvement (2003) identified a very similar list of issues in the early 2000s, suggesting a considerable lack of progress over time:

- the isolated nature of services;
- institutional environments;
- low staffing levels and high use of bank and agency staff;
- closed cultures; and
- poor clinical leadership and supervision.

Conclusion

Despite recent positive developments, acute mental health services seem to be starting from a low base with a recent history characterised by relative policy neglect. Following official commitments to community care, the nature and quality of acute services has attracted less attention, with evidence of a range of serious issues rising over time. Thankfully, this is now beginning to change, and a number of new initiatives have sought to tackle some of the long-standing issues at stake. However, the long-standing nature of these issues suggests that there are few 'easy answers' and that the way forward may lie in taking a whole systems approach that considers the full range of mental health services. Many of the problems of over-occupancy, poor-quality acute care and delayed discharges cannot be resolved in isolation, but require concerted action across the full range of available services. Ultimately, as Higgins *et al.* (1999: 61) observe:

> Without close examination of what is happening in hospitals … and without suitable remedial action, it is conceivable that hospital care might once again be subject to the scrutiny and criticism that cast a shadow over psychiatric services in the 1960s and 1970s. Nurses and other mental health professionals need to work together to prevent such circumstances arising and to develop the full spectrum of services required in each locality.

While much of this is about resources, collaboration and policy focus, it is also about values and attitudes – and these may be even harder to change. Despite some recent grounds for optimism, it remains to be seen whether the recent 'rediscovery' of acute care and the many shortcomings that exist in inpatient services will be sufficient to tackle the scale and complexity of the problem. As a psychiatrist in Hardcastle *et al.*'s (2007: 82–3) study of the views of service users, carers and professionals has suggested:

> Many of our hospitals are now frankly scandalous. We can only guess at the horror of patients and carers as they walk (or are dragged) into a ward that is filthy, offers no sexual privacy and has an atmosphere of predatory violence. Partly this is a matter of resources. The impression has grown that community care equals success and in-patient care equals failure; so all the fancy new money and creative thinking has gone into community teams. Hospital staff and patients have been left behind, demoralised and institutionalised, cut off from the worlds outside the walls. Ideally, hospital and community should be complementary parts of one mental health service, equally well resourced, with the integration of patients' and carers' needs, across the boundaries. And there are plenty of examples now of in-patient care broken down into smaller, modern, short-stay units nearer to patients' homes. We should not have to put up with old-style, isolated 'bins', where I did most of my training decades ago. But it is also a matter of attitudes too.

Reflection exercises

1. Hospital services (*exercise for all practitioners*)

Arrange a visit to your local mental health hospital:

- How old or new is the building – and what impression does it give from outside?
- How did you feel when you went it – was it welcoming or intimidating, for example?
- How clean was it?
- Did it feel a good place to be delivering support to people in crisis?
- What were staff doing and how much interaction was there between staff and patients?
- What was there to do for patients?
- Would you like to work there, visit a friend or be a patient there?

2. Hospital services (*exercise for hospital staff*)

- Why did you choose to work in a hospital setting and what do you like about your job?
- What do you find difficult/what frustrates you?

- What impact do you feel you have – both as an individual and your service generally?
- How could the service be improved for service users, families and staff?
- Even in a small way, what could you do personally as an individual or as a team?

3. Hospital services (exercise for community staff)

- How well do services support people as they move in and out of hospital?
- How much contact do you have with hospital services – and how much of your time do you spend in inpatient settings? How much time do hospital staff spend in community settings – and are there any ways of increasing contact or knowledge of each other's roles?
- How did service users with whom you work experience hospital and what could be done to improve services?

Further resources

1. National overviews of mental health inpatient care are provided by the former Healthcare Commission (2008), the National Patient Safety Agency (2006) and the Sainsbury Centre for Mental Health (2004). From a service user and voluntary sector perspective, Rethink, Sane, the Zito Trust and the National Association of Psychiatric Intensive Care Units (2006) have produced their *Behind Closed Doors* summary of the current state and future recommendations for acute mental health care.

2. Although dated, the Sainsbury Centre for Mental Health's *Acute Problems* (1998b, 2004) provides a key analysis of the quality of care in acute psychiatric care.

3. The DH's *Mental Health Policy Implementation Guide: Acute Adult Inpatient Care Provision* makes a series of recommendations about future policy and practice (Rooney, 2002). An additional guide focuses on education, training and continuing professional development (Clarke, 2004). A 2006 update on the National Acute Inpatient Project summarises both actions and aspirations around service improvement in acute inpatient care (CSIP/National Mental Health Partnership/DH, 2006). CSIP's (2007) *A Positive Outlook* provides a good practice toolkit to improve discharge from inpatient mental health care. Where localities have used out-of-area services to reduce demand on acute care, a series of national bodies have collaborated to produce a toolkit to take stock and

potentially reduce reliance on such short-term solutions (Ryan *et al.*, 2011).

4. The Royal College of Psychiatrists' Centre for Quality Improvement has developed a system of accreditation to identify and acknowledge wards that have a high standard of organisation and patient care (Accreditation for Acute Inpatient Mental Health Services (AIMS) – www.rcpsych.ac.uk/pdf/Standards%20for% 20Inpatient%20Wards%20-%20Working%20Age%20Adults%20- %20Fourth%20Edition.pdf). The Royal College also runs a Quality Network for Inpatient Child and Adolescent Mental Health Services (QNIC) (www.rcpsych.ac.uk).

5. Above all, the user-centred accounts of hospital services cited in this chapter give a clear indication of users' priorities for change and provide very powerful and graphic descriptions of people's experiences as inpatients (see, for example, Sainsbury Centre for Mental Health, 1998b; Goodwin *et al.*, 1999; Baker, 2000; Kumar *et al.*, 2001; Quirk *et al.*, 2004; Mind, 2004). An excellent resource is Hardcastle *et al.*'s (2007) *Experiences of Mental Health In-patient Care* – an edited collection of accounts by service users, carers and mental health professionals.

6 Forensic Mental Health Services

In this chapter we discuss:

- The 'mad' vs 'bad' debate.
- Forensic mental health services.
- Mental health needs in prison.
- Inappropriate placements in secure services.
- Possible ways forward.

The 'mad' vs 'bad' debate

We know from the wider literature that people with mental health problems face considerable discrimination, poverty and social exclusion (see Chapters 4 and 9), factors known to contribute to criminal activity in the wider population. Moreover, some people with mental health problems probably commit some crimes knowing that what they are doing is illegal – in such situations, the criminal activity may be little different from crimes committed by people without mental health problems and should be punished through the criminal justice system. According to Sayce (2000: 226), therefore, there are a number of key messages which we need to test out on the public and the media:

- Most crime is committed by people without mental health problems.
- People with mental health problems often commit crimes for the same reasons as everyone else (poverty, drink and drugs, family/relationship frustrations).
- It is extremely rare for people with mental health problems to attack someone they don't know.
- People with mental health problems are more often victims than perpetrators of crime.
- People with mental health problems can usually be held responsible for their crimes.

When someone commits a crime that the public finds particularly hard to understand, an immediate response is often to question whether the person concerned is either 'mad' or 'bad': did they behave as they did because they are 'evil', or are they experiencing some form of mental health problem? Whereas many would see the need to punish the 'bad', they may often feel that someone with a mental health problem may not have been 'in their right mind' and hence not responsible for their action. As a result, such a person should receive treatment and care in the health service, rather than punishment in prison.

In practice, such distinctions are sometimes hard to make (especially where the crime is horrific and difficult to comprehend). Examples include infamous figures such as Ian Brady, Myra Hindley, Harold Shipman and Ian Huntley. While these are extreme cases, they nevertheless illustrate the complexities at stake, as someone with a mental health problem assessed as not responsible for their actions will 'escape' prison and be treated in a health rather than a penal setting. Of course, whether entering the mental health system in such circumstances is an 'escape' is a moot point. Arguably, the stigma of using forensic mental health services is so significant that some would consider it as bad as or worse than the stigma of having been in prison. However, the fact remains that the initial assessment is crucial to establish why someone acted as they did, whether or not they were responsible for their actions and what should happen to them next.

Forensic mental health

While the association between mental health problems and violent crime is vastly overstated in the public imagination, there is a small minority of people with serious mental health problems who do pose a risk to the public and who do commit crimes – sometimes very serious ones. Although high-quality community and hospital services will be sufficient to meet the needs of many people, there may always be a small group of people who require even greater levels of support and supervision than is possible in these settings. These people fall under the remit of forensic mental health services. As McFadyen (1999: 1436–7) explains:

> Forensic mental health services deal with those mentally ill people whose presentation has been assessed as requiring a more focused level of expertise and/or increased levels of physical security. Some of these people will have exhibited behaviours which present major challenges, with or without associated violent conduct, beyond the capabilities of general psychiatric services. Others will be mentally disordered offenders who have broken the law or who are deemed to have the propensity to do so. Some patients will have been identified at the level of general NHS psychiatric services and some via the criminal justice system. Of the latter, some will be on remand … Others, however, will be convicted prisoners … who are subsequently transferred from prison during the course of their penal sentence.

From this initial extract, a number of key issues are immediately apparent that are explored in more detail later in this chapter:

- Forensic mental health services are extremely complex, with different routes in and a wide range of service users.
- Forensic services potentially involve a large number of agencies (such as health care, social care, probation and the prison service).
- By definition, forensic services will be working with people who may display extremely challenging behaviour and who may have been found to be too difficult to work with in other settings.

This complexity is also emphasised by McCann (1999: 65):

> Mentally disordered offenders ... span the range of mental health problems and diagnoses, and the spectrum of criminal offences. Often their needs are complex and involve a number of agencies ... Invariably there is also an element of political or media interest ... This pressure on services to make the 'right' decisions, often with inadequate information, places professionals in a vulnerable position, both clinically and personally. It is understandable therefore that professionals are cautious, treading carefully the narrow path between their roles as therapist and custodian. Generally however the needs of mentally disordered offenders are no different to any other individual with mental health problems, and they require access to a similar range of services.

As McCann (1999) continues, forensic mental health services are typically divided into three different categories depending on the level of service users' needs:

1. Low security services tend to be based near general psychiatric wards in NHS hospitals, but often have higher staffing ratios (also known as psychiatric intensive care units or PICUs).
2. Medium secure services often operate on a regional basis and usually consist of a number of locked wards with a greater number and a wider range of staff.
3. High security services are provided by the three special hospitals (Ashworth, Broadmoor and Rampton). These are characterised by much greater levels of security and care for people with mental health problems who pose an immediate and serious risk to others.

There are currently around 6,000 people in secure mental health services in England (680 in high security, 2,800 in medium security and 2,500 in low security) (Joint Commissioning Panel for Mental Health (2013).

In addition, a range of services has been developed to meet the needs of mentally disordered offenders in the community, either with a forensic specialist working with a community mental health team (an *integrated* model) or with forensic specialists working as a separate specialist team (a *parallel* model) (Judge *et al.*, 2004; Mohan *et al.*, 2004; Mohan and Fahy, 2006). These received particular impetus following the creation of Multi-agency Protection Arrangements (MAPPAs), statutory local partnerships introduced and then strengthened under the 2000 and 2003 Criminal Justice Acts to assess and manage the risk of violent and sexual offenders.

Over time, a series of official reviews have emphasised the principles that should underpin forensic services, often building on concepts first articulated as part of the Reed Report (DH/Home Office, 1992: 7). This stated that services should be provided:

- With regard to the quality of care and proper attention to the needs of individuals.
- As far as possible, in the community, rather than institutional settings.
- Under conditions of no greater security than are justified by the degree of danger they present to themselves or others.
- In such a way as to maximise rehabilitation and the chances of sustaining an independent life.
- As near as possible to their own homes or families.

In seeking to deliver these aspirations, policy has also tended to emphasise:

1. The concept of 'equivalence' (DH/HM Prison Service/National Assembly for Wales, 2001: 5) – a recognition that people in prison should 'have access to the same range and quality of services appropriate to their needs as are available to the general population through the NHS'.
2. Diversion schemes to ensure that people with mental health problems are moved away from the criminal justice system towards the NHS so that their needs can be more appropriately met (Home Office, 1990). This can happen at a number of key stages, including on arrest, during interview, after a court appearance or while on remand/bail. Although such schemes can be effective and are often well regarded, there is ongoing evidence of a failure to identify and refer relevant people, problems around training and a lack of knowledge, and more general concerns about the experience of people with mental health problems within the criminal justice system, both as suspects and as witnesses (see, for example, Independent Police Complaints Commission, 2008; NACRO, 2005; Thompson et al., 2004; Vaughan et al., 2001; Watson, 1997; Bradley, 2009; Pakes and Winstone, 2010; HMI Probation et al., 2009).

In many ways, this chapter reflects similar themes to the rest of the book. As with hospital services, there is considerable evidence to suggest that many people in forensic mental health services may be inappropriately placed. At the same time, delivering effective forensic services requires a high degree of partnership working, and raises particular issues with regard to gender and ethnicity (Chapter 9). In many ways, forensic services are at the 'extreme' end of the mental health system, and any findings from general psychiatric services will probably apply to an even greater extent in forensic mental health, where the issues at stake are even more complex and high profile. To supplement this material, the remainder of this chapter explores three key issues:

1. the prevalence of mental health needs in prison;
2. inappropriate placements in secure services; and
3. possible ways forward.

Mental health needs in prison

Despite attempts to divert people with mental health problems away from the criminal justice system, research for the Ministry of Justice (2009) suggests that adults with mental health problems are overrepresented in the prison population (see also Table 6.1), that linked factors such as homelessness and substance misuse increase the risk of offending, that prejudicial attitudes within the criminal justice system can result in negative justice outcomes for people with mental health problems and that discrimination may prevent people from disclosing their mental health status and from seeking support. When people need access to specialist mental health services outside prison, moreover, there can often be significant delays – and an estimated 3,000–3,700 people in prison have problems serious enough to need urgent transfer to hospital (Rickford and Edgar, 2005; Olumoroti et al., 2009). All this contributes to a situation where, according to the Prison Reform Trust, we are doing 'too little too late' (Edgar and Rickford, 2009: 63):

> A significant number of prisons receive people who have a series mental illness and for whom prison in not a suitable environment. Caring for these people places intolerable strains on prisons, and exhausts disproportionate amounts of resources and staff time. From the perspective of many boards [Independent Monitoring Boards that monitor prison services], these prisoners should not have been sent to prison, and were not diverted when they should have been by police and court liaison services, or supported adequately by mental health services in the community. Many prisons lack the resources they would need to conduct full psychiatric assessments of those they receive ... the shift of commissioning responsibility to PCTs has resulted in an improvement ... However, there remains a huge gap, as the mental health needs of prisoners have expanded in numbers, severity and complexity. There are some signs of improvement in the capacity to transfer mentally ill people in prison to suitable services outside. However, intolerable delays were reported by some boards. A wider concern is that far too often, prisons use segregation units to hold people who are seriously ill until a transfer can be arranged.

Clearly, this raises serious questions about the role that prisons may be being asked to play in caring for people with mental health problems and the extent to which prison staff are equipped to fulfil this role. While a detailed consideration of prison health care is beyond the scope of this book, the government has recognised that this is a real problem (DH/HM Prison Service/National Assembly for Wales, 2001: 5; see also Box 6.1):

Table 6.1	Mental health needs in prison	
	Prevalence among prisoners (16 years +) (Singleton *et al.*, 1998) (%)	Prevalence in general population (16–64) (Singleton *et al.*, 2001) (%)
Psychosis	8	0.5
Personality disorder	66	5.3
Neurotic disorder	45	13.8
Drug dependency	45	5.2
Alcohol dependency	30	11.5

Source: Sainsbury Centre for Mental Health (2009c: 2)

The way mental health services are currently organised ... do not meet prisoners' needs. Ineffective and inflexible services that do not match identified health needs inevitably result in poor outcomes for prisoners, wasted resources and demotivated staff. There are too many prisoners in too many prisons who, despite the best efforts of committed prison health care and NHS staff, receive no treatment, or inappropriate treatment ... from staff with the wrong mix of skills and in the wrong kind of setting.

While the numbers in Table 6.1 are dated, the Joint Commissioning Panel for Mental Health (2013: 10) observes that:

Despite the relative increase in secure services over the 10 years since some of these studies, it is likely that these figures have not changed substantively, while the prison population over the same period has increased by 66%.

In response, there have been a number of policy initiatives to improve prison health care, including:

- *Changing the Outlook*, a joint DH/Prison Service programme to improve mental health care in prisons.
- The transfer of responsibility for commissioning health services for prisoners from the Prison Service to the NHS (from 2006).
- The development of in-reach services to support prison-based staff and to focus on prisoners with the most severe mental health problems.
- The creation of a National Health and Social Care in Criminal Justice programme.

■ An ongoing series of reviews of the experience of people with mental health problems in prison and in the criminal justice system more generally (see, for example, Ministry of Justice, 2009; Edgar and Rickford, 2009; Bradley, 2009).

Box 6.1	Safer prisons

According to a study of 157 prison suicides, the *National Confidential Inquiry into Suicides and Homicides by People with Mental Illness* (Shaw *et al.*, 2003) concluded that:

■ 30 (21 per cent) were known to have been victims of bullying.
■ 32 (21 per cent) did not take part in any prison activities.
■ 57 (42 per cent) had received no visits prior to death.
■ 19 (18 per cent) had experienced a recent family bereavement or terminal illness in a family member.
■ 110 (72 per cent) had at least one psychiatric diagnosis.
■ 95 (62 per cent) had a history of drug misuse.
■ 46 (31 per cent) had a history of alcohol misuse.
■ 78 (53 per cent) had a history of self-harm.
■ 89 (57 per cent) had symptoms of psychiatric disturbance on reception to prison.
■ 46 (30 per cent) had a history of contact with NHS mental health services.

While many of these people had been referred to a health professional, admitted to the prison health care inpatient unit or placed on medium or high levels of observation, there were a number of concerns. For example:

■ It was unusual for information to be requested from a GP or from mental health services.
■ 15 per cent had no further contact with health care staff after reception.
■ 22 (15 per cent) of suicides were seen by health staff as preventable.
■ There was a range of antecedents, including expressions of suicidal ideas, deliberate self-harm, adverse life events, bullying, bereavement and family/relationship problems.
■ In seven cases a transfer to an NHS hospital was awaited.
■ Between 1996 and 2000, 354 people died within a year following release from prison. Eighty (23 per cent) died within the first month following release, suggesting the need for better follow-up in the community.

Altogether, 141 (90 per cent) of the 157 suicides in this study could have been seen as 'at risk' at reception to prison because of a history of previous NHS mental health care, a lifetime history of mental disorder, current symptoms, current treatment, a history of drug misuse, alcohol misuse or self-harm (p. 43).

However, a key risk in the current economic climate is that increases in poverty, unemployment and financial pressures coupled with cuts to front-line health, social care and criminal justice services could reduce access to support in the community and lead to more people in future falling through the gap in current services and ending up in prison (as the one 'service' which can't really turn people away).

The level of inappropriate placements in secure services

An additional factor that may contribute to high levels of unmet mental health needs in prison may be an inappropriate use of existing bed capacity in secure services. With the current system having developed piecemeal over many years, there remains something of a fragmented approach. According to a number of commentators, somewhere between 37 and 75 per cent of patients in maximum-security hospitals may not need the services provided there (see, for example, Coid and Kahtan, 2000; McCann, 1999; McKenna et al., 1999; Vaughan, 1999) – and similar problems of inappropriate placement seem to exist within low- and medium-secure services too (see, for example, Dabbs and Isherwood, 2000; Dolan and Lawson, 2001; McIntyre, 1999; Beer et al., 2005; McClean, 2010). When capacity problems occur, patients have to wait to access the services most appropriate for their needs and increasing use is made of independent sector provision (Coid et al., 2001; Lelliott et al., 2001; Polczyk-Przybyla and Gournay 1999), often some distance away from the area in which the individual concerned lives. This is not only expensive, but also contravenes the stated aim of supporting service users in their own homes or under conditions of no greater security than are justified by the degree of danger they present to themselves or others. As McIntyre (1999: 382) observes:

> The inappropriate placement of people in … secure services has long been recognised. The need to develop services that more appropriately meet the needs of these people … has similarly long been recognised. However progress is slow … Absence of [alternative service provision] represents a significant drain on precious financial resources; it forces people needlessly and without clinical justification to be required to live in conditions of significant security and curtailment of liberty, potentially in breach of civil rights. It has to be asked how much longer this will continue unchallenged.

Possible ways forward

As highlighted throughout this book, the provision of effective mental health services requires a wide range of agencies to work closely together (see also Box 6.2 for additional quotes illustrating this issue). A good example is provided by Vaughan et al. (2000), whose study of community teams providing support to mentally disordered offenders found that this user group had complex and multiple needs which often fell outside the range of skills and services that individual teams could offer. As a result, community mental health teams felt deskilled,

> **Box 6.2   Partnership working in forensic mental health**
>
> The system of care for offenders with mental disorders in the United Kingdom has developed piecemeal over the years, and responsibilities have been divided between the criminal justice system, the National Health Service, and ... social services departments. The specialized secure facilities have also evolved in an ad hoc way throughout the country, without standardized models of service delivery.
>
> *Source*: Badger *et al.* (1999: 627)
>
> In this survey, most community services were not organized in a way that facilitates contact with mentally disordered offenders, who tend to shun services. For the most part, teams ... operate within their own strict boundaries and there is a general reluctance to work with other client groups. Each group has its own distinctive cohort of mentally disordered offenders but often cannot meet all of their needs due to limitations within each service. Because of the compartmentalized nature of the services, gaining access to a wider range of skills is difficult. Accordingly, many mentally disordered offenders are denied a comprehensive range of interventions and sometimes get only partial help for their problems.
>
> *Source*: Vaughan *et al.* (2000: 583)
>
> Effective screening of mentally-ill defendants in the criminal court system requires cooperation between legal professionals in the criminal justice system and health and social care professionals in the mental-health system. This inter-agency working, though, can be problematic ... [In this study] results showed that both agencies were uncertain of their ability to work with the other and there is little training that supports them in this.
>
> *Source*: Hean *et al.* (2011: 196)

unsupported and frustrated by the reluctance of some support services to accept referrals for this group. Team members also highlighted a lack of interagency communication and cooperation, with each agency reluctant to accept ownership of mentally disordered offenders. From the perspective of probation teams, however, mental health services were seen as difficult to access, slow to respond and poor at sharing information. As a result, many individual teams adopted something of a 'siege mentality', reluctant to offer a service to people outside their normal referral criteria and spending a significant amount of time disputing responsibility for 'borderline' cases (pp. 580–1). Similar findings also emerge from Hean *et al.*'s (2011) study into the potential for joint training between criminal justice and mental health staff, which found that collaboration between the legal/criminal justice system and the health and social care system may be damaged by a lack of joint awareness and could be improved by greater inter-professional training.

Similar themes have also emerged from Hill *et al.*'s (2007) study of psychiatrists' attitudes towards forensic psychiatry, with some of the former feeling that forensic services should have a lower admission threshold, that they have been over-funded compared to other services, that they should integrate more closely with non-secure psychiatric services and that they should offer more community services rather than focusing on inpatient care. As one psychiatrist commented (p. 223):

> Are forensic services and prisons the new asylums? Society is increasingly risk averse and forensic services are the 'beneficiaries' of the increased money being spent to allay these anxieties. How this affects perceptions and stigma of mental illness and medicalisation of character traits can only be negative. It also means that other more preventive measures remain under resourced and developed.

In response, there is an increasing recognition that the issues at stake are so funda-mental that only a whole systems approach will suffice. For Maguire (1999: 21), there is a need for 'a clear pathway from the point of entry into a service, through to the point of discharge, incorporating community and mainstream mental health services' (see also Markham, 2000; McFadyen, 1999). This is echoed by Vaughan (1999: 562), who suggests that 'in order to facilitate a flow-through of patients in the system as a whole, adequate provision is required at every stage of a person's illness'. Unfortunately, such a spectrum of support may be a long way from fruition in some areas, with a range of ongoing pressures preventing a more holistic approach from being developed. As an example, Coid and Dunn (2004) describe a forensic mental health system in one health and social care commu-nity only able to respond reactively to referrals from other agencies, making no sessional commitments to probation services, prisons or court diversion schemes, providing no dedicated aftercare, relying heavily on private sector provision, accumulating growing waiting lists and unable to reduce the number of people detained in maximum security hospitals who no longer require this level of supervision.

In addition to a whole system approach, there is also a need for a longer-term perspective which moves away from episodic approaches to ones which support people over time as their needs change. As an example, Davies et al. (2007) explored the long-term outcomes of people admitted to a medium secure unit from 1983 to 2003. Of 554 people, the researchers found (p. 73) that:

> After discharge the outcome for patients was poor, with a mortality rate that was six times that which one might expect; that almost half of those discharged had at least one reconviction; that almost two-thirds were readmitted within 5 years after discharge; and that their capacity to obtain and retain gainful employment was very limited.

Perhaps most significant of all is the need to develop approaches which draw more fully on the experience of service users and their families. In other chapters in this book, there are detailed accounts from a service user and/or carer perspective that provide a powerful critique of some aspects of current services. In contrast, serv-ice users and carers often only appear in the forensic mental health literature as statistics in large-scale audits of patient populations, and (with a few notable exceptions) hardly ever as real people with feelings, preferences and experiences to contribute to the debate about what works and what does not work in mental health. As McCann (1999: 67) observes:

> There is a need to foster closer working relationships with the people for whom … services are being provided. For too long forensic services have ignored the views of users and excluded their families from becoming involved. Future work should aim to build mechanisms and services that seek the involvement of users and carers, and respond to their views. It is to be hoped that this will improve as services take steps to meet their obligations to be sensitive to the needs of the communities they serve.

Against this background, there seem a number of possible areas for further exploration. Although user and carer involvement is even harder in forensic services, there are a number of studies that have managed to achieve a degree of meaningful engagement, illustrating the power of this way of working (Durcan, 2008; Spiers *et al.*, 2005; see Canning *et al.*, 2009 for an insight into the needs of carers of people in secure services). As but one example, Brooker *et al.*'s (2009) review of the service development and organisational literature on prisoners with mental disorder found only four papers describing the views of prisoners with mental health problems (in a review that looked at research since 1983 – see Morgan *et al.*, 2004; Nurse *et al.*, 2003; Spudic, 2003; Vaughan and Stevenson, 2002). While more user and carer-focused research feels important in its own right, it is also possible that such an approach will yield different results to more traditional studies. As one illustration, Walsh *et al.*'s research (2011) with young people attending a youth offending service suggests that key barriers to services were not necessarily lack of provision, but the result of 'psychological, social, structural and cultural barriers to accessing those services, including issues of understanding, stigma and confidentiality' (p. 420). Understanding such perspectives may therefore be crucial in improving future services. Even more fundamentally, there seems very little emphasis in the literature on the scope for preventive work (despite the fact that people in secure services have often had significant contact with mental health services in the past and have sometimes committed a number of crimes prior to their admission to forensic services; see, for example, Lelliott *et al.*, 2001; Maden *et al.*, 1999a, 1999b). Against this background, a fascinating insight is provided by MacInnes (2000), whose review of the literature suggests that carers often detect changes in users' behaviour before offending or admission to forensic services, but that health services do not react to carers' concerns as users are beginning to become unwell. A similar insight is provided by a small exploratory study by Ryan (2002), who examines the risk management strategies developed by carers. Although it must remain conjecture, both these contributions raise the possibility that more genuine user and carer involvement might be a way of gaining an insight into more effective means of preventing a crisis in the person being cared for.

Conclusion

Overall, there is clear evidence of a need for reform in forensic mental health services. Despite significant recent attention, there remains a sense that too often we have the wrong people in the wrong settings at the wrong time. While there seems to be greater recognition than in the past of the need for a long-term and whole systems approach that builds on the expertise of service users and carers, long-standing concerns about unmet mental health needs in prison, inappropriate placements in secure services and insufficient interagency collaboration remain. Ultimately, these overarching issues are probably more to do with ongoing debates about risk, public protection and 'mad vs bad'. Until we can achieve a degree of consensus about these as a society, then solutions to some of the more service-specific tensions within forensic mental health care may well remain elusive. Ultimately, forensic mental health seems in part the product of tensions elsewhere in the system and in broader society, and the challenges identified in this chapter are unlikely to be resolved in isolation.

Reflection exercises

1. Mental health and risk (*exercise for all practitioners*)

- Think of someone you know who has a mental health problem. How dangerous are they, and how does their mental health status affect the way you relate to them?
- When mental health is mentioned in the media, what kind of language is used and is the coverage predominantly positive or negative?
- To what extent does the image portrayed in the media reflect your experience of working with people with mental health problems?

2. Prison and/or secure services (*exercise for community services*)

- Have you ever visited a prison or a secure unit? (If so, is there opportunity to do so?)
- What do colleagues or service users tell you about what it feels like to be placed in such settings?
- How much contact does your team or profession have with such services, and how can you improve relationships?

3. Partnership working (*exercise for all readers*)

- What contact with/how much knowledge do you have of local mental health, forensic and criminal justice services?
- How can you find out more and do any local opportunities exist for people from different agencies to come together to learn more about each other?
- Given we work in a very divided system, what could you do in practical terms to promote more effective interagency working?

Further resources

1. The *National Confidential Inquiry into Suicide and Homicide by People with Serious Mental Illness* is a key resource, with a series of useful publications which shed light on issues of risk, dangerousness and suicide (www.national-confidential-inquiry.ac.uk).

2. The Sainsbury Centre for Mental Health has published a series of helpful overviews (Rutherford and Duggan, 2007; Sainsbury Centre for Mental Health, 2006b–d, 2007b–c, 2008, 2009a–c).

3. Changing the Outlook is a former government strategy for improving the quality of mental health services in prisons (DH/HM Prison Service/National Assembly for Wales, 2001), while the Bradley report (2009) reviews the extent to which people with mental health problems or learning disabilities can be diverted away from prison. The DH/NIMHE (2005) have produced an offender mental health care pathway to provide best practice guidance for providers and commissioners. Detailed policy and practice guidance is also available on the management of people with mental health problems and substance misuse problems in prison (Ministry of Justice/DH, 2009), working with personality disordered offenders (Ministry of Justice/DH, 2011), improving access to psychological therapies for offenders (DH, 2009b), diversion services for people from Black and Minority Ethnic (BME) communities (NACRO, 2009) and on police responses to people with mental health problems.

4. Work by the Prison Reform Trust provides a series of critical overviews of key policy and practice issues (see, for example, Edgar and Rickford, 2009; Rickford and Edgar, 2005).

5. Of all the sources cited in this chapter, one of the most powerful remains Durcan's (2008) study of prison mental health care, based on the experiences of prisoners themselves.

7 | User Involvement

In this chapter we discuss:

- Different definitions of the term 'mental health service user'.
- The history and current status of user involvement in mental health services.
- The importance of user involvement.
- Key barriers and examples of positive practice.
- The importance of organisational culture and personal attributes.
- Future directions.

One of the most important changes in recent years in mental health services has been an emerging voice for people who have used services – with such people being increasingly seen as 'experts by experience' (Beresford, 2003) rather than simply as passive recipients of services designed and delivered by professionals. To quote Peter Campbell, a long-term system survivor and activist:

> Living with mental distress is, and is likely to remain, a difficult experience. Nevertheless there are grounds for believing that it is a better time to be a mental health service user in the UK (and numerous other countries) than it was 25 years ago … . One important aspect to these positive changes is the greater involvement of service users in their own care and treatment, in the development of better mental health services and in social change more generally. (Campbell, 2008: 291)

One landmark in breaking down the hierarchical barrier between professionals and users of services was the public declaration by the then President of the Royal College of Psychiatrists, Mike Shooter, that he was himself a long-term user of services in relation to his experiences of depression (Crane, 2003).

What is meant by the term 'mental health service user'?

The language used to describe service users is perhaps more varied in mental health than in other areas of health and social care. User, survivor, patient, customer, citizen, consumer: all imply different notions of the roles and responsibilities of people with mental health problems and the relationship between services and users. Pilgrim and Rogers (2010) have described a useful four-part typology of users as consumers, survivors, providers or, perhaps most commonly, as patients.

'Consumerism' is a relatively new ideology within public service, linked to the rise of general management principles in the NHS and the development of a market economy through the introduction of an internal market (see Chapter 2). It is also linked to the growing acknowledgement of the importance of customer satisfaction with users of health and social care seen as 'customers' who can exercise informed choice about the services they receive and, if not satisfied, take their 'business' elsewhere. However, as Rogers and Pilgrim (2001: 169) point out:

> Many psychiatric patients do not ask for what they get – it is imposed on them. Various sections of the 1983 Mental Health Act, like its legal predecessors, are utilised to lawfully impose restraints and treatments on resentful and reluctant recipients. In such circumstances, mental patients could be construed to be consumers if being dragged off the street and force fed was a feature of being a customer in a restaurant.

Poverty can also limit choice with private sector mental health services out of bounds, while, at times of crisis, the ability and motivation to obtain information about a range of services and select between them can be difficult (Lester *et al.*, 2004). Choice also implies a possibility of exit from the system, a notion that is difficult to sustain in a society whose courts have recognised the validity of advanced directives only when they prospectively authorise treatment, not when they are used to reject the possibility of treatment (Szasz, 2003). Choice, then, appears to be a relative concept if you are a mental health service user.

In contrast, the user as 'survivor' is linked to the growth in the early 1970s of collective activities of mental health service users, initially in the Netherlands and the USA. Recognising the wisdom of the dominant trade union philosophy of the time that 'Unity is Strength', organisations such as the Campaign Against Psychiatric Oppression and the British Network for Alternatives to Psychiatry were formed. The image and term 'survivor' is very particularly chosen by groups such as Survivors Speak Out, the UK Advocacy Network (UKAN) and the Hearing Voices Network to portray a positive image of people in distress as those who had the strength to survive the mental health system. 'Survivor' also implies a notion of rejecting forms of professionally led and produced information.

Linked to this, the conceptualisation of users as 'providers' is reflected in the development of user-led services that are found in the voluntary and statutory sector across the UK. The range of user-led activities includes a spectrum of involvement from patients being mutually supported in professionally led services to projects that are managed and staffed by users themselves. The latter include safe houses and drop-in day centres and often reflect the user movement priorities of voluntary relationships, alternatives to hospital admissions and personal support.

Box 7.1	Elements of citizenship

Marshall (1950) defined citizenship rights as comprising:

- Legal or civil rights which enable the individual to participate freely in the life of the community. These rights include property and contractual rights, and rights to freedom of thought, freedom of speech, religious practice, assembly and association.
- Political rights which entitle the citizen to participate in the government of the community: the right to vote and to hold political office.
- Social and economic rights to the circumstances which enable the individual to participate in the general well-being of the community. They include rights to health care, education and welfare.

Source: Barnes and Bowl (2001: 14)

However, Pilgrim and Rogers suggest that the main way in which users have been portrayed is as 'patients' – as 'objects of the clinical gaze of mental health professionals' (2010: 217). Here, users are seen in terms of their illness, perceived as irrational and therefore as incapable of having a valid view. Patients and relatives are assumed to share the same perspective and where they do not, relatives' views often take precedence.

A further way of thinking about the meaning of the word 'user' is as a citizen. This is a fluid concept that incorporates a cluster of meanings including defined legal and social status; a means of signifying political identity; a focus of loyalty; a requirement to perform duties; expectations of rights; and a yardstick of behaviour (Heater, 1990). Marshall's (1950) classic influential analysis of the development of the meaning of citizenship over time is summarised in Box 7.1. A recent shift in the meaning of citizenship is that it entails not only rights but also a moral duty to 'to take part in constructing and maintaining the community' (Meehan, 1993: 177). Barnes and Walker (1996) similarly suggest that citizenship is closely allied to the concept of empowerment rather than consumerism, and includes the right to interactive participation and to share power with health and social care professionals.

However, with respect to mental health service users, we would argue that citizenship rights are eroded in a number of different ways. The potential for compulsory detention, community treatment orders and medical treatment administered without consent are all constraints on legal and civil rights. Above all, aspects of the social exclusion experienced by many people with mental illness severely impact on their social and economic rights (Sayce, 2001).

The history of user involvement in mental health services

Although user involvement became more prominent in the late twentieth century, protest and dissent have been a feature of the relationship between

Box 7.2	Early user voices

In 1838, John Perceval published 'A narrative of the treatment experienced by a gentleman during a state of mental derangement: designed to explain the causes and the nature of insanity and to expose the injudicious conduct pursued towards many unfortunate sufferers under that calamity'.

He described how, as a patient in Brislington House, 'men acted as though my body, soul and spirit were fairly given up to their control, to work their mischief and folly upon … I mean that I was never told such and such things we are going to do: we think it advisable to administer such and such medicine in this or that manner. I was never asked, Do you want anything? Do you wish for, prefer anything?'

Source: Perceval, 1838, quoted in Porter (1999: 182)

madness and medicine throughout the ages. Campbell (1996), for example, cites 'The Petition of the Poor Distracted People in the House of Beldam' in 1620 as an early example of collective protest. The Alleged Lunatics' Friends Society, a lobbying and campaigning organisation, was formed by 'ex-patients' in 1845 and is credited with extricating the poet John Clare from a Victorian asylum, possibly one of the first examples of peer advocacy. Occasionally, users' voices have also been heard in terms of individual experiences and treatment in early asylums (see Box 7.2). It is interesting, if disheartening, to note that despite the passage of nearly two hundred years, hopes and desires for treatment remain essentially unchanged.

During the early part of the twentieth century, individual descriptions of life in asylums continued to emerge, often in the context of the treatment of shell-shock following the First World War. However, most were again individual accounts and there was little sense of a collective user voice. It was not until the 1960s and early 1970s that the convergence of a number of different related influences from both within the UK and internationally led to a slow but progressive change in the way in which users perceived themselves, and were perceived by society. For example, social movements such as the women's movement started to develop powerful critiques of the assumptions underpinning social policy. Academic analysis of the nature and impact of the institution (Goffman, 1961) also created an impetus to think differently about patients and their environment. Parallel developments, particularly a series of reports on hospital scandals, similarly focused on the poor care and inadequate living conditions of institutionalised patients (see Chapter 2). The 1960s also saw the rise of the anti-psychiatry movement, a largely professionally led movement that opposed the traditional medical model of thinking about mental illness and suggested that the symptoms of mental distress reflected an individual's life experiences. The anti-psychiatry movement proposed that the focus should move from symptoms, to the meaning behind them, and that this could only be achieved by listening to the voice of the people experiencing the distress. In the 1970s, a rising concern about individual freedom and the civil rights of the individual, with the National Campaign for

Civil Liberties taking a leading role in this respect in the UK, also helped to shape the form and function of the mental health service user movement.

By the mid 1980s, user-based organisations included the Nottingham Advocacy Group, Survivors Speak Out and the UK Advocacy Network, while more traditional voluntary organisations also began to include a greater number of user representatives in their work. Patient councils and user groups became increasingly widespread within mental health services as service providers sought feedback directly from users. However it is also important to remember that, in 1985, the total number of mental health service user groups only numbered around a dozen (Sainsbury Centre for Mental Health, 2005).

The recent policy context of user involvement

The last 20 years have been characterised by a rapid growth in a range of different user involvement activities underpinned by a plethora of policy directives. Since the establishment of community health councils in 1973, the rhetoric of user involvement has become a central component of UK health and social policy. In 1990, the NHS and Community Care Act was the first piece of UK legislation to establish a formal requirement for user involvement in service planning. Subsequent key policies included *The Patient's Charter* (DH, 1991) and *Local Voices* (NHS Management Executive, 1992) which aimed to make services more responsive to patients' needs, but stressed consumerism rather than partnership or participation. Encouragement for user involvement in the context of mental health at that time was provided in documents such as *The Health of the Nation* (DH, 1992), the Mental Health Nursing Review, *Working in Partnership* (DH, 1994) and *Building Bridges* (DH, 1995). Indeed, *Working in Partnership* declared:

> The work of mental health nurses rests upon the relationship they have
> with people who use services. Our recommendations for future action
> start and finish with this relationship. (DH, 1994: 5)

Since 1997, 'patient and public involvement' in health care became one of the central tenets of New Labour's reforms. This has been driven by a number of different agendas, including:

- democratic right as taxpaying citizens;
- consumerist principles and the patient choice agenda;
- the desire to increase accountability within the NHS; and
- the cross-policy partnership agenda.

The justification for user involvement can be made on the basic democratic principle that, since 1948, the NHS has been paid for by taxpayers, so they should have a choice in what is funded and how services are delivered. However, as noted earlier in this chapter, the principle of consumerism has also been a strong justification for user involvement for at least two decades, with users as consumers enabled to exercise choice to ensure their needs are met. More recently, the patient choice agenda fuelled by the wider availability of information, more treatment options, a slowly growing private sector as well as consumerism (Appleby *et al.*, 2003) has become a particularly strong political imperative. *Building on the Best* (DH, 2003f) set out a series of measures to extend patient choice across primary, secondary and community care (although mental health was mentioned only briefly), and the 2012 Health and Social Care Act has been seen by many as an attempt by the Coalition to develop New Labour's market reforms yet further. In contrast, another driver is the notion of partnership – and this includes ensuring that partnerships include engaging users and other local people in ways that make sense to them and that have an impact on resources and decision making.

Under New Labour, the user involvement agenda was formalised in policy terms through *The NHS Plan* (DH, 2000a), which emphasised the government's commitment to creating a more patient-centred NHS (see also Box 7.3):

> Patients are the most important people in the health service. It doesn't always appear that way. Too many patients feel talked at, rather than listened to. This has to change. NHS care has to be shaped around the convenience and concerns of patients. To bring this about, patients must have more say in their own treatment and more influence over the way the NHS works. (DH, 2000a: 88)

In 2007, the Local Government and Public Involvement in Health Act introduced new Local Involvement Networks (LINks) in each local authority. Their role was to find out what citizens want from local services, to monitor and review the care they provide and to tell those who run and commission services

---

Box 7.3 | **Policies to encourage patient and public involvement in the NHS**

- Statutory duties placed on NHS organisations by the Health and Social Care Act 2001 ensure that patients and the public are consulted at an early stage about the planning and organisation of services.
- Local authority overview and scrutiny committees, made up of elected councillors, have powers to scrutinise the NHS. The committees can review any aspect of NHS care locally and call NHS managers to account for their actions. They have the power to refer significant changes in service provision to the secretary of state for health for a final decision.
- A national network of independent complaints advocacy services provided locally but operating to national standards was set up in 2003 to support people when they want to complain about the NHS.
- The public can become involved in the running of NHS foundation trusts by becoming members, eligible to vote for board members.
- From April 2008, LINks were developed in each local authority (replaced from 2013 by local Healthwatch organisations).

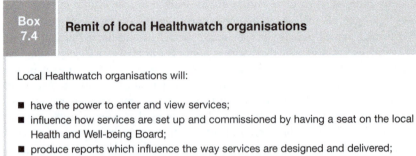

Local Healthwatch organisations will:

- have the power to enter and view services;
- influence how services are set up and commissioned by having a seat on the local Health and Well-being Board;
- produce reports which influence the way services are designed and delivered;
- provide information, advice and support about local services; and
- pass information and recommendations to Healthwatch England and the Care Quality Commission.

what the community thinks. Under the Coalition, LINks have been replaced with Healthwatch.

However, despite the new raft of policies and legislation, a series of intended and unintended consequences are beginning to emerge. A national survey in 2008 on the current state of patient and public involvement in NHS trusts across England found that implementation of LINks had caused the stalling of PPI activity more generally. Definition of and the resources underpinning these activities varied greatly and there were few examples of genuine impact from patient and public involvement (NHS Centre for Involvement, 2008). In turn, LINks have been superseded by the local organisations of Healthwatch England in April 2013, with the implementation of the Health and Social Care Act 2012. These have increased powers and the opportunity to input directly into the new Health and Well-being Boards convened by local authorities (see Box 7.4). The coalition government has also stressed the principle of 'no decision about me without me' and a series of reforms have sought to give people more transparent information about the quality of care they receive and seek more immediate feedback on service provision. While improving choice has enormous popular and political appeal, the entire agenda raises a number of additional issues and creates particular tensions for people with mental health problems who, as we have already discussed, are rarely seen or treated as 'consumers' of services.

Mental health service user involvement in theory and practice

User involvement, like the concept of user itself, encapsulates a range of different ideas (Braye, 2000) from active participation at the micro level of individual decision making, to more macro-level involvement in service planning and evaluation and, increasingly, in training and research. A range of different models to describe and conceptualise user involvement has been proposed. The four-way Pilgrim and Rogers formulation discussed at the beginning of the chapter reflects in part Arnstein's classification of citizens' participation (1969) along an eight-point ladder of participation from being informed (patient) through consultation and negotiation (consumer) to co-production or partnership, and on to the transfer of power (user-led services). There can be an implicit assumption within Arnstein's formulation that higher levels up the ladder are intrinsically more desirable. However, it may be more helpful so see that different sorts of involvement may be more suitable for particular individuals at particular times and in relation to particular situations or issues – but it should be service users and not services that should have the opportunity to choose how they would wish to be involved.

For involvement to be genuine rather than tokenistic, service users must have influence, and must be able to see how their influence is making a difference. Whether it is in terms of individual decisions relating to treatment, or wider issues around service delivery, three models of meaningful participation are possible, depending on where responsibility for outcomes is located (see Table 7.1). What is excluded from this typology are 'one-way' models of consultation in which service users are simply asked to respond to or choose between ideas already formulated by services or practitioners. In addition, Hoggett (1992: 9, quoted in Means and Smith, 1998: 89) distinguishes between the degree of participation/

Table 7.1	Models of user involvement	
Model	**Features of model**	**Examples**
Collaborative engagement	Service users can input their own ideas and respond to the ideas of others (i.e. it is a two-way process) Final responsibility for outcome rests with service commissioner/ provider or practitioner Service users receive feedback in terms of how their contribution may have influenced the final decision that was made	Developing a CPA care plan Commissioning a new service
Coproduction/ partnership	Service users are full partners in the process from the outset Responsibility for final outcome is shared No party can proceed without the agreement and participation of the other	Jointly agreed crisis plan involving service user, family and friends and service providers Service user involvement in management group
User control	Full responsibility for process and outcome rests with service users Practitioners and others may contribute support or expertise – but only by invitation	Personal budget User-led group or service (e.g. Hearing Voices Network)

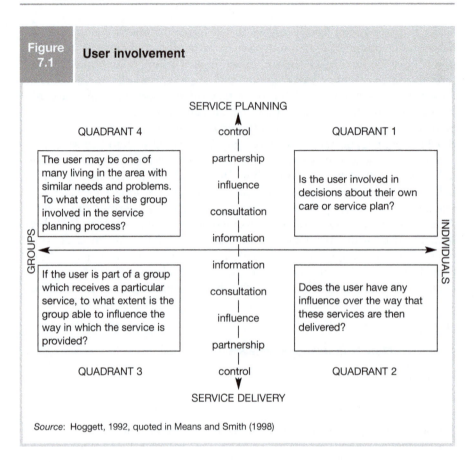

Figure 7.1   **User involvement**

SERVICE PLANNING

QUADRANT 4   control   QUADRANT 1

partnership

The user may be one of
many living in the area with   influence   Is the user involved in
similar needs and problems.   decisions about their own
To what extent is the group   consultation   care or service plan?
involved in the service
planning process?   information

GROUPS ← — — — — — — — — — — — — — — — — — — → INDIVIDUALS

information

If the user is part of a group
which receives a particular   consultation   Does the user have any
service, to what extent is the   influence over the way that
group able to influence the   influence   these services are then
way in which the service is   delivered?
provided?   partnership

QUADRANT 3   control   QUADRANT 2

SERVICE DELIVERY

Source: Hoggett, 1992, quoted in Means and Smith (1998)

control available and whether a user is involved as an individual or through collective action (see Figure 7.1).

Although 'user involvement' is the current 'buzz word' and appears regularly in policy documents, in mission statements and in the academic literature, it may be less meaningful in practice. This view is supported by Wallcraft and Bryant's (2003) survey of the mental health service user movement in England which identified 318 user groups and found that 'local service user groups play a very important role in mutual support, combating stigma, helping people to recover and stay out of services and participating in local service planning and development' (p. 1). However, most groups were small, recently formed, poorly funded and non-representative of BME communities, all of which limited their capacity to achieve change. There also appeared to be tensions between centrally determined agendas that failed to acknowledge local needs and choices, perhaps reflecting a wider debate regarding the need for local responsiveness within a system of considerable central government control.

Webb *et al.*'s (2000: 281) survey of 503 patients across five NHS trusts also found a failure to respond to several prominent and long-standing criticisms from the user movement:

On the face of it ... the results of this study point to the old chestnuts that mental health user campaign groups have raised again and again in the past two decades, and that previous studies have reported on: a lack of information, communication and consultation. It would seem that the National Health Service still has some way to go in meeting these basic principles of good quality care.

So, while it is true that there are now hundreds of user groups where there used to be tens, it appears that their influence may still be limited, with an emphasis on information sharing rather than partnership or user-led services.

Why is user involvement important?

There are a number of interrelated reasons for believing that mental health service user involvement is more than a politically mandated 'good thing' but is a worthwhile activity with a range of practical and ethical benefits (see Box 7.5).

First, there is growing recognition that service users are experts, with an in-depth knowledge of mental health services and of living with a mental health problem. By definition, no one else, no matter how well trained or qualified, can possibly have had the same experience of the onset of mental illness, the same initial contact with services or the same journey through the system. These experiences are an important resource that can help to improve individual packages of care as well as services more generally. Borrill (2000), for example, emphasises the way in which users can predict when they are about to become unwell and formulate appropriate responses at an early stage. If mental health professionals can tap into this expertise, they make their own jobs much easier and more productive by focusing on users' considerable strengths.

Box 7.5	Benefits of user involvement

1. Users are experts about their own mental health difficulty and what this means to them.
2. Users may have knowledge and creative ideas as to what may assist them and other service users in managing or recovering from their mental health difficulty.
3. User involvement may increase the existing limited understanding of mental distress.
4. Users are able to develop alternative approaches to mental health and illness.
5. User involvement may of itself be therapeutic.
6. User involvement may encourage peer relationships between service users and wider social engagement.

In addition, service users and mental health professionals often have very different perspectives. Lindow (1999: 154), for example, highlights the way in which users and service providers may have very different priorities:

> Our discussions are seldom about new styles of management, or changes
> in service organisations: I have heard little interest [among users] in the
> idea of a GP-led National Health Service. There is, rather, much
> discussion of poverty, employment, housing; about services that control
> and rob our experiences of meaning and about dangerous treatment.

Involving users can therefore provide insights that prompt practitioners to reevaluate their work, challenge traditional assumptions and highlight key priorities that users would like to see addressed. May (2001) suggests that the inclusion of users' experiences and knowledge will elaborate the existing limited understanding of mental distress. User involvement in this sense may also lead to a new way of thinking about the nature of evidence itself, with what was sometimes seen as anecdotal experience given new validity through viewing it as 'human testimony' (Glasby and Beresford, 2006).

At the same time, users have been able to develop alternative approaches that can complement existing services. The Strategies for Living group, for example, have highlighted the importance of alternative and complementary therapies (Faulkner and Layzell, 2000; Mental Health Foundation, 2003) while the Hearing Voices Network encourages positive working practices with people who hear voices and works to promote greater tolerance and understanding of voice hearing (www.hearing-voices.org). For some people, moreover, user involvement can be therapeutic. Helping to shape services, particularly when users work together collectively, can help users increase their confidence, raise self-esteem and develop new skills (Clark et al., 2004; Mental Health Foundation, 2003).

The barriers to user involvement in mental health services

Despite the benefits of user involvement and the significant political encouragement in recent years, levels of user involvement in mental health services remain patchy and there are a range of barriers to overcome. First and foremost, accessible information is an essential prerequisite for meaningful involvement, yet there is long-standing evidence of a lack of information for service users, including a lack of information about the nature of mental health problems, the side effects of medication, alternative forms of treatment and mental health law (Carpenter and Sbaraini, 1997; Hogman and Sandamas, 2001; Morrissey 1998; Webb et al., 2000). As an example, the User's Voice project, which included interviews with over 500 users in seven geographical areas across England, found very low levels of involvement in individual care planning and in the planning and delivery of services more generally, and suggested this was often related to a lack of information. As Rose (2001: 6) observed:

Mental health service users need information to make informed choices about their care. Around 50 per cent of users interviewed for this work felt they were not getting enough information on a range of issues and therefore felt themselves to be recipients of rather than involved in their mental health care.

User involvement, if done properly, can also be expensive and time consuming for the organisation and service users themselves. A good example is provided by Carpenter and Sbaraini (1997: 27), whose account of user involvement in the care management process identified time constraints as a major barrier:

> The main disadvantage [of user involvement] perceived by staff was that the process took more time than previously. The assessment and planning meetings themselves took between 45 minutes and one-and-a-half hours, depending on the amount of preparatory work which had been done, the complexity of the user's needs and their ability to contribute to the discussion. In some cases this was longer than the participants and care manager had allowed. To this must be added the time involved explaining the purpose and procedures to the user, liaising with carers and other professionals, and in setting up the meetings themselves. Following the meetings, the forms had to be written out clearly for typing, typed, checked with the user and distributed. In the event that the user's condition had deteriorated severely, or for some reason the care programme had proved difficult to implement, all the preceding work could sometimes be seen by the care manager as time wasted.

In addition, the results of a survey of 46 mental health trusts around payments to mental health service users and carers found that only 12 (26 per cent) made transport available to users and 14 (30 per cent) to carers, while only 15 (33 per cent) paid service users and 12 (26 per cent) paid carers for their time. The authors concluded:

> There is considerable desire to develop practice in this area and the issue of payments is viewed as important in addressing user and carer participation. Significantly, many organisations employed unwritten policies based on custom and practice and were most likely to relate to basic expenses and payments rather than payments for time given. (Ryan and Bamber, 2002: 635)

At the same time, professionals wishing to promote user involvement have frequently expressed concerns about the 'representativeness' of individual service users, sometimes suggesting that particular users may be 'too well', 'too articulate' or 'too vocal' to represent the views of users more generally. However, Lindow (1999) suggests that the concept of 'representativeness' may be used as a subconscious method of resisting user involvement. This also seems to create something of a 'catch 22' situation, with users either 'too well' to be 'representative' or 'too ill' to be involved (Lindow, 1999: 166):

> When workers find what we [users] are saying challenging, the most usual strategy to discredit user voices is to suggest we are not to be listened to because we are too articulate, and not representative. Workers seem to be looking for someone, the 'typical' patient, who is so passive and/or drugged that they comply with their plans. We are developing our own strategies to respond to these challenges in an attempt to reveal to such workers their double standards:
>
> We ask how representative are they, and the others on the committee? We point out that as they are selected for their expertise and experience, so are we. Indeed, we are more likely to have been selected by a group than they are.
>
> We ask, would workers send their least articulate colleague to represent their views, or the least confident nurse to negotiate for a change in conditions?
>
> We ask, if a person's criticisms are valid, what relevance has representativeness?
>
> We point out that it is very rude to suggest that someone is not a 'proper' service user (that is, so disempowered and/or medicated that they cannot speak).
>
> We could ask, but do not, that the challenger produce his or her credentials, their certificates of qualification.

Finally, some professionals may find it difficult to view service users as experts and resist moves towards greater involvement. Although there is some evidence to suggest that professionals are generally supportive of user involvement, there are also dissonances between expressed support and actual practice (Campbell, 2001). This could reflect professionals genuinely perceiving themselves to be more supportive than users do (Peck *et al.*, 2002), resistance to the notion of sharing and transferring power to users, or a clash of professional 'scientific' and users' more 'social' ways of thinking and working (Summers, 2003). At the same time, involvement may be difficult from users' perspectives, because of differences in perceived and actual power between users and professionals. As an example, Morgan's work on user involvement in three London boroughs revealed a number of worrying findings in this regard, particularly around the difficulty of feeling empowered (Morgan, 1998: 184):

> Where they did come into contact with staff ... a worrying feature ... was the extent of the feelings of powerlessness and fear that emerged. The anxieties expressed, and the need for reassurance that speaking up would not put them personally at risk, was too common to be put down merely to individual paranoia. People who have experienced compulsory admission to hospital, ECT and having to take medication that they have neither chosen nor understand, know what it is like to be subject to the

power of the system and of another person ... The way that some of those in authority had managed this, and the legacy of fear this had left, was disturbing to us.

Examples of positive practice

Despite the rhetoric–reality gap and barriers to user involvement, there are emerging examples of positive practice in terms of involvement in:

- prioritising and conducting research;
- staff selection;
- employment as paid mental health workers;
- planning and redesigning services;
- education and training; and
- on governing boards.

Although mental health professionals are perhaps less familiar with the concept of service users as active participants in the research process than those working in the disability field or engaged in emancipatory research (research with the aim of empowerment at its core), user involvement in research is important for a number of different reasons. Service users' priorities for research are often different from those of academics, health and social care professionals or funding bodies. A consultation exercise organised by the South London and Maudsley NHS Trust with service users, for example, found that highly ranked research topics included discrimination and abuse, social welfare issues and arts as therapies (Thornicroft et al., 2002). Unfortunately, user-led research projects are still relatively rare but key contributions have included the Strategies for Living projects (Faulkner and Layzell, 2000; Mental Health Foundation, 2003) and Rose's (2001) work on users' experiences of mental health services. These projects highlighted the importance of training service users to undertake research and the added value as participants 'visibly relaxed and opened up once they realised the interviewer had 'been through the system' and understood their own situation' (Rose, 2001: 4). More recently, the mental health research network has established the Service Users in Research Group for England (SURGE) to coordinate service user-led research in mental health and collaborative initiatives (Telford and Faulkner, 2004).

Second, some mental health service users are being involved in recruiting staff. This is not only a symbolic statement about the importance of user involvement, but can also improve the appointment process. Newnes et al. (2001: 12) describe an attempt to involve service users in recruiting a clinical psychologist. An evaluation suggested that some participants felt that questions from the service user were 'wise and thought-provoking'. In particular, the user was seen as being able to offer a human perspective that was well respected: 'she came up with questions none of us professionals would ever have thought of and got a much stronger sense of what the candidate was like as a person'.

Third, changes to the mental health workforce have included the development of STR workers (DH, 2003e, 2008c), who come from different walks of life (including volunteers and existing and former services users who have the ability to listen to people without judging them). They work as part of a team that provides mental health services and focus directly on the needs of service users, working across boundaries, providing support, giving time and promoting recovery. It was originally envisaged that up to 3,000 STR workers would be trained and working by 2006. This proved to be a significant overestimate and in spite of an Accelerated Workforce Programme introduced in 2003, numbers remained lower than anticipated.

Fourth, involving users in the planning and delivery of services has grown considerably over the last decade, with a systematic review (Crawford *et al.*, 2002) identifying 337 relevant studies, including a number in the field of mental health. As an example, Collaboratives, part of the government's modernisation agenda as outlined in *The NHS Plan* (DH, 2000a), used an approach based on the principles of continuous quality improvement and service redesign. They involved a network of organisations working together for a fixed time period on a specific clinical area. The government saw Collaboratives as a method of redesigning services so they are responsive to the needs of patients rather than the organisation. Within mental health, 37 organisations across two former northern NHS regions participated in the Mental Health Collaborative on inpatient care from October 2000 to November 2001. An evaluation of the user involvement in the Collaborative (Robert *et al.*, 2003) found a strong involvement ethos across services and evidence of the positive effects of user involvement. Users were invited to join project teams as members, to attend learning sessions and to be closely involved in all aspects of work. Improvements made through service user involvement included changes to process issues such as improved documentation. Some of the improvements suggested by service users were not the changes that staff themselves might have prioritised but were perceived as valuable. Many staff also felt that user involvement had challenged their own assumptions and led to new insights about patient care. However, the evaluation also noted scope for future improvements and the need to increase the level of user involvement.

Fifth, there has been recent policy support for greater involvement of both mental health service users and carers throughout the whole education and training process (DH, 2001f) – and this has been reflected in good practice guidance (Tew *et al.*, 2004) and a quality improvement tool (Brooker and Curran, 2006). Involving users in training also has the potential to challenge some of the myths around mental illness, enabling those responsible for delivering mental health services to gain an insight into what it is like to be on the receiving end of such services (Repper and Breeze, 2006). Beyond this, it gives practitioners-in-training the opportunity to develop and experience co-productive relationships with service users and carers, learning through processes of dialogue and challenge in which all forms of knowledge and experience can be valued (Tew *et al.*, 2011). Such learning experiences may be seen as crucial in preparing a workforce that can enable people to work towards self-management and recovery, and to make use of opportunities such as personal budgets.

Finally, there are growing numbers of service users represented on the governing boards of local and national organisations. As an example, a report published by SCIE on the roles and responsibilities of a small number of services users in senior governance positions on governing boards of the bodies set up to regulate service, workforce, education and training standards in social care found that the experience of user members on national boards was overwhelmingly positive. Users reported that 'every effort was made to include them' (SCIE, 2003: 6) and interviews with other stakeholders found that 'users were felt to contribute a vital perspective to the work' (SCIE, 2003: 7). Overall, organisations were perceived to be listening to and learning from the users on their boards. However, a personal account from a mental health service user on the board of an integrated mental health trust shows how isolating and difficult it can be to be the only service user on a governing board and suggests the need for much more planning and forethought about the need for training, support and clarity of role (Brodie, 2003).

The importance of organisational culture and personal attributes

Meaningful user involvement requires organisations to think about their own cultural environment. Service cultures that encourage involvement share a number of common characteristics, including a commitment to genuine partnerships between users and professionals and to the development of shared objectives. As the National Schizophrenia Fellowship (now Rethink) (1997: 10) observes:

> Everyone involved in the delivery of care, including service users and carers, should be treated as equal partners. Occasionally, some professionals may initially feel threatened by the involvement of service users and carers and if this is the case, then it is important that this issue is addressed so that all of the parties involved can work well together. It is essential to remember that every care partner brings something different, but equally valuable, to the relationship and that successful delivery of care depends on effective collaboration between the care partners.

The approach and value base of individual practitioners are also crucial. Thus, for service users in a study by Breeze and Repper (1998: 1306), individual attributes were a crucial feature:

> All the informants [in our study] were able to identify 'good' relationships that had developed with 'helpful' nurses. A good nurse–patient relationship included the nurse: treating the patient with respect, essentially as a person, but, more than that, as a valued person (for example, exuding warmth, displaying empathy and holding 'normal' conversations with the patients); enabling the patient to have some meaningful control over their own care, for example, working with the patients to develop an appropriate and realistic care plan directed towards achieving the patient's own goals; and listening to and, especially, believing the patient.

Future directions: from patient to citizen?

In late 1997, a former British prime minister announced measures aimed at improving life for an estimated 5 million citizens affected by crime, unemployment, low educational attainment and poor housing: 'we are passionately committed to making Britain one nation, giving every single person a stake in the future and tackling chronic poverty and social division' (Tony Blair, quoted in *The Independent*, 7 December 1997). It is against this political background that mental health service users have increasingly campaigned for more generalised reform on the grounds that every individual is a citizen with a series of political, civil and social rights. As Campbell (1996: 224) eloquently suggests: 'Madpersons as empowered customers of services and madpersons as equal citizens are two quite different propositions.' Campbell also points out (2001: 81):

> The great irony about service user action in the past 15 years is that, while
> the position of service users within services has undoubtedly improved,
> the position of service users in society has deteriorated. As a result, it is at
> least arguable that the focus of service user involvement needs adjustment.
> Service users and service providers should accept that the quality of life of
> people with a mental illness diagnosis in society, indeed their proper
> inclusion as citizens, depends on education and campaigning. Although
> the quality of mental health services will continue to be a dominant issue
> for service providers, it might no longer have such a place in the agendas
> of service user organisations. The climate may be changing – the
> Disability Rights Commission, the Human Rights Act, bioethics etc. We
> should not expect service user involvement not to change.

This agenda will almost certainly require partnerships with other groups who face similar challenges to their citizenship status, including people with physical impairments within the wider disability movement. The former Disability Rights Commission, which started work in 2000, brought over 150 legal actions under the Disability Discrimination Act in its first two years, as well as campaigning to make it harder for employers to justify discrimination and to improve access to business premises and transport. This legislation has provided mental health service users with opportunities to pursue their rights. The first legal case backed by the Commission was that of Pravin Kapadia, a man with severe depression who had been compulsory retired by his employers. The ruling that Kapadia was disabled under the terms of the Disability Discrimination Act enabled him to bring a case under the Act for discrimination and unfair dismissal (Valios, 2000) (see Chapter 8 for further discussion of discrimination issues and links between mental health and a social model of disability).

Perhaps the single biggest shift in policy that will impact on service user involvement will be opening up opportunities for personal budgets (Coldham, 2007). There is nothing as potentially influential as direct control over funding in terms of changing the power relationships between service users and professionals. On an individual basis, service users can determine what will be most helpful to them and have some control over how this is provided. If service users are encouraged to use this resource more collectively, it may open up the way for developing formal and informal alternatives to current service provision, including activities that are entirely user run. Alternatively, armed with their own budget, service users may choose to engage with services on a co-productive basis, in order to create new forms of therapeutic opportunity, rather than simply purchasing existing services off an 'à la carte' menu.

Conclusion

Meaningful involvement should not be a one-off intervention or a discrete programme of work, but a much broader and more empowering way of working which affects every aspect of mental health provision. As Hutchinson (2000: 26) explains:

> If users are to regain some control over their lives there needs to be a shift in the balance of power between themselves and mental health professionals ... The key element to achieving this shift is to involve service users at all levels of the mental health system: in the planning of their own support; in the design and running of statutory and independent services; in the recruitment of staff; in the training of mental health professionals; in monitoring the effectiveness of services; in researching and evaluating services; and finally, in the establishment of user-run or user-led services.

However, despite a plethora of policy reforms and pockets of good practice, it appears that a fundamental shift in the balance of power between users and professionals has still not quite come about.

Reflection exercises

1. User involvement within your own organisation (*exercise for all practitioners*)

You have been asked to organise a service user reference group. You have a budget to pay for travel costs and a small honorarium. Think through the issues that you will need to address before and during the first meeting. For example:

- How and where are you going to advertise for members?
- What size should the group be?
- What is the most appropriate location for the first meeting?
- What could the remit of the group be and who should decide this?
- What issues will need to be thought through to ensure that the first meeting is structured, paced and chaired in an appropriate manner?

- Devise an agenda for the meeting
- How will you judge the success of the meeting?

2. The role of Healthwatch (*exercise for all readers*)

Local Healthwatch organisations aim to give citizens a stronger voice in how their health and social care services are delivered in each local authority area. Find out about your local Healthwatch organisation and then make contact with the group to explore how they run and how issues affecting mental health can be prioritised on their agenda.

Further resources

1. Carr, S. (2004) *Has Service User Involvement Made a Difference to Social Care Services?* London: SCIE.

   Accessible review of the evidence and emerging good practice.

2. Sainsbury Centre for Mental Health (2005) *Beyond the Water Towers: The Unfinished Revolution in Mental Health Services 1985–2005.* London: Sainsbury Centre for Mental Health.

   Edited collection examining key issues facing mental health services (with a particularly insightful chapter from Peter Campbell on the mental health service user movement).

3. Campbell, P. (2008) Service user involvement, in T. Stickley and T. Basset (eds) *Learning about Mental Health Practice.* Chichester: Wiley.

   Excellent overview from the perspective of a survivor and a long-term campaigner for service user rights.

4. Weinstein, J. (ed.) 2009 *Mental Health, Service User Involvement and Recovery.* London: Jessica Kingsley.

   Overview of user involvement in mental health services, its origins and implications for policy and practice.

5. It is also worth taking a look at the websites of the National Survivor User Network (www.nsun.org.uk) and Shaping Our Lives (www.shapingourlives.org.uk/ourpubs.html) for the latest news and resources in relation to service user involvement.

Social Inclusion, Stigma and Anti-discriminatory Practice

In this chapter we discuss:

- Social inclusion and mental health.
- The impact of stigma and how this may be challenged.
- Discrimination in society and in mental health services.
- Anti-discriminatory practice.
- Policy responses and prospects for the future.

There is a complex relationship between mental health difficulties and experiences of social exclusion or discrimination. On the one hand, there is substantial evidence that adverse social experiences, including social isolation, abuse or discrimination, can be a contributory factor leading to the onset of mental health difficulties (see Chapter 1). On the other, once people become identified as suffering from mental health difficulties, they may become subject to a range of stigmatising or discriminatory responses, not only from society at large but also within the mental health system. These may, in turn, serve to exacerbate the impact of previous negative experiences, potentially leading to a further worsening of people's mental health (Tew, 2011).

Particularly in the years following the introduction of the NSF in 1999, these issues have been taken much more seriously in the formulation of mental health policy. Standard 1 of the NSF aimed to 'ensure health and social services promote mental health and reduce discrimination and social exclusion associated with mental health problems'. As will be discussed in more detail below, the government went on to produce guidance in relation to mental health and social inclusion in general, and particular guidance for more sensitive and helpful service responses in relation to factors such as race and gender. However, what is less clear is the degree to which these policies have been reflected in significant changes in service delivery and professional practice.

Social exclusion and mental health

Morgan *et al.* (2007) reviewed the conceptual and methodological literature in this area and concluded that social exclusion is an enforced lack of participation in key social, cultural and political activities. On virtually any indicator of social exclusion, people with serious mental illness are among the most excluded in British society (ODPM, 2004; Sayce, 2001). Part of the difficulty in teasing out what we mean by and how we can address issues of social exclusion within the context of mental illness is that many of the precipitating factors for social exclusion such as unemployment, lack of social networks and poverty can be both a cause and a consequence of mental illness.

Promoting the social inclusion of people with mental health problems has been a key focus of UK government policy (ODPM, 2004; 2006). However, social exclusion is both poorly defined and hard to measure. Sayce (2001: 121) has focused attention both on the impact of impairment and societal responses, and has described social exclusion as:

> The interlocking and mutually compounding problems of impairment, discrimination, diminished social role, lack of economic and social participation and disability. Among the factors at play are lack of status, joblessness, lack of opportunities to establish a family, small or nonexistent social networks, compounding race and other discrimination, repeated rejection and consequently restriction of hope and expectation.

The reality of social exclusion for many service users is that of multiple interlocking factors that can impact on every aspect of life. People with mental health problems also have fewer social networks than average, with many of their contacts related to health services rather than sports, family, faith, employment, education or arts and culture. One survey found that 40 per cent of people with ongoing mental health problems had no social contacts outside mental health services (Ford *et al.*, 1993). Fear of stigma and discrimination can also lead to severe loss of confidence. Perhaps the biggest issue for people with mental health problems is that of unemployment and the consequent risk of financial hardship. In the general working age population, 70–90 per cent of people are economically active. However, in England, only 24 per cent of people with mental health problems are in work (the lowest employment rate of any group of people), and only 8 per cent of those with severe mental health problems are in employment (ONS, 2003). People with mental health problems also earn only two-thirds of the national average hourly rate (ONS, 2002). The costs to society of workforce exclusion are also considerable. Mental illness costs employers an estimated £26 billion each year; over £8 billion a year in sickness absence; £15.1 billion a year in reduced productivity at work; and £2.4 billion a year in replacing staff (Sainsbury Centre for Mental Health, 2007a).

Studies show a clear interest in work among users of mental health services, with up to 90 per cent wishing to go into or back to work (Grove and Drurie, 1999). In 2001, however, fewer than four in ten employers said they would consider employing someone with mental health problems compared to over six in ten for a physical disability (ODPM, 2004). Read and Baker (1996) found that 34 per cent of people with mental health problems had been dismissed or forced to resign from their job, and that almost four in ten people with mental health problems felt they had been denied a job because of their previous psychiatric history.

Employment also provides latent benefits such as social identity and status, social contacts and support, a means of occupying and structuring time and a sense of personal achievement (Shepherd, 1998). Lack of work therefore exacerbates the paucity of available social contacts and networks. It is also interesting to reflect that in 1995, a MORI public attitudes survey found that while the public are most likely to accept people with mental illness as road sweepers, actors and comedians, they are less likely to accept them as doctors or police officers (that is, with jobs requiring greater 'responsibility').

Overall, the government's former Social Exclusion Unit has identified five key reasons why people with mental health difficulties face social exclusion (ODPM, 2004):

1. Stigma and discrimination.
2. Low expectations from professionals as to what people with mental health difficulties can achieve.
3. Lack of clear responsibility within NHS and local government for promoting social and vocational outcomes for people with mental health difficulties.
4. Lack of ongoing support to enable people to take up and sustain mainstream employment.
5. People face barriers to engaging in the community – e.g. in accessing education, arts and leisure activities.

Since the publication of this report there has been some progress in addressing these issues, including a nationally coordinated action plan in relation to stigma (see below) and a range of initiatives aimed at supporting people back into education, employment and voluntary work. People with long-term mental health problems can work effectively given the right support and adjustments (for example, someone to talk to or a quiet space). Prevocational training (a period of preparation before entering competitive employment) and supported employment (placement in competitive employment while offering on the job support) are both ways of helping people with severe mental illness obtain work. A systematic review of the evidence in this area found that supported employment is more effective than prevocational training in helping people obtain and keep competitive employment (Crowther et al., 2001) and there is also some evidence that supported employment is cost-effective (Grove et al., 1997). Initiatives like Support Time and Recovery workers (DH, 2003e) offer positive examples of developing jobs where lived experience of mental illness is a positive asset rather than a gap in the curriculum vitae. Where employment initiatives have been properly established and supported, UK and European evidence has shown that they are generally successful for people with serious mental health difficulties – not just in terms of enabling people to find and hold down mainstream jobs, but also in bringing about wider improvements in social functioning and clinical symptoms (Burns et al., 2008). However, despite this evidence base, such activity has tended to be quite small scale and has remained marginal rather than central to service delivery – and hence impact has not as great as might have been anticipated. Focusing on the social care workforce, a recent review of the evidence (Seymour *et al.*, 2011) found that:

- Mental health problems are widespread in the working-age population.
- Mental health stigma and discrimination remain common in the workplace.
- Employers are largely unaware of the levels of mental health need among employees, line managers lack confidence in supporting people with mental health problems and co-workers have mixed views about mental health.
- Policy on mental health and employment does not provide a coherent framework to support the recruitment and retention of people with mental health problems.
- People with mental health problems do not have to be completely recovered to remain in or return to work.
- Good practice means collaboration between professionals, practitioners and employees.
- There is sufficient evidence to inform the development of services and interventions so that people with mental health problems can find and keep work.

Stigma

Alongside the social processes that serve to disadvantage or oppress people on the basis of gender, race, class or other aspects of social identity, people who are identified as having mental health difficulties may face a particularly extreme and pernicious version of this. Both service users and those involved in providing services have generally agreed that this may best be described using the term 'stigma' and this has been the focus for policy initiatives in this area. In seeking to understand stigma, Link and Phelan (2001) have suggested the following process of exclusion for people with mental illness: we label a person as different, and then, at least in the context of mental illness, associate that label with negative attributes (that is, we negatively stereotype the person as being dangerous or incompetent). In doing so, we separate out 'them' from 'us' and so differentiate ourselves from people we perceive as 'other.' Finally, 'they' become the thing that they are labelled, so they become not a person with schizophrenia, but a 'schizophrenic'. This leads to a loss of status and discrimination, and then, quite quickly, to exclusion. As Miller (cited in Laurance, 2003: 43) describes:

> There is a vast and very complicated unwritten constitution of conduct which allows us to move with confidence through public spaces, and we can instantly and by a very subtle process recognise someone who is breaking that constitution. They are talking to themselves; they are not moving at the same rate; they are moving at different angles; they are not avoiding other people with the skills that pedestrians do in the street. The speed with which normal users of public places can recognise someone else as not being a normal user of it, is where madness appears.

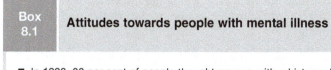

Box 8.1   Attitudes towards people with mental illness

- In 1993, 30 per cent of people thought anyone with a history of mental problems should be excluded from public office and that 43 per cent thought that most women who were once patients in a mental hospital could not be trusted as babysitters. However, 92 per cent of people agreed that we need to adopt a far more tolerant attitude towards people with mental illness in our society (DH, 1993).
- In 1997 (DH, 1997b), the survey found strong support for community care services but only 13 per cent of people would be happy if their son or daughter were going out with somebody with schizophrenia.
- In 2000, just under 20 per cent of respondents were frightened to think of people with mental illness living in residential areas (compared to 25 per cent in 1997). However, 90 per cent also agreed that we need to adopt a far more tolerant attitude towards people with mental illness in our society and 92 per cent believed that virtually anyone can become mentally ill (DH, 2000b).
- The proportion of people agreeing 'people with mental illness have for too long being the subject of ridicule' has dropped from 82 per cent in 1994, to 72 per cent in 2007 (ONS, 2007).
- In 2003, only 83 per cent of people agreed that we need to adopt a far more tolerant attitude towards people with mental illness in our society (DH, 2003d).

The DH has been tracking popular attitudes to mental health since 1993 and, although certain aspects of the British public's attitudes have become a little more positive, there are still many examples of negative stereotyping (see Box 8.1).

These figures are backed up by individuals' experience of distrust, hostility and even violence, as quotes from a *Journal of Mental Health* editorial suggest (Clement *et al.*, 2011: 219–22):

> I remember the day they physically assaulted myself and my sister, physically and verbally assaulted us and we had to call the police and it was just shocking to see grown people not only attacking you but encouraging their children to. I just lived in fear.

> I did say to I think the inspector or whatever well 'this train is overcrowded and I can't breathe' then I heard one bloke saying 'oh the lunatic is asking about the overcrowding'.

> I had dog mess pushed through my letterbox, closely followed by paint stripper thrown over the door.

> The gentleman came from upstairs, he came down and told me 'you are mad, you are mental that is why you are sweeping [the hall]'. And then he started beating me yeah ... he kicks me.

> I do feel unsafe coming out of my flat, and going down the road and whatever. It's difficult to explain … I suppose it's fear of people, you know, shouting abuse.

> I am really upset at people thinking I am violent … It is a really lonely feeling.

What can be particularly damaging for people is when they find themselves unable to resist the impact of negative labelling and internalise the belief that they are indeed dangerous, unworthy and deserving of the abuse they receive. Such injury to people's identities and self-esteem can seriously inhibit their chances of recovery (Tew et al., 2012).

Unfortunately, there is evidence that mental health services themselves may inadvertently play a part, both in feeding into wider processes of social stigmatisation, and in rendering people more vulnerable to internalising stigma. It was widely thought that educating the public that mental illness was 'an illness like any other' would allay public anxieties and break down stigmatising barriers – and this was an approach promoted by the Royal College of Psychiatrists. However, evaluation of the impact of such campaigns has shown that medicalising mental health difficulties can actually reinforce public perceptions of people as intrinsically 'other' – and therefore not to be seen as belonging to mainstream society (Read et al., 2006). Similarly, other research has shown that being admitted to a hospital environment and accepting a mental illness diagnosis can lead to greater likelihood of people losing their positive 'ordinary life' identities and taking on the identity of a 'schizophrenic', and internalising the stigma that goes along with this (Sibitz et al., 2009). When people may also be facing devaluation or oppression in relation to other aspects of their identities – e.g. race – the overall impact can be particularly devastating (Keating et al., 2002; Ferns, 2005).

Instead, research would suggest that promoting direct contact within positive and collaborative contexts can be the most effective strategy for breaking down barriers of prejudice and stigma (Corrigan, 2004; Pinfold et al., 2005) and this can be particularly successful if it is located within wider community development activity designed to mobilise social capital and benefit all sections of local communities (Seebohm and Gilchrist, 2008). It is important that public campaigns include positive images and messages of active contribution and participation, rather than depicting people with mental illness as victims (Thornicroft, 2006a). At a national level, anti-stigma activity has been led through the Time to Change Campaign (www.time-to-change.org.uk) in England and See Me Scotland (www.seemescotland.org). The Stigma Shout survey that was carried out at the beginning of Time to Change in 2008 showed that 87 per cent of people with mental health problems reported the negative impact of stigma and discrimination, and follow-up surveys are indicating significant reductions in this (Time to Change, 2011). A range of activates have been promoted under the umbrella of Time to Change (see Box 8.2).

Box 8.2	Anti-stigma activity as part of Time to Change

A national **high-profile marketing and media campaign**, aimed at reaching 29 million adults, to change attitudes and behaviour towards people with mental health problems

- **Community activity and** *events* that bring people with and without mental health problems together
- Work with **children and young people** to change their attitudes and behaviour towards mental health
- A **£2.7m grants scheme to fund grassroots projects**, led by people with mental health problems, that will engage communities in meaningful conversations about mental health
- A programme to **support a network of people with experience of mental health problems** to take leadership roles in challenging discrimination, within their own communities
- Strategic **work with organisations from all sectors** to improve policy and practice around mental health discrimination
- A programme of **media engagement** to improve media reporting and representations of mental health issues
- Focused work with **BME communities**, starting with African and Caribbean audiences
- Develop a networking and peer learning programme to support organisations to tackle workplace stigma and discrimination.
- Deliver 10 events which will challenge stigma and discrimination in communities around England. The events will enable people with mental health problems to develop leadership skills.

Source: www.time-to-change.org.uk

Discrimination

As sociological research has demonstrated over many years, certain groups in society, such as women and members of BME groups, have experienced unequal opportunities in relation to areas such as education, employment and housing, and this has reflected wider discriminatory attitudes and practices that have permeated formal and informal social relations in Britain. Some of this may be implicit and covert, such as the 'glass ceilings' that certain groups have faced in terms of promotion opportunities at work. Some of this may be overt in terms of verbal or physical abuse, ridicule or other forms of oppression which permeate everyday social interactions – from racist jokes through to homophobic hate crime (see, for example, Otis and Skinner, 1996). In response, there have been a series of official attempts over time to promote greater equality – generally focusing on one aspect of discrimination at a time, as in the Race Relations Act or the Disability Discrimination Act. While the different statutes and regulations have traditionally been overseen by separate bodies, these have since been amalgamated into a single Equality and Human Rights Commission (www.equalityhumanrights.com) with a single Equality Act. This brought together a series of previous laws and identifies a series of 'characteristics' that are protected by law – including age, disability, gender reassignment, marriage and civil partnership, pregnancy and maternity, race, religion and belief, sex and sexual orientation. Although this should help to link the struggles of different marginalised groups and emphasise the cross-cutting nature of discrimination, there is also a risk of diluting existing campaigns with regard to race, gender and disability, and opinion is divided on the best way forward.

Discrimination in mental health services

Social class

It is interesting the degree to which social class has disappeared as an explicit consideration within health and social care policy discourse since the latter part of the twentieth century. In the 1960s, a number of studies highlighted strong negative correlations between socio-economic status and the incidence of many mental health difficulties such as a diagnosis of schizophrenia (Srole *et al.*, 1962; Goldberg and Morrison, 1963) – although there was debate as to the relative importance of social disadvantage as a contributory factor leading to the initial onset of mental health difficulties, as against low socio-economic status (and living in socially deprived neighbourhoods) being the consequence of prolonged mental distress. Although more recent analyses have pointed to levels of income inequality as still being a major factor in explaining poorer mental health and health outcomes in developed societies (Wilkinson and Pickett, 2009), social class has not featured as an identified dimension of possible discrimination within any recent policy initiatives in mental health. Nevertheless, social class remains an issue, with working class people being overrepresented in services and more likely to receive biological and/or coercive rather than psychological/voluntary forms of treatment (Pilgrim and Rogers, 2010). Such unequal treatment may be seen to be occurring within a wider social context in which universal and freely accessible public services are in decline in the current climate of public spending, and therefore social and economic opportunities are increasingly becoming only available to those who have the ability to pay – making it harder for working-class people to access such resources in support of their recovery, and hence more likely that they will stay as long-term users of mental health services.

Gender

Both women and men may find that mental health services respond to them either on the basis of 'gender blindness' or of gender stereotyping. Some men, and in particular African-Caribbean men can be assumed to be dangerous and become disproportionately subject to compulsory detention in general and to more coercive practices, such as physical restraint, in particular. Some women may be current or recent victims of rape or domestic violence, and an approach to care which focuses too much on their medical diagnosis may be experienced as completely inappropriate to their needs (Ramsay et al., 2001; Halliday 2005). This was highlighted in the strategy document *Women's Mental Health: Into the Mainstream* which was issued by the government in 2002:

> Women say they want recognition that their psychological vulnerability is not rooted in their 'biology' but in the context of their lives. (DH, 2002e: 10)

Research indicates that as many as 70 per cent of women and 60 per cent of men with psychosis have been sexually or physically abused as children (Read et al., 2005) – predominantly by men in positions of relative power. This may be seen to have major implication in terms of what may or may not constitute a safe relationship or a safe place when people are in a state of acute vulnerability – but is not always taken into account if services tend only to view people's experience in terms of medical diagnosis. Some mental health workers may lack awareness of gender issues, with Black and Shillitoe (1997) citing examples of male workers entering women's rooms unannounced. More seriously, many women (and some men) report abuse or harassment while under the care of psychiatric services – and for some, this will be replicating abuse that they may have suffered in the past:

> There has been recent recognition that women in acute mental distress may be poorly served by existing mental health facilities where there is a lack of privacy, assaults are common and the atmosphere highly aroused. Female patients' vulnerability to sexual harassment and assault has been highlighted by [a number of commentators] ... Many women admitted to psychiatric wards have experienced childhood sexual abuse or domestic violence and their vulnerability on the ward is especially worrying. (Killaspy et al., 2000b: 102)

A particular ongoing issue has been women's experience of harassment (or even worse) in mixed-sex wards. A survey of hospital patients conducted by Mind found that almost one in six female patients had experienced sexual harassment, and that 72 per cent of those who complained felt that no action was taken (Baker, 2000). Similar concerns were raised in a 1996 national visit of 118 mental health trusts carried out by the Mental Health Act Commission and the Sainsbury Centre for Mental Health (Warner and Ford, 1998). Here, the researchers found that 162 out of 291 mixed wards (56 per cent) reported problems of sexual harassment of women patients, ranging from sexual assault in a small number of cases to exploitation, inappropriate touching, exposure and sexually disinhibited behaviour. While ward staff identified a range of policies and practices designed to protect women, only 34 wards had written procedures and only 26 of these were able to supply a copy to the researchers. Some policies were out of date and others were not always enforced due to pressures on hospital wards. Thus, there was

Box 8.3	Ongoing concerns about sexual safety

A national analysis of patient safety issues in mental health services focused in more detail on concerns about sexual safety. This found 122 incidents, including allegations of:

- rape (19 cases);
- consensual sex (20 cases);
- exposure (13 cases);
- sexual advances (18 cases);
- touching (26 cases); and
- other incidents (26 cases).

Of the 19 allegations of rape, the alleged perpetrator was another patient in 8 cases and a member of staff in 11 cases.

Unfortunately, 'it is not possible to make firm judgements on the veracity of the reported allegations' (as incidents were often sent to the former NPSA soon after the event before an investigation had reported). In addition, the NPSA noted that 'NHS Litigation Authority data … include 13 clinical negligence claims between 1995 and August 2005 that involve allegations of harm to patients resulting from sexual activities with other patients, including three cases of unwanted pregnancies' (NPSA, 2006: 38).

sometimes insufficient female staff to have a female worker on duty each shift, male patients who had persistently harassed women patients could not always be transferred to another ward and male patients were placed in women-only areas if no beds were available elsewhere. Also of concern was the layout of some wards, which made it difficult to observe patients at all times and which did not always allow sufficient space to defuse potential tensions. That concerns persist is demonstrated by more recent analysis of patient safety issues in mental health services (see Box 8.3).

In response, commentators propose a number of possible solutions. Most prominent has been the call for more women to be able to access women-only services if they so wish – not just in terms of segregated accommodation in hospital, but also in terms of specialist women's services in the community (see Box 8.4 for an early good practice example). Certainly, this has been the official direction of policy, with a pledge to eliminate mixed-sex accommodation (DH, 1999a: 2002). However, progress has been inconsistent with many hospitals being under intense pressure to place people in urgent need wherever a bed space is available. Not all patients prefer single sex wards, and the culture of male-only wards may raise issues and concerns of their own (see Thomas *et al.*, 2009 for an interesting insight into workers' experiences on a male ward after single-sex wards were introduced).

While the debate about gender appropriate services will continue, it seems likely that the issues at stake are so significant and so engrained that they will

Box
8.4 **Case study**

Drayton Park has been cited as a good practice example by a range of commentators (see, for example, Killaspy *et al.*, 2000b; McMillan, 1997; Payne, 1998). According to a Camden and Islington Mental Health NHS Trust (2001) leaflet:

> Drayton Park is an alternative to hospital admission for women … It has been open since December 1995. The service recognises the need for women to have a safe place in which they can recover from crises and it focuses on issues that cause mental health problems for women. It was inspired and supported nationally by government recommendations and work such as the [1994 Mind] Stress on Women campaign. In 1999, it became a Beacon Service as part of the NHS Learning Network … A management advisory group consisting of women who have used services and women who work in mental health organisations within Camden and Islington guided [Drayton Park] in its first few years. This group maintained an alternative focus and supported the project in its development stages. In 1999, users of the service, in partnership with staff developed a Women's User Forum. This group has taken over some aspects of the advisory group along with other responsibilities.

In the same Trust researchers and practitioners also set up a Women's Social Network, facilitated by the occupational therapy service. The OTs then evaluated service users' needs and experiences within rehabilitation and residential services in order to explore the gender sensitivity of provision. In particular, the team concluded that: 'Although many of the national and local strategic objectives to improve services for women were being met by the mental health rehabilitation service in this survey, there was inadequate provision of women-only sleeping areas in inpatient settings and insufficient take-up of women-only groups and activities. Collaboration between staff and service users is needed to identify and provide a variety of groups and activities in which women service users would like to participate in order to encourage their engagement in meaningful occupation' (Taylor, *et al.*, 2010: 480). While the study found some areas to improve, this process of evaluating services from a service users' perspective/with service users seems an important way forward.

require much concerted action (see later in chapter for further discussion). Many would argue that the difficulties women experience when accessing and using mental health services are much more fundamental than simply introducing women-only areas. In particular, guidance from the Royal College of Nursing and CSIP called for a fundamental shift in thinking away from asking 'What is wrong with this woman?' to 'What has happened to this woman?' (RCN/CSIP/NIMHE, 2008: 5). While this might only seem like a minor change in wording, the shift in mindset that it entails is potentially revolutionary (and applying the same thinking in relation to men as well might be even more revolutionary).

People from minority ethnic communities

There is overwhelming evidence to suggest that people from BME communities experience mental health services in a very different way to white people – and with different ethnic groups having very different experiences from each other. In particular, African-Caribbean, African and mixed-heritage people are overrepresented in mental health services, tend to receive more coercive forms of treatment and suggest that existing services are too culturally insensitive to meet their needs (see Box 8.5). Certain white minorities, such as Irish people, also experience overrepresentation. By contrast, there is no consistent pattern of over-representation of people from South Asian backgrounds within mental health services.

Elevated rates of hospital admission for black people may result from a number of different factors. Taking into account other possible variables, such as social class and living circumstances, the large AESOP study demonstrated that African-Caribbean people can be up to nine times more likely to be diagnosed with schizophrenia than white British people (Fearon *et al.*, 2006). Although part of this may be explained on the basis of misdiagnosis (perhaps due to a lack of understanding of cultural context), the greater part of this would seem to relate to people's specific experience of living in Britain – as there is no similar pattern of high rates of diagnosis in the Caribbean. Given that admission rates for British-born people have been found to be higher than for migrants (McGovern and Cope, 1987), it would seem that it is not primarily the migration experience that is the main cause. Rather, it is people's pervasive experience of racism and unequal

---

Box 8.5	**Black people's experiences of mental health services**

In 2010, a national census of mental health inpatients found that (Care Quality Commission, 2011: 3–4):

- Rates of admission to hospital were two to six times higher than the average for various black and mixed-heritage groups.
- Rates of referral for some black groups were lower than average from GPs and community health teams, but higher than average from the criminal justice system.
- Rates of detention under the Mental Health Act were between 19 per cent and 32 per cent higher than the average for various black groups.
- Detention rates under section 37/41 (imposed by the courts) were also higher in these groups.
- Rates of seclusion were higher than average for various black groups.
- The rate of hands-on restraint was higher than average in the 'other white' and 'white/black Caribbean mixed' groups.

It was also noted that there were no signs of improvement since the first such census in 2005 (see also Sainsbury Centre for Mental Health (2006d) for further discussion).

opportunity that would seem to be the key factor. This hypothesis is further supported by research which has shown the impact of an 'ethnic density' effect: black people tend to fare less well in terms of their mental health in 'better off' areas where they are a small minority than in 'rougher' areas where they have more of a critical mass (Boydell *et al.*, 2001).

In contrast, Patel and Shaw (2009) explore the under-representation of people from the Gujarati community in mental health services, despite having experienced some of the same underlying social stresses as members of the African-Caribbean community. They highlight three possible causes: genuinely low rates of mental illness, different health-seeking behaviours and GP failure to detect mental illness in Asian patients. They conclude that all three possible explanations have a degree of credibility, that the issue is multifaceted and that more research is therefore required to understand these issues in more detail.

Overall, people from non-white UK backgrounds are less likely to enter the mental health system in a planned and consensual manner via a GP referral. Disproportionate numbers enter after being picked up by the police or through the court system, or through presenting at accident and emergency departments. This may reflect a number of factors, including a disjunction between western medicine and cultural ways of viewing certain experiences (e.g. as due to possession by spirits of Djinn) and wider distrust or lack of understanding of mental health services. Specific issues that have been identified include:

■ Primary care should provide an arena in which mental health problems can be identified at an early stage before a crisis has occurred. Unfortunately, this opportunity is often lost as a result of the failure of some GPs to diagnose mental health problems in some of their Afro-Caribbean patients and to over-diagnose in the case of other African and African-Caribbean groups (see, for example, Bahl, 1999; Browne, 1997; Koffman *et al.*, 1997; Thornicroft *et al.*, 1999).
■ A failure to appreciate the importance of religious beliefs in shaping people's attitudes to mental health and their willingness to seek help from western services (Copsey, 1997a, 1997b).
■ A lack of understanding of or knowledge about mental health issues in particular minority ethnic communities (see, for example, Li *et al.*, 1999; Tabassum *et al.*, 2000).

Once in the mental health system, further issues of potential discrimination have emerged:

■ In 1999, a national visit conducted by the former Mental Health Act Commission and the Sainsbury Centre for Mental Health found that many patients from minority ethnic communities were not receiving care sensitive to their cultural backgrounds (Warner *et al.*, 2000b). Despite several examples of good practice, many wards had no policies on dealing with racial harassment or race equality training, and many lacked access to trained interpreters. Although most units recorded the ethnicity of patients, this information was seldom put to great use.

- Research by the former National Schizophrenia Fellowship (2000) suggests that BME service users were more dissatisfied with the care they received than white respondents, were more likely to feel that their cultural needs had not been met, were more likely to disagree with the diagnosis they had been given, experienced far more detentions under the Mental Health Act and had been forcibly restrained more often.
- Wilson and Francis's (1997: 33) survey of 100 African and African-Caribbean users across England and Wales found that 'a significant proportion of [respondents] feel they are largely misunderstood within the mental health system – either because they are feared, stereotyped or ignored. The stereotypes interact in complex ways and appear to have a powerful impact, as people are seen as black, as mad, as dangerous, as inadequate. This can reduce people's trust in the services on offer, and potentially damage their sense of identity and thus their mental health.'
- The risk of discriminatory attitudes among mental health workers. As Webbe (1998: 12) observes, many practitioners have preconceptions of African and African-Caribbean people as 'big, black and dangerous'. Whereas mental illness is often equated with 'danger', African and African-Caribbean mental illness is equated with 'danger x 2' (see also Browne, 1997).
- A frequent complaint from BME service users is the lack of accessible information about the services available, the nature of their mental health problem and their legal rights (see, for example, Arshad and Johal, 1999; Grant-Pearce and Deane, 1999; Li et al., 1999).
- A lack of BME staff in mental health services (Pierre, 1999). Often, the small numbers of BME staff that do exist can experience just as much discrimination as BME service users (Webbe, 1998).
- Often, ethnicity can interact with gender. Thus, Asian women may have different needs than white women and Asian men (see, for example, Arshad and Johal, 1999; Tabassum et al., 2000).

Above all, there is evidence to suggest that all of these factors may combine to create a 'vicious circle' (Parkman et al., 1997: 264), whereby people from BME communities have negative experiences of mental health services and are therefore less inclined to seek help at early stage in the future or to comply with medication. This can then lead to relapse and readmission to hospital, where existing negative expectations are reinforced. This has been described by the Sainsbury Centre for Mental Health (2002b) in terms of a downward spiral or a 'circle of fear' (see Box 8.6).

Such issues reached a head in 2003 with the publication of the Independent Inquiry into the death of David Bennett (Norfolk, Suffolk and Cambridgeshire Strategic Health Authority, 2003). A 38-year-old African-Caribbean man, David Bennett died in a medium-secure unit in 1998 after being forcibly restrained by staff face down on the floor for some 25 minutes. According to some commentators, Bennett may have been one of at least 27 black people since 1980 to die while in psychiatric services and this case is 'typical of the poor care' received by 'black' people (Leason, 2003a, 2003b: 12). One of the key

Box 8.6	Circles of fear

Stereotypical views of Black people, racism, cultural ignorance, and the stigma and anxiety associated with mental illness often combine to undermine the way in which mental health services assess and respond to the needs of Black and African Caribbean communities. When prejudice and the fear of violence influence risk assessments and decisions on treatment, responses are likely to be dominated by a heavy reliance on medication and restriction.

Service users and carers become reluctant to ask for help or to comply with treatment, increasing the likelihood of a personal crisis, leading in some cases to self-harm or harm to others. In turn, prejudices are reinforced and provoke even more coercive responses, resulting in a downward spiral, which we call 'circles of fear', in which staff see service users as potentially dangerous and service users perceive services as harmful.

Black people see using mental health services as a degrading and alienating experience: the last resort.

Source: Sainsbury Centre for Mental Health (2002b: 8;
see also Keating and Robertson, 2004)

recommendations of the subsequent inquiry was for 'Ministerial acknowledgement of the presence of institutional racism in the mental health services and a commitment to eliminate it' (p. 67). This concept is particularly associated with the 1999 Macpherson Inquiry into the murder of a young black man, Stephen Lawrence. Macpherson's definition of institutional racism was directly quoted by the Bennett Inquiry, which also included a statement from the then chief executive of NIMHE that the NHS is racist in parts and that 'institutional racism was a true accusation that should be levelled at the NHS who should have no tolerance of it' (p. 43):

> Institutional racism is the collective failure of an organisation to provide an appropriate and professional service to people because of their colour, culture, or ethnic origin. It can be seen or detected in processes, attitudes and behaviour which amount to discrimination through unwitting prejudice, ignorance, thoughtlessness and racist stereotyping, which disadvantage minority ethnic people. (Norfolk, Suffolk and Cambridgeshire Strategic Health Authority, 2003: 43)

While many commentators have found the concept of institutional racism helpful (see, for example, McKenzie and Bhui, 2007a, 2007b), some have described this analysis as 'a vague, meaningless, yet insulting accusation' (Singh and Burns, 2006: 650). In particular, McKenzie and Bhui (2007b: 650) identify four tactics that can be used to deny the painful feelings which this issue raises:

1. Shooting the messenger (i.e. that the problem is being overstated by people with 'a chip on their shoulder').
2. Misunderstanding the message (taking offence as if this was a personal accusation rather than a focus on systems).
3. Focusing on whether racism is intentional (and vindicating inequity if no proof of intent can be found).
4. Ignoring the urgency of the problem (and asking for more research).

For many commentators, the way forward may require a dual approach – working *inside* mental health services to make them more appropriate for people from minority ethnic communities, while at the same time working *outside* mental health to tackle wider discrimination and to build capacity within BME communities and the voluntary sector for dealing with mental ill-health. This has been usefully summarised in an NIMHE (2003a) report which highlights these concepts in its title: *Inside Outside*. At a very basic level, the provision of effective interpretation services with workers trained in mental health issues could help to make services more accessible (Tabassum *et al.*, 2000; Warner *et al.*, 2000a). In addition, a key contribution has been made by the voluntary sector, which has traditionally been able to provide more flexible, responsive and culturally sensitive services (La Grenade, 1999; Sashidharan, 1999; Bhui *et al.*, 2000). However, developing specialist culturally sensitive services is only part of the solution, and several commentators emphasise the mixed messages that this can create. Rather than promoting the needs of black service users, there is a danger that specialist services can marginalise people from minority ethnic communities even further, suggesting to workers that ethnicity is a fringe rather than a mainstream issue. Often, moreover, there is a tendency for workers to assume that ethnicity will be addressed by black staff – an approach which many black workers feel can deskill them and fails to recognise the importance of ethnicity for all workers irrespective of their own skin colour (La Grenade, 1999).

To ensure that culturally sensitive services become a mainstream feature of mental health services rather than an 'optional extra', the majority of commentators emphasise the central importance of training. For some, this would enable staff to explore their own attitudes to people from minority ethnic communities, understand the health beliefs and lifestyles of different communities and provide more culturally sensitive services (see, for example, Bahl, 1999; Koffman *et al.*, 1997; Webbe, 1998). Another key issue is the need for meaningful two-way communication between service providers and minority ethnic communities to ensure that minority ethnic users are involved in the planning and provision of services (Pierre, 1999; see also Bhui and Bhugra, 1999; Copsey, 1997a, 1997b). Above all, a number of commentators emphasise that good-quality, responsive mental health services will benefit all service users, irrespective of their ethnicity. Thus, for Bhui and Bhugra (1999: 231) 'all services need to be local, accessible, comprehensive, flexible and consumer-oriented, empowering those using the services'. For La Grenade (1999: 188), moreover, good services should be 'available, affordable, accessible, adaptable and acceptable' – principles that may well apply to black people and white people alike.

Unfortunately, our knowledge of black people's experiences of mental health – although extremely well documented – is limited by two key shortcomings in the current literature. First, the majority of documents focus on the African-Caribbean community, with fewer attempts to consider groups such as South Asian people and very few attempts to explore the needs of refugees and asylum seekers, Irish people and smaller minority ethnic communities such as Chinese or Vietnamese people (for exceptions, see Bracken *et al.*, 1998; Li *et al.*, 1999; Rethink, 2007; Bowl, 2007; Bradby *et al.*, 2007). Second, is the tendency for the majority of documents focusing on ethnicity and mental health to *describe* ethnic differences in service provision, without necessarily considering the experiences and views of service users from different minority ethnic communities. As Thornicroft *et al.* (1999: 163) explain:

> Substantial differences have been demonstrated in the pattern of contacts with psychiatric services of patients from different ethnic groups, especially between those who are White and Black Caribbean ... So far, these are largely expert-reported differences, or are aggregated data from inpatient service contacts. It is striking that information is largely absent in the psychiatric literature from the perspective of the patients themselves, of whatever ethnic group. Since types of contact with services vary so much, it is reasonable to hypothesise that service users' views of services prior to, during and after such contact may also differ substantially by ethnic group. These views may then affect how such people use services in the future. In this way the experiences that patients accumulate from using services progress in ways which reflect their expectations, satisfaction, perception of illness and 'harder' aspects such as the number of admissions, particularly those which are compulsory. The ways in which such psychiatric 'careers' develop in relation to ethnic group, and their implications for how services can be sensitised to ethnic issues, are yet to be properly understood.

People with physical impairments, people with learning difficulties and older people

In contrast to the extensive body of literature on women and people from minority ethnic communities, the experiences of people with physical impairments, people with learning difficulties and older people have often been neglected. Despite this, more recent research and campaigning have suggested that each of these user groups may face particular difficulties when seeking to access mental health services:

1. While some *people with physical impairments* may also develop mental health problems, attention has tended to focus primarily on sensory impairments. For example, the mental health charity, Mind (2003a), has drawn attention to the emotional and mental health problems which can develop as a result of difficulties coming to terms with loss of sight and feelings of anxiety, depression,

isolation and uncertainty. Also significant are the barriers faced by many deaf people who have mental health problems, including the failure of staff to communicate effectively with deaf people, a subsequent risk of misdiagnosis and a lack of specialist service provision (Clark, 2003; Evans, 2003; Mind, 2003b; Sign, n.d.). In addition, Morris's (2004a) study of 25 people with physical impairments and mental health problems reveals a range of difficulties with physical access and with workers not recognising the 'whole person', with both physical and mental health needs (see Box 8.7).

2. *People with learning difficulties* have more mental health problems than the general population (NHS Executive, 1998), yet may experience difficulties accessing services. This may be to do with communication barriers and a lack of accessible information produced by mental health services. However, also significant is a lack of clarity about who should take the lead in meeting the needs of people with mental health problems and learning difficulties. In the past, some mental health services have been reluctant to work with people with learning difficulties, while learning disability services sometimes lack the expertise to work with mental health problems. In response, the government's learning disability strategy, *Valuing People*, argued that people with learning difficulties should have full access to general psychiatric services like everyone else in society, but that specialist learning disability workers could help to facilitate and support this process (DH, 2001h). This may require substantial changes before mainstream mental health services are able to work as effectively with people with learning difficulties as they do with members of the general population. In addition to this, the former Disability Rights Commission (2006) produced a challenging study into the physical health inequalities experienced by people with learning difficulties and/or mental health problems which highlights a range of more general barriers to accessing the same quality health care as other members of the population.

3. *Older people* (often defined as people aged 65 and over) with mental health problems are sometimes considered to be the 'Cinderella' of mental health and often nobody's priority. This is despite the fact that older people with mental health problems form a significant user group (and that current numbers are set to rise dramatically as a result of demographic changes). According to the National Inquiry into Mental Health and Well-being in Later Life, this is both morally wrong and a poor use of scarce resources, with a massive negative impact on society and the economy (Age Concern, 2007: 4):

> Older people's mental health is an increasingly important area of public policy that does not get the attention it deserves. Three million older people in the UK experience symptoms of mental health problems that significantly impact on quality of life, and this number is set to grow by a third over the next 15 years. This represents an enormous cost to society and the economy, in direct costs to public services and indirect costs in lost contributions from older people who boost the UK economy by over £250 billion each year as workers, volunteers, unpaid carers and grandparents. At a time when the Government wants to

Box 8.7	People with physical impairments and mental health problems

- The majority of respondents said they had difficulty accessing mental health services because of their physical impairments. The majority also had difficulty using physical disability services because of inadequate recognition of mental health needs and negative attitudes among staff towards mental health issues.
- Inpatient experiences were often characterised by inaccessible physical environments and a lack of assistance for even simple things.
- Medication required for a physical condition was commonly withdrawn on admission to a psychiatric ward and was not always available when needed.
- Community mental health staff were often unfamiliar with needs relating to physical impairment and this could be associated with unhelpful attitudes.
- There was commonly poor or no communication between mental health and physical disability services.
- Medication given for mental health needs often had an impact on physical impairment, but most people said they had not been warned about these potential effects.
- Talking treatments received the highest rating of any service, but it was often difficult to find an accessible and, within the private sector, affordable therapist or counsellor.
- When people were asked about what they wanted from services, they said they wanted to be seen as 'a whole person', with attention paid to both mental health needs and those relating to physical impairment. They wanted services and professionals to communicate and work together, and easy access to flexible services which could address individual needs. Above all, they wanted to be listened to and treated with respect.

Source: Summarised from Morris (2004b: 1)

> make the most of older people's contributions to society, the neglect of older people's mental health needs represents a waste of human potential that we cannot afford.

However, responding to these needs of older people with mental health problems can be particularly difficult, as adult social care tends to include this user group as part of their generic older people's services, while NHS provision tends to include this group as part of its mental health services, making interagency working all the more complex (Glasby and Littlechild, 2004).

Uniting all these groups is the concept of a social model of disability (see also Chapter 2). In contrast to traditional medical approaches (which see disability in terms of individual physiological and biological conditions), the social model acknowledges that disabled people have *impairments*. However, rather than focus on individual medical factors, many disabled people define disability in terms of the discrimination and exclusion they face as a result of the way in which society is organised. As UPIAS (1976) has argued (quoted in Oliver and Sapey 2006: 30):

In our view, it is society which disables physically impaired people. Disability is something imposed on top of our impairments by the way we are unnecessarily isolated and excluded from full participation in society. To understand this it is necessary to grasp the distinction between the physical impairment and the social situation, called 'disability', of people with such an impairment. Thus we define impairment as lacking part or all of a limb, or having a defective limb, organism or mechanism of the body; and disability as the disadvantage or restriction of activity caused by a contemporary social organisation which takes no account of people who have physical impairments and thus excludes them in the mainstream of social activities. Physical disability is therefore a particular form of social oppression.

Using this approach, the emphasis shifts from medical intervention and cure for the individual to tackling the way society discriminates against disabled people. As an example, a person who uses a wheelchair may be unable to use public transport – however, depending on the model of disability we adopt, we could attribute this to the person's impairment (they need to use a wheelchair) or to social causes (buses are not always designed for people in wheelchairs). With the current state of medical technology, intervening at a social level can be more effective – thus, it would probably be easier to raise the curb of a bus stop so that a wheelchair user can get on than it would be to intervene individually (working with the individual to try to 'heal' their impairment). Such an approach is also more cost-efficient – by altering the bus stop, planners and policy makers could make the bus accessible for all wheelchair users as well as for other groups.

In theory, a social model also has the potential to develop a common cause between people with mental health problems, people with physical impairments, older people, people with learning difficulties and others. While the disability movement has not always been as inclusive of some of these groups as it perhaps could have been, a social model emphasises the way in which all these people are disabled not by their impairment, frailty, learning difficulty or mental distress, but by the way in which society responds to such people and issues. While much more work is required to develop these links, there is at least scope for a much broader and potentially very powerful coalition of groups whose focus is not on individual impairments, but on the way society is organised and the way in which discrimination operates.

Gay men, lesbians and bisexuals

Prohibited since legislation in 1885, homosexuality was only legalised in 1967 when men over 21 were permitted to have sexual relationships with each other (although it was not until 1992 when the Isle of Man came into line). In contrast, lesbianism has never been included in legislation and has therefore never been illegal (see Mind, 1996, for all dates quoted in this section). Despite this, homosexuality has traditionally been seen as a form of mental illness, and was not declassified as such by the American Psychiatric Association until 1973 and, by the WHO, until 1992. Even as late as 1989, the *Oxford Textbook of Psychiatry* could include homosexuality under 'problems of sexuality and gender' and discuss ways of 'curing' homosexual people. While such overt discrimination no longer exists, much of the misunderstanding and prejudice behind these statutes and practices remain. As Mind (1996) emphasises:

> Although blatant examples of bigoted, misinformed theory are no longer common in psychiatric writing, evidence shows that homosexuality continues to be referred to as a mental disorder in some psychiatric texts, and anecdotal evidence shows that homosexuality continues to be thought of as a mental illness per se by society in general and by some mental health professionals.

That gay men, lesbians and bisexual people continue to have negative experiences of mental health services is demonstrated by a small number of key research studies (see Box 8.8).

Box 8.8	**The experiences of lesbian, gay and bisexual service users**

Golding's (1997) interviews with 55 gay, lesbian and bisexual service users identified some positive experiences of mental health care, but also found that 73 per cent said they had experienced some sort of prejudice or discrimination in connection with their sexuality:

- 88 per cent of people experiencing discrimination felt unable to challenge it, largely because of feelings of fear or vulnerability.
- 22 per cent said they had experienced direct victimisation in connection with their sexuality in the form of violence (including instances of rape or sexual assault).
- 38 per cent experienced additional discrimination due to their religious beliefs, race, physical ability or age.
- 16 per cent had partners at the time when they were using mental health services. Two-thirds of these people felt that their partners had not been treated on an equal par with the partners of heterosexual service users.
- 51 per cent said that their sexuality had been inappropriately used to explain the cause of their mental distress.
- 7 per cent of participants said that they felt they were forced to have a blood test for HIV.

Price's (1997) review and in-depth interviews emphasise:

- The prevalence of suicide and self-harm within the gay/lesbian community.
- The discriminatory nature of the 'nearest' relative regulations, which discriminate against gay or lesbian partners.
- The distress caused by homophobia and harassment.
- Professionals seeking to blame or cure people's sexuality.
- The value which gay/lesbian users place on 'out' workers.

- The tendency for gay or lesbian workers to be seen as 'the gay expert'.
- Workers ignoring or responding inappropriately to people's sexuality.

McFarlane's (1998) research with 35 service users and 35 mental health workers concluded that (p. 117): 'lesbian, gay and bisexual mental health services users are discriminated against and oppressed, not only by the attitudes and behaviour of society at large, but also from within mental health services. Judgement is made on the basis of their sexual identity and their identity as service users. Not only that, they are also discriminated against from within lesbian, gay and bisexual communities, again on the basis of their use of mental health services.'

King *et al.* (2003) conclude that gay men, lesbians and bisexual people are more likely than heterosexuals to: experience psychological distress; harm themselves; experience harassment or bullying because of their sexuality; have contact with the mental health system; and experience negative reactions from professionals. A subsequent systematic review (King *et al.*, 2007) concluded that lesbian, gay and bisexual people are 'at significantly higher risk of mental disorder, suicidal ideation, substance misuse and DSH [deliberate self-harm] than heterosexual people' (p. 3). For a more personal view of this, see Carr (2005).

A more general review of the health, social care and housing needs of lesbian, gay, bisexual and transgender older people (Addis *et al.*, 2009) suggests that managing long-term stigma in the form of heterosexism and homophobia can contribute to this group of people being more at risk of depression, suicide, deliberate self-harm addictions and substance misuse than members of the general population.

Policy responses

Over time, the research findings above point to a poor track record with regard to tackling discrimination in mental health services. However, there are signs that issues of discrimination and equality are beginning to become more of a mainstream feature of the policy agenda, with a series of key policy initiatives, including:

- Official guidance on women's mental health (DH, 2002e, 2003g; see also RCN/CSIP/NIMHE, 2008; CSIP, 2006).
- Official policy documents on the experience of minority ethnic communities and on race equality in mental health (DH, 2003h, 2004a–c, 2005a, 2005b; NIMHE, 2003a, 2003b, 2004a).
- A national strategy for dementia (DH, 2009a).
- An increased focus on tackling stigma and discrimination (see, for example, NIMHE, 2004b).
- The creation of a new Equality and Human Rights Commission and a new Equality Act.
- Work to improve health and social care services for lesbians, gay men and bisexual people (Ward *et al.*, 2010).

While these policies all place a welcome focus on tackling discrimination, many of the issues highlighted in this chapter are longstanding, complex and seem unlikely to be resolved easily. Moreover, some accounts appear to cast doubt on the extent of official commitment to the radical action required to promote anti-discriminatory practice. Thus, progress in creating women–only hospital settings has sometimes been slow (Copperman and Knowles, 2006), and current approaches to race equality training have been described as 'inappropriate and inadequate in addressing racial inequality in mental health services' (Bennett *et al.*, 2007: 7). The social work and medical press have also criticised the government for apparently rejecting some of the Bennett Inquiry recommendations, refusing to acknowledge the existence of institutional racism (Community Care, 2004; Gillen, 2005; McKenzie and Bhui, 2007a). In addition, there have been claims of a watering down of a critical report into mental health services for people from minority ethnic communities (see also findings by the former Commission for Racial Equality, 2007, for broader discussion). According to the report author (quoted in Leason, 2003c: 8):

> They [the Department of Health] tried to dilute it as much as they could. We had to fight all the way … The experience of working with the DH around this document, and subsequently, has reinforced my view that this is an example of institutionally racist attitudes and behaviours on its part. As a result, it may well be that discrimination in mental health services persists and that the negative experiences of some of the groups set out above continue.

Conclusion

Overall, the particular forms of discrimination addressed in this chapter have a number of themes in common. For example, individual forms of discrimination can interact. Thus, BME women may have very different experiences to white women, while gay, lesbian or bisexual service users may face additional discrimi-nation due to their age, physical ability, religion or ethnicity. While specialist serv-ices that are sensitive to the needs of a particular marginalised group of people may be welcome, this may actually hinder change in more mainstream services. There is also an additional danger that staff from a particular group may be perceived as the 'expert' on a particular issue (e.g. BME staff members as 'experts' on ethnicity and gay staff as 'the gay expert'). This not only deskills and exploits these staff members, but also takes the responsibility away from other workers for making services more responsive to the needs of service users from particular backgrounds.

Above all, many of the negative experiences cited throughout this chapter are long-standing issues which policy makers and practitioners have known about, but have so far been unable to resolve. This suggests either a lack of political will or that the issues concerned are so complex and deep-seated that they are extremely difficult to put right (or both). As we discussed at the beginning of this chapter, discrimination not only exists within mental health services, but also in wider society. Also, discrimination cannot be tackled simply by changing the way individuals behave. Instead, attempts to root out discrimination in mental health services need to be accompanied by efforts to root out discrimination in wider society at personal, cultural and structural levels. Discrimination, in short, is pervasive and multifaceted, and only an equally multifaceted response will suffice. Of course, this is not to deny that mental health services can do a range of things to tackle discrimination. However, it may mean that changes within mental health should take place alongside more widespread and fundamental action to ensure that services and wider society function in a non-discriminatory manner.

Reflection exercises

1. Promoting social inclusion (*exercise for all practitioners*)

Think about the ways in which your organisation and you as an individual can promote access and inclusion for people who use your service:

■ What skills do you think are key to building a positive and affirming relationship with your service users and patients?
■ What strategies can you use and what resources can you call on or direct people towards to help them feel more included within their local community?
■ How would you measure whether your ideas for improving inclusion for service users have had any effect?

You may find it helpful to look at the Inclusion website (www.ndt.org.uk/projectsN/SI.htm) and to read Hacking and Bates's (2008) description of issues around the measurement of social inclusion.

2. Experiencing discrimination (*exercise for all readers*)

Think of a situation where someone made a judgement about you based on a preconception of who you are or how you look:

■ How fair did the judgement feel?
■ How did you respond?
■ Were you able to challenge or change their preconceptions (and, if so, how)?
■ What impact did it have on your subsequent relationship or ability to work together?
■ What lessons can you draw to inform how you approach others?

3. Experiencing discrimination in mental health services (*exercise for all practitioners*)

How would someone using your service feel if they were:

■ A woman?
■ A person from a minority ethnic community?

- A person with a physical impairment?
- A person with a learning difficulty?
- An older person?
- A gay man, lesbian or bisexual person?

Do you collect patient stories or experiences to help you understand this in more detail? If so, do you analyse these with some of the key social divisions in mind? What can you do to make services more sensitive to the needs of diverse service users? Where you work with a colleague from a different professional background, share these answers and explore how service users' experiences would vary in different organisational/professional settings.

4. Institutional racism (*exercise for all readers*)

Using Macpherson's definition of institutional racism, discuss this concept with colleagues from different professional backgrounds or with fellow students. To what extent do you and they find this a helpful concept when seeking to work with people from minority ethnic communities? Do some of your views or those of colleagues reflect the defensive tactics identified by McKenzie and Bhui (2007b) above?

Further resources

1. Pilgrim, D. and Rogers, A. (2010) *A Sociology of Mental Health and Illness* (4th edn), Buckingham: Open University Press; Rogers, A. and Pilgrim, D. (2003) *Mental Health and Inequality* Basingstoke: Palgrave.

   Comprehensive overviews of social inclusion issues from a sociological perspective

2. Repper, J. and Perkins, R. (2003) *Social Inclusion and Recovery*. London: Bailliere Tindal.

   Focuses on social inclusion from more of a practice perspective.

3. Social Exclusion Unit (2004) *Mental Health and Social Exclusion*. London: Office of the Deputy Prime Minister.

   Although a few years old, the comprehensive catalogue of evidence remains highly relevant today.

4. Thornicroft, G. (2006b) *Actions Speak Louder: Tackling Discrimination against People with Mental Illness*. London: Mental Health Foundation.

   Useful guide to practical approaches to tackling stigma against people with mental health difficulties.

5. Women

In addition to official policy documents on mental health and gender (DH, 2002e, 2003g), helpful guides include *Informed Gender Practice* (RCN/CSIP/NIMHE, 2008) and *The Mental Health of Women in Contact with the Criminal Justice System* (CSIP, 2006).

6. People from minority ethnic communities

Key introductions to the experiences of people from minority ethnic communities include the Sainsbury Centre for Mental Health's (2002b) *Breaking the Circles of Fear*, the inquiry into the death of David Bennett (Norfolk, Suffolk and Cambridgeshire Strategic Health Authority, 2003) and NIMHE's (2003a) *Inside Outside*. Mind also publishes a number of factsheets on mental health and the African-Caribbean, Chinese and Vietnamese, Irish and South Asian communities (www.mind.org.uk/Information/Factsheets/Diversity), while the DH (2004 e–g) has produced guides to mental health promotion and particular minority ethnic communities. The Mental Health Foundation's *Black Spaces Project* (2003) reviews the learning from a series of innovative black voluntary sector projects working with mental health issues, while a second report on *Keeping the Faith* (Mental Health Foundation, 2007) explores issues of spirituality within mental health services.

7. People with physical impairments, people with learning difficulties and older people

Key sources include factsheets by Mind (www.mind.org.uk) on visual impairments and deafness, and research by Sign (n.d.) into mental health services for deaf people (see also www.signcharity. org.uk). For older people, the former Audit Commission (2000a, 2000b, 2002) has produced a number of key reports, while the *National Service Framework for Older People* included a specific standard about older people with mental health problems (DH, 2001i). National overviews by the UK Inquiry into Mental Health and Well-being in Later Life (Age Concern, 2007) and the national dementia strategy are also useful resources (DH, 2009a). The previous government's learning disability strategy, *Valuing People*, summarises official policy and introduces the concept of health facilitation to support people with learning difficulties to access mainstream community services (DH, 2001h). This was subsequently updated with the publication of *Valuing People Now* (DH, 2007c). Although dated, *Signposts for Success* provides a good practice guide to commissioning and providing health services (including mental health services) for people with learning difficulties (NHS Executive, 1998), while the former Valuing People Support Team (2004) have produced a toolkit for improving mental health services for people with learning difficulties. In addition, *Equal Treatment: Closing the Gap* is a powerful review of the physical health inequalities experienced by people with learning difficulties and/or mental health problems produced by the former Disability Rights Commission (2006).

8. Sexuality

In addition to the studies cited in the main body of the chapter, good practice guidance is available via the website of PACE, a London-based counselling and mental health project working to promote lesbian and gay health and well-being (www.pacehealth. org.uk).

9 Families and Carers

In this chapter we discuss:

- Family members' experience of mental health difficulties and involvement in services.
- Parents with mental health difficulties and their children.
- The importance of carers.
- The policy context.
- The neglect of carers of people with mental health problems.
- The needs of carers.

Mental health and family life

Over time, there has been an unfortunate tendency within mental health services to focus on the needs and difficulties of the individual without any serious appreciation of the relationships context(s) in which these difficulties may be taking place. This tendency may result from the influence of a number of factors:

- A biomedical approach tends to foreground physiological processes that are seen as internal to the person.
- The legislative framework for social care in the community prioritises individual assessment – although subsequent carers' legislation has sought to redress this to some extent.
- The training of most mental health professionals does not equip them with the skills to work with family groups.
- Protecting confidentiality has been widely used as a rationale for assuming that friends and relatives should be excluded from anything more that very general information about the service user – without checking out whether such practices are actually in the service user's best interests.

At its worst, this leads to an approach to practice in which distressed individuals are suddenly plucked out from their family and social context when they are admitted to hospital, leaving behind family members who may be bewildered, frightened, guilty or upset. It is not seen as anyone's responsibility to engage with these people in order to help them to come to terms with what has happened and prepare them for the sorts of situation that they may have to face once the person is discharged. Visiting a loved one in hospital may be intimidating, especially if staff seem to treat visitors as 'getting in the way' rather than providing a lifeline in terms of maintaining contact with the outside world. There may be limited options in terms of quiet and confidential spaces in which to talk – and visiting may be particularly traumatic for children who need to maintain contact with a parent in hospital.

From the perspective of family members, discharge can be just as sudden. The reality of shorter hospital stays and limited bed availability is that many people are still quite unwell when they leave hospital. Such early discharge may not, of itself, be a bad thing. However, it becomes a problem if those who were close to them are frightened and unsure how to handle everyday interactions with someone who is manifestly not the same as the person they once thought they knew. Unsupported and without relevant knowledge, family members' best efforts to cope may actually turn out to make things worse – perhaps through appearing resentful or overprotective. There is a substantial body of research evidence to show that if people recovering from psychosis are exposed to relationships characterised by intrusiveness or (covert) hostility, they will be more likely to relapse and require readmission to hospital (Wearden et al., 2000).

Where more family-inclusive service approaches have been piloted, results have been very positive, both in terms of family members feeling more confident and competent, and in terms of better outcomes for service users and reduced need for hospital stays. This was the philosophy of the experimental Buckinghamshire service headed up by Ian Falloon in the 1980s (Falloon and Fadden, 1993) which was able to operate successfully with minimal use of hospital beds. It is also the philosophy of the Open Dialogue approach that has been developed in Finland and is achieving wider international recognition (see Box 9.1).

Even within more conventionally organised services, there is strong evidence that involving family members through approaches such as behavioural family therapy can be beneficial both for family members and for service users in terms of less frequent relapse or need for readmission to hospital (Fadden, 2006a) – and this forms part of recommended NICE guidelines for the treatment of schizophrenia. However, due in part to the ingrained individualised focus within many UK mental health services, even when staff are trained in family approaches, there may be barriers to offering this as a routine part of service packages (Fadden, 2006b). Nevertheless, recent research has shown that a number of different whole-family approaches are being offered in particular areas, although there is little consistency across England as a whole (Tew et al., 2013). Approaches include not just behavioural family therapy, but also systemic family therapy and family group conferencing – all of which can be effective, particularly if they are offered early on at a time of crisis, rather than in response to longer-term entrenched situations.

Box 9.1	Open Dialogue Approach for working with people with psychosis

Principles of service model:

- All staff are trained in working with families.
- An initial crisis response meeting is convened within 24 hours and includes the service user and those close to them, as well as relevant professionals.
- Presumption that the person can be treated and supported at home, although brief hospital stays (usually of a few days only) available as an option.
- Integrated professional team around the family and frequent family meetings to ensure everyone's safety during period of crisis.
- Professional team make sure that all family members are heard.

Reported outcomes at two-year follow-up (Seikkula *et al.*, 2003; 2011):

- 81 per cent of patients did not have any residual psychotic symptoms;
- 84 per cent had returned to fulltime employment or studies;
- Only 33 per cent had used neuroleptic medication; and
- relapses occurred in 24 per cent of the Open Dialogue cases compared to 71 per cent in the comparison group.

Parents with mental health difficulties and their children

Around 50 per cent of those being treated for mental health difficulties (and 25 per cent of people being treated in hospital) are parents of dependent children. This may raise particular issues for children if they take on the role of 'young carers' (Aldridge and Becker, 2003) and there is substantial evidence that children of parents with mental health difficulties are more likely to experience behavioural or mental health difficulties in their own right – either as a child or subsequently in adult life (Bates and Coren, 2006). However, this is not a necessary consequence and there is also strong evidence that difficulties can be mitigated by ensuring that children have social support and a life of their own (and they are not subject to stigmatisation by their peers or others), that they can trust the professional system to provide all necessary support to their parent, and that they are supported in maintaining their relationship with their parent throughout the time that they are unwell (Evans and Fowler, 2008; Gopfort *et al.*, 2004).

Except for specialist mother-and-baby services for women experiencing postnatal depression or puerperal psychosis, UK mental health services have a poor track record in terms of being able to provide holistic support to parents *and* their children. Adult mental health services can tend to ignore the needs and safety of children altogether – although this has finally been recognised in the most recent CPA guidance (DH, 2008b). Liaison with local authority children and family services can be poor, as can be their response in terms of delayed responses and low prioritisation. Conversely, local authority Children and Family Services find that a substantial proportion of their child protection referrals involve families where a parent has a mental health difficulty, but this has either not been picked up by the GP or they are deemed not to meet the threshold of service eligibility.

This inability to assess and respond to the needs of a family as a whole was highlighted in the Think Family initiative led by the Cabinet Office Social Exclusion Unit (Morris *et al.*, 2008; Cabinet Office, 2007). A specific outcome of this was the commissioning of a series of pilots within local authorities to explore more effective approaches to joint working between children's and mental health services (SCIE, 2012). However, achievements have been modest as very substantial organisational barriers were encountered in terms of a lack of alignment between the priorities, targets and ways of working between the respective agencies – exacerbated by issues such as incompatible information systems. Positive change was only possible if there was a strong commitment to developing systems for joint working from both the top and the bottom of participating organisations.

The emergence of the term 'carer'

The term 'carer' is a relatively recent one that emerged in the late twentieth century out of a need to recognise the sheer level of physical and emotional support that many family members, most frequently women, put into looking after or supporting other adult relatives or family members. For some this may be a positive choice. For others, this may have been a major and stressful burden, particularly if the person had to juggle caring with employment, childcare or other responsibilities. In the 1980s, a series of research studies, often influenced by feminism and the gendered nature of caring, began to highlight this (see, for example, Baldwin and Twigg, 1990; Finch and Groves, 1983; Ungerson, 1987). In 1989, the *Caring for People* White Paper provided one of the first official acknowledgements of the substantial role played by carers, and made support for carers a key priority (DH, 1989a: 4):

> The government acknowledges that the great bulk of community care is provided by friends, family and neighbours. The decision to take on a caring role is never an easy one. However, many people make that choice and it is right that they should be able to play their part in looking after those close to them. But it must be recognised that carers need help and support if they are to continue to carry out their role.

While this was an important statement of government intent, the White Paper and 1990 Act did little to deliver any substantial support or recognition for carers in practice. However, this marked the start of a process in which carers started to achieve legal recognition, although the framing of the legislation tended to impose an implicit model in which each service user had a single identified carer (who was then entitled to have their needs assessed or be included in decision making). This did not reflect the more complex realities of family life and (somewhat unintentionally) tended to put all the burden of responsibility onto one person. While this may have delivered administrative simplicity, it flies in the face of experience that good and sustainable support systems generally involve a number of family members or friends each making a contribution – and potentially providing support for one another as well as for the service user.

Family members and friends who provide care can often feel ambivalent about being redefined as 'carers'. On the one hand, this can provide recognition for what they do – and a label which means that they have to be listened to by services where previously they may have been ignored. On the other hand it distorts the construction of family relationships. If one is a carer, does this diminish one's role as spouse, parent, sibling or son or daughter – and, in particular, the reciprocal expectations that would normally be associated with such relationships? There can be particular issues in relation to mental health where it is much more emotional support rather than physical labour that is provided – and some have suggested that the term 'ally' feels much more comfortable and appropriate (Tew, 2011: 77).

The importance of carers

The vast majority of care is (and always has been) provided by carers: family members, friends and neighbours who support someone else as a result of a personal relationship with that person, not as a paid job or as part of a statutory service. In England, it has been estimated that there are 5.2 million carers, with over 1 million people caring for more than 50 hours per week (HM Government, 2008: 33). This saves public services an estimated £87 billion per year (House of Commons Work and Pensions Committee, 2008: 5). Without this support – often unseen and unheard – statutory services would be unable to function. In a more recent calculation, Carers UK has estimated the economic value of the contribution made by carers in the UK as £119 billion a year – equivalent to £2.3 billion per week, £326 million per day and £13.6 million per hour or over £18,000 for every carer in the UK (Buckner and Yeandle, 2011: 2). As former Prime Minister, Tony Blair, stated in the UK's first national carers' strategy (DH, 2000c: 3):

> When I talk about the importance to Britain of strong communities and
> of people having responsibilities towards each other, I'm not speaking of
> abstract ideas, but of real people and real events: the things many people
> do to make things better for those around them. The extraordinary
> work which carers do may well be the best example of what I mean.
> Extraordinary not in ways which make headlines, but in ways which really
> matter and which really make a difference to those they are caring for.
> Carers devote large parts of their own lives to the lives of others – not as
> part of a job, but voluntarily ... For the sick, the frail, the vulnerable and
> the elderly, carers provide help and support in ways which might
> otherwise not be available. By their effort, their patience, their knowledge,
> their understanding, their companionship, their determination and their

compassion, carers very often transform the lives of the people they're caring for ... Carers are among the unsung heroes of British life.

In many respects, therefore, this chapter is in the wrong place in this book – it should not be last after primary, community and hospital services, but should come first, because carers provide the bulk of support. However, as explained below, it is only in the last 20 years or so that we have come to recognise the needs and contribution of carers, and, until relatively recently, this has often been a neglected area – with the needs of carers under-researched and undervalued.

The policy context

In 1995, the Carers (Services and Recognition) Act gave people providing care on a regular basis to someone eligible for community care services the right to an assessment of their needs, but with a number of limitations (Mandelstam, 1998: 45; see also DH, 1996a):

- Entitlement to an assessment depended on the carer either providing or intending to provide a substantial amount of care on a regular basis.
- Entitlement depended on the carer requesting an assessment.
- Carers' assessments could only take place if the person being cared for was themselves being assessed under the Community Care Act – carers had no independent right to an assessment.
- Any services provided would be offered to the 'service user', and carers were not entitled to any services to meet their own assessed needs.
- Social services were not given any additional funding to implement the Act.

In recognition of some of these previous shortcomings, the 1998 *National Strategy for Carers* underlined the government's commitment to improving information, support and care for carers (DH, 2000c). This was followed in 1999 by the *National Service Framework for Mental Health* (DH, 1999a), which included a specific standard about the needs of carers. Standard Six stated that all individuals who provide regular and substantial care for a person on CPA should:

- Have an assessment of their caring, physical and mental health needs, repeated on at least an annual basis.
- Have their own written care plan which is given to them and implemented in discussion with them.

Interestingly, it was local authorities rather than the NHS which was tasked with delivering this standard. However, while this gave local authorities an area of responsibility within the field of mental health service provision, it also served to marginalise the needs of carers as local authorities themselves became less and less significant players within overall service provision over the subsequent decade.

In 2000, the Carers and Disabled Children Act strengthened the entitlement to an assessment by giving carers aged sixteen or over the right to an assessment (even where the person they care for has refused an assessment by social services or has refused services following an assessment). Policy guidance also emphasised that workers should give carers verbal and written information about their right to an assessment. In addition, local authorities were given the power to supply certain services direct to carers (such as short-term break

---

Box 9.2   The 2008 and 2010 carers' strategies

In 2008, the government's updated carers' strategy set out a new vision for carers: 'by 2018, carers will be universally recognised and valued as being fundamental to strong families and stable communities. Support will be tailored to meet individuals' needs, enabling carers to maintain a balance between their caring responsibilities and a life outside caring, whilst enabling the person they support to be a full and equal citizen' (p. 9). Key commitments included:

- Providing every carer with access to comprehensive information.
- £150 million to increase breaks for carers from caring.
- Pilots to enable the NHS to better support carers (including pilots to improve GP support and pilot annual health checks for carers).
- Up to £38 million to support carers to combine employment and caring and to re-enter the job market after their caring role has finished.
- Improving the emotional support offered to carers.
- Over £6 million to improve support for young carers.
- Training carers to strengthen their caring role and empower them in their dealings with professionals.
- Additional training for welfare professionals.
- Extension of third-sector support for carers.
- Providing data to help commissioners and policy makers provide better support for carers.
- Establishing a standard definition of carers across government.

This is claimed to represent a total of £255 million additional investment (2008–11) above and beyond £22 million previously committed (HM Government, 2008: 10–12).

In 2010, the coalition government built on these policies and committed to a range of activities, including (HM Government, 2010):

- Making £1 million available to voluntary organisations for a Reaching out to Carers innovation fund.
- Additional resources for GP training to increase GP awareness of carers' issues.
- A new training framework on supporting carers.
- Promoting good practice around carers and personalisation.
- Exploring how to extend rights to more flexible working.
- Extra NHS funding for short breaks for carers.

voucher schemes or direct payments) (DH, 2001j). In 2004, the Carers (Equal Opportunities) Act sought to ensure that all carers are informed of their right to an assessment, that councils take account of carers' outside interests (such as wishes to work, undertake education or training and leisure activities), and that the NHS and social services work together more effectively to provide support for carers. More recently these measures have been boosted by a range of additional policies and initiatives, including greater rights to flexible working and a new carers' strategy to update the previous 1998 version (see Box 9.2). Despite this emphasis on the needs of carers, however, there is evidence to suggest that such policy measures have not always been translated fully into practice. In particular, a large body of research demonstrates that carers may be unaware of their rights to an assessment, that they may feel unsupported in their role as carers and that some public services may not always perceive support for carers as a high priority (see, for example, Carers UK, 2003, 2004, 2006; and below for further discussion).

The neglect of carers of people with mental health problems

In 2001, the case of James Lawson provided a powerful example of the lack of support which some carers of people with mental health problems receive and the sense of helplessness which they may experience (see Box 9.3).

Shortly after this case, the DH and the National Schizophrenia Fellowship (since renamed Rethink) launched their Commitment to Carers campaign to coincide with National Carers Week (DH/National Schizophrenia Fellowship, 2001). Figures published by the National Schizophrenia Fellowship (n.d.)

Box 9.3	**The pressures facing carers**

The assisted suicide of Sarah Lawson brought the plight of people caring for those with mental health problems sharply into focus. The reality of looking after people with such severe problems means they often live under unimaginable pressures with very little support. When Sarah Lawson committed suicide in April last year, it was a desperate act by a severely depressed young woman. The fact that her father, James Lawson, assisted in her suicide by placing a bag over her head as she lay dying from an overdose is shocking – even appalling. But few of the estimated 1.26 million people caring for a friend or relative with some form of mental illness are going to be appalled by the actions of this man – an exhausted, distraught and desperate parent. Caring for someone in these circumstances can be tough, unremitting and lonely. Every year, a few people are inevitably pushed beyond the limit of their endurance (Winchester, 2001). James Lawson later received a two-year suspended sentence.

Source: Community Care (2001)

suggest that almost one in four of Britain's carers (22 per cent or 1.26 million people) are caring for someone with a mental health problem, often with only limited support from statutory services. Traditionally, the needs of carers of people with mental health problems have received even less attention than carers of people from other user groups. This was initially highlighted in the ground-breaking study *Families Caring for People Diagnosed as Mentally Ill* (Perring *et al.*, 1990) funded by the DH. In particular, Perring *et al.* argued that the carers of people with mental health problems had been neglected for two main reasons:

1. The literature tends to focus on physical caring tasks.
2. Mental health services have tended to focus on the person with mental health problems, without necessarily recognising the needs and contributions of the user's family and friends. This may be partly because of the strong medical influence within mental health practice and research which had tended to focus on definitions and theories of mental illness and neglected 'the more general non-medical, societal and familial aspects' of living with a mental health problem (Perring *et al.*, 1990: 3). Even where families have been considered, this is often only as an adjunct to helping 'the patient'. On other occasions, families have been seen as 'part of the problem' rather than 'part of the solution' – either contributing to the mental health problem in the first place or exacerbating it (personal communications, mental health workers).

Despite these limitations in the literature, Perring *et al.* were able to identify a number of key issues for the carers of people with mental health problems, including the considerable stresses and strains of the caring role and a lack of support from formal services (see Box 9.4).

Many of these themes have since been developed in more recent studies. In 1995 the National Schizophrenia Fellowship published a national survey of carers' needs on behalf of the DH's Mental Health Taskforce (Hogman and Pearson, 1995). For the research authors, the carers of people with mental health problems had become 'silent partners' in community care: so used to the difficulties associated with caring and with lack of support from formal services that they see this way of life as the norm and do not ask for help (see Box 9.5). As a result, the study began with 'four facts you need to know about carers' (p. 4):

1. Every carer has individual caring responsibilities and individual needs. Carers cannot be classified as one group with a shared set of needs.
2. Carers are experts in severe mental illness.
3. Carers do not always want to care.
4. Carers have a low ceiling in terms of demands for services. They are not a group that make unrealistic demands.

Of course, both these studies took place prior to more recent carers' legislation, and considerable progress might have been expected given the policy initiatives

Box 9.4	The carers of people with mental health problems

Perring *et al.*'s (1990) review of the literature suggests that:

- Carers of people with mental health problems face 'difficult' behaviour, including social withdrawal, uncontrollable restlessness, threatened or actual suicide or hypochondriacal preoccupations. Often carers are uncertain how to respond, wanting to be sympathetic, but feeling baffled and frustrated.
- Carers often take on unexpected new roles, from personal care to household and financial responsibilities.
- There can be a substantial impact on every aspect of family life (marital and parental relationships, domestic routine, social life, leisure activities, employment and financial circumstances).
- Caring can provoke a range of emotions (including negative feelings such as fear, anger, resentment and a sense of being overloaded, as well as positive emotions such as warmth and love).
- Caring can have a negative effect on health and mental health.
- Carers are concerned about the low quality and quantity of their contact with formal services. Key issues include frequent staff changes and a lack of continuity, family concerns being ignored until a crisis is reached, unsympathetic workers and poor communication between workers and families.
- There are high levels of unmet need.

Overall: 'the ability of families to cope against a background of inadequate formal support does not mean that services to families need no improvement. The issues of unreported need, the continuing evidence that care by the family is associated with various indicators of stress, and criticisms that families make of their experience with professional workers all underline the fact that some effective intervention for families with a mentally ill member is essential, for the benefit of the family and identified patient alike' (Perring *et al.*, 1990: 44).

set out earlier in this chapter. Despite this, Wright *et al.*'s (2000) thematic review of NHS-funded research suggests that there are significant variations in the amount of support available to carers, with many not receiving the services they need to continue in a caring role or to maintain their own health. Research by the Mental Health Foundation (2001) also highlights the emotional difficulties and the lack of support which respondents experienced when trying to support a friend with mental health problems. Similar themes are echoed by a number of other commentators, who suggest that the contribution of carers is often undervalued and their needs unrecognised. As Allen (1997: 34) suggests: 'Carers are the invisible corner-stone of community care. For the relatives and friends of someone with a severe and enduring mental health problem, community care represents a 24-hour burden with serious, often unacknowledged consequences.'

Box 9.5	The silent partners

- 71 per cent said that caring had resulted in health problems such as stress, depression, heart trouble, sleep problems and anxiety: 'Don't you know anyone it hasn't affected? You live on a knife edge all the time.'
- 58 per cent said that caring led to significant extra expense: 'We are doing the government's job for them for free without it being acknowledged.'
- 42 per cent said that time spent caring had prevented them from working as much as they would have liked: 'As a carer I had to go part-time and also had to have time off ... Therefore I did not reach my full potential in work, and therefore could not demand a higher salary, thus affecting my pension on retirement.'
- Many carers wanted more services than they were receiving to help them continue in their role: 'The problem is that there are not enough facilities within the community, and many people do not know how to gain access to what little there is.'
- Information is crucial for carers, yet is often neglected: 'I have had to search for all the information regarding services, sections and care management, nothing has been offered.'
- Many carers had experienced a crisis and felt that there was insufficient support: 'I found it very frustrating that nothing was being done to help when she was ill.'

Overall, many people found caring without adequate support extremely difficult:

It has been a nightmare which I wouldn't wish on any living soul. It has broken a part of my heart, which I feel will never heal.

The carer is almost as much a victim of the illness as the patient.

I know how to care – but I have had enough. I want to be able to live whatever life I have left – my way – and know my daughter is safe and will be helped.

Sources: Summarised from Hogman and Pearson (1995): assorted quotes; sample: 400 carers

More recently, the needs of the carers of people with mental health problems have received renewed attention from the national voluntary organisation Rethink (2003b, 2003c). According to a survey of 1,451 users and carers, around half of carers felt that improvements were taking place in mental health services, but that there was still a long way to go, with many people not receiving a proper break from caring, not sufficiently involved with health and social care professionals and concerned about the availability of relevant services. Many carers also felt that caring had adverse affects on their health, their social life and their family relationships, and that access to and take-up of carers assessments was low (see Box 9.6). Similar issues have also been raised by monitoring undertaken on behalf of the DH, which emphasises the adverse effect which caring can have on carers' own mental health (Singleton *et al.*, 2002). As the Rethink chair and chief executive suggested in their introduction to one of these reports (2003c: 2):

| Box 9.6 | **Rethink survey 2003** |

- 92 per cent of carers want contact with a professional, but only 49 per cent say they are in regular contact all or most of the time. A key barrier was concerns about 'patient confidentiality', which many carers felt was used by professionals in an unhelpful way to block the sharing of information (see also Pinfold *et al.*, 2004; Rapaport *et al.*, 2006; Gray *et al.*, 2008, for further discussion).
- One in four carers said they had been denied access to help during the past three years. For one person, a 'lack of beds and resources locally means my son doesn't get help until a crisis', while for another carer 'no one ever phones back when I make a call requesting help. [It] usually takes seven or eight calls to get hold of anyone'.
- Key frustrations for carers include shortage of adequate service provision locally (30 per cent), difficulty accessing crisis services (16 per cent), difficulty getting access to mental health professionals (14 per cent), concerns about the quality of mental health staffing (11 per cent) and a feeling of not being listened to or valued by professionals (10 per cent).
- One in four carers feel that they don't have any information to help them.
- 41 per cent of carers said that caring had moderately or significantly affected their physical or mental health.
- 60 per cent of carers say that their ability to have a social life outside the home is significantly or moderately affected.
- 50 per cent of carers feel that they never have any choice about whether they continue to provide help and support.
- Only one in four carers had received a carer's assessment.

Sources: Summarised from Rethink (2003b, 2003c)

Mental health carers ... are recognised now in a way that they were not 20 years ago. More carers than ever before are involved not just in one-to-one care but also in the planning of mental health services. On paper, carers have never had it so good. And yet the reality of caring today is to see a deterioration in your own mental and physical health, reduced finances and career prospects, strained family relationships and lost leisure. There are regional variations in the availability of information, help and support. Too many carers find the present legal right to an assessment of their needs a sham because identified needs go unmet. Pockets of good practice for supporting carers are emerging but the challenge is to see these vital supports and services extended to all.

Another significant contribution has been Arksey *et al.*'s (2002) review of the literature and consultation with key stakeholders – which suggests that services should be underpinned by four key principles:

1. Positive and inclusive: mental health professionals should have a positive approach to carers, involve them in decision making and recognise them as partners or 'co-experts'.

2. Flexible and individualised: services should be person-centred, reflecting the diversity of carers.
3. Accessible and responsive: services should be available at all times, including outside 'office hours', and offer a rapid response.
4. Integrated and coordinated: services should be 'joined up'; carers' services should be embedded within mainstream mental health services.

Overall (Arksey *et al.*, 2002: 40):

> Support for carers of people with mental health problems needs to be offered in the form of a flexible package of services that is tailored to suit the individual carer–care recipient dyad; that is underpinned by key principles of service delivery such as inclusiveness, responsiveness and co-ordination; and that takes account of local contexts. The content of these packages will vary, and will reflect the diversity of carer experience in terms of geography, socioeconomic variables, patient diagnosis and stage of illness, as well as differing delivery methods provided by both the statutory, private and voluntary sectors.
>
> A consensual view emerged ... that ... interventions should be tailored to the needs of both individual carers and care recipients; disregarding care recipients can lead to unanticipated outcomes, as well as hindering the full realisation of benefits ... On this basis, we feel that it is important to identify and examine what carers, and care recipients, believe is effective in terms of the range of services available and explore how best these can be delivered in order to lead to improved outcomes for both carers and care recipients.

Marginalised groups

A key criticism of some of the existing literature is the implicit assumption that carers are a single category of people, each with similar needs. As the quote from Arksey *et al.* above suggests, this is an oversimplistic view that runs the risk of neglecting the needs of individual carers. In particular, we know relatively little about (Arksey *et al.*, 2002: 11):

- BME community carers;
- carers of people with dual diagnosis;
- carers supporting more than one person; and
- less-common caring situations (for instance, caring in gay and lesbian relationships or caring at a distance).

An additional group traditionally neglected in the literature are young carers – children and young people caring for a parent with a mental illness. This issue has been particularly highlighted in recent years as a result of a general growth in our awareness of the needs of young carers (through research and campaigning carried out by academic bodies such as the Young Carers Research Group at Loughborough University and by other key stakeholders – see Aldridge and Becker, 2003; Barnado's, n.d.; Royal College of Psychiatrists, 2011). Although estimates vary, there may be some 68,000 young carers in Britain, with anywhere between 6,000 and 17,000 young carers looking after mentally ill parents. Overall (Aldridge and Becker, 2003: 137):

> The findings [of this study] suggest that, where professionals engage in effective intervention procedures (recognising children's caring roles, acknowledging needs, making appropriate assessments and referrals), these can be crucial in preventing crises and allowing children (and parents) some degree of choice in undertaking informal care responsibilities. Furthermore, when professionals offer sensitive and non-demeaning assistance, this help is also highly valued by families. However, in most cases it seems that professionals fail to engage in these effective intervention procedures and to offer needs-led assistance.

The needs of carers

From the growing literature, it is clear that caring for someone with a mental health problem can have significant implications for almost every aspect of daily life. While some people describe positive aspects of caring (such as increasing self-confidence and putting other issues into perspective), negative aspects of caring include the potential impact on the carer's family and social life, work and health (see Box 9.7). Such difficulties can also be exacerbated if the person being supported is placed in a service out of the local area (see, for example, Rethink/CSIP, 2007). More generally, there is significant evidence to suggest that caring can have a significant impact on the physical and mental health of carers (see Box 9.8 for a summary).

In response to these issues, carers have expressed a desire for a range of support services to enable them to carry on in their caring role. In Leeds, for example, a carers' support service identified the importance of emotional support, respite, advocacy, 24-hour crisis support and good quality information (Allen, 1997). Also in the north of England, an evaluation of voluntary sector family support workers found that carers valued the workers as a counselling, information, listening and advocacy resource, providing both emotional and practical support (Weinberg and Huxley, 2000). Research into carers' experiences of assertive outreach suggests that carers value services perceived as flexible and responsive, close relationships with the team and practical support for the person they cared for (Hughes *et al.*, 2011). Similar findings have also emerged from Hill *et al.*'s (1998) study of the carers of people with manic depression. When asked to rate the importance of 17 areas of need and whether they had experienced any difficulties in accessing services in these areas, the carers concerned gave a very clear indication not only of the support they wanted, but also of the significant unmet need which continues to exist. In particular, carers said they saw as a high priority:

Box 9.7	The impact of caring

Hill *et al.*'s (1998) survey of 1,113 carers of people with manic depression found that many participants saw caring as having a negative effect on their friends and social life, with some also reporting a negative impact on their self-esteem, their family relationships and their work/work prospects.

Huang and Slevin's (1999) review of the literature on carers who live with someone who has schizophrenia suggests that many carers may experience:

- Physical problems (such as sleeping problems, headaches and chest tightness).
- Social difficulties (such as economic problems, stigma, social alienation and loss of leisure time/employment).
- Relationship difficulties (such as the disruption of family life, marriage problems or loss of friends).
- Psychological or emotional difficulties (such as anxiety about the future, grief reactions, mental health problems such as depression, loneliness and loss of motivation).

Leavey *et al.*'s (1998) study of 50 carers in north London found that 56 per cent saw caring as moderately stressful and 36 per cent considered it very stressful. Fifty-six per cent sometimes felt unable to cope with the person being cared for and 20 per cent often felt unable to cope.

In one evaluation of voluntary family support workers, interviews with 62 carers revealed the stressful nature of caring (Weinberg and Huxley, 2000: 500–1). Of the 62 people, 21 had consulted their GP for help with an emotional problem in recent months and a further 20 had received treatment for a potentially stress-related illness (such as high blood pressure, chest pains and palpitations). Carers also reported significant restrictions on their social and leisure activities, hidden expenses, a lack of understanding from family or friends and difficulties engaging in paid employment.

Black carers may have particular unmet needs as a result of culturally insensitive services and the difficulty of obtaining information in languages other than English (Arshad and Johal, 1999).

Carers in Gloucester said that they had given up various things to be a carer, including careers, independence, finances, holidays, health, social life and, for two people, 'everything'. Problems included tiredness, the unpredictability of the person cared for, emotional stress, physical and mental strain, isolation, relationship difficulties, financial pressure, boredom and worry about the future (Gregory *et al.*, 2006).

Although the focus is often on the risk that people with mental health problems may or may not pose to wider society (see Chapter 6), carers also face potential risk and little is known about the risk management strategies that they adopt (see Ryan, 2002, for an exception).

- 24-hour professional support seven days per week (valued by 67 per cent but with 67 per cent reporting difficulties accessing such support).
- Information about the illness of the person they cared for (valued by 61 per cent but with 55 per cent finding it difficult to obtain this).
- Opportunities to learn personal coping strategies (valued by 41 per cent but with 70 per cent finding this difficult to access).
- Regular updates from professionals (valued by 35 per cent but with 60 per cent finding this difficult to access).
- More education about manic depression (valued by 31 per cent but with 53 per cent finding it difficult to access).

Box 9.8	**The physical and mental health needs of carers**

Results from the General Household Survey (ONS, 2000) suggest that:

- Over one-third (35 per cent) of carers reported that their physical or mental health had been affected as a result of their caring responsibilities.
- Among carers devoting at least 20 hours per week to caring, half reported having a long-standing illness and over one-third (35 per cent) stated that their illness limited their activities.
- One-fifth of this group reported that their health over the past 12 months was 'not good'. Older carers spending 20 hours or over per week caring reported still higher levels of health problems; just under half (47 per cent) reported a limiting long-term illness (compared with 41 per cent in the general population).
- One-fifth of carers (20 per cent) reported feeling tired and the same number reported that they had a general feeling of stress.
- 17 per cent reported being short tempered.
- 14 per cent reported feeling depressed.
- 14 per cent reported having disturbed sleep.

Further ONS analysis of the mental health of carers (Singleton *et al.*, 2002) found that:

- 53 per cent of carers said their caring responsibilities caused them to worry a little or a lot of the time.
- 33 per cent said that caring made them depressed at least a little of the time.
- 48 per cent said that caring made them tired.
- The prevalence of mental health problems was highest among those caring for a spouse or partner, while carers who spent the least time caring had the best levels of mental health.
- Carers who were able to take a break from caring had lower levels of neurotic symptoms than those who had not.
- 13 per cent of carers reported having consulted a GP about being anxious or depressed or about a mental, nervous or emotional problem – 1 per cent had done so in the last two weeks.

Crucially, many of the priorities expressed by carers are also highly valued by service users (see Chapter 7) – and it may well be that a good quality service for users is also a good quality service for carers. Similar issues have also been raised by Huang and Slevin (1999: 91–2) in their review of the literature on the carers of people with schizophrenia. According to this review, carers particularly value:

- Advice and guidance on the use of medication.
- Education in the use of cognitive and behavioural strategies.
- Education of the total family regarding the need for family support.
- Contact information for external support groups.
- Family and individual counselling if required.
- Education about schizophrenia to improve family knowledge.
- Practical advice and guidance, including financial advice.
- Education on the use of stress-management techniques.
- Access to adequate respite services.
- 24-hour access to professionals in emergencies.
- Carer and client involvement in care planning.
- Access to multidisciplinary services via a key worker.
- Access to specialist mental health services when required.

Focus groups with users and carers carried out by Rethink (2005) suggest a similar list, with carers wanting to feel valued and respected by professionals, to be seen as a full and equal partner, to get better access to short breaks and to have their own personal support needs recognised more fully. As with user involvement (see Chapter 7), ensuring that services are responsive to the needs of carers is likely to require an explicit commitment to carer involvement, both in designing individual care packages and in shaping services more generally. As an example of the importance of carer involvement, Allen (1997) describes the development of a carers' service in south Leeds, emphasising the following guiding principles:

- The participation of carers in service provision, service development and service evaluation.
- Involvement that gives carers the power to influence policy and practice.
- Carer-led rather than service-led provision.
- Commitment to a continuing process rather than a one-off activity.
- Flexibility in the face of the diverse and potentially conflicting needs of users and carers.
- The strategic development of carer involvement in all aspects of the agency's work.

As in other chapters, by far the most powerful evidence comes from carers themselves, and Box 9.9 cites an example from the former Princess Royal Trust for Carers of someone talking directly about their experience of caring for a partner with mental health problems. Above and beyond the issues discussed in this chapter, this quote captures just some of the practical and emotional struggles that being a 'carer' for someone with a mental health problem involves, as well as the many positives, hopes and loving relationships.

Box 9.9	John's story

John has been caring for his partner since she suffered a breakdown two years ago

I first met my partner when she was working as a hospital portering assistant and was attracted by her cheerful personality and forthright nature. It was in November 2005 that she first fell ill, quite dramatically. She had a breakdown and ran away to 'live rough' in Brighton, although she was located the next day by the police. When this happened I was left feeling guilty and wondered what I had done wrong.

Now I keep my mobile on at work in case she experiences a crisis and also make several calls throughout the day to make sure she is okay. The only immediate family near us is my partner's sister and her family, who have a young family of their own to tend to and my partner would not be willing to have strangers caring for her. This means I don't have any respite, but when she takes her medication consistently, things calm down and I can take a breather.

The main casualty in our relationship has been trust. My partner often thinks that my concerns, although innocent, are a just way for me to get her into hospital. I often find myself questioning things like 'has she taken her medication?' or 'is she about to run away/attempt to take her own life'? There have also been times when members of my family have felt that there is nothing wrong with my partner; that she is only attention seeking. This has been hurtful, maybe even offensive at times.

Obviously my partner is no longer able to work and relies on benefits and I am unable to work extra hours due to my domestic obligations. All this has had a dramatic impact on our finances. In order to cope, I have had to put our unsecured debts onto a debt management plan and to budget the finances very carefully each month in order to meet priority bills.

My health has also suffered due to the pressures of caring; I suffer bouts of depression diagnosed as secondary to my partner's illness, which has caused me to take time off work.

When my partner first became ill I consulted my GP for loss of sleep and was referred to my local Carers' Centre. I must confess to feeling rather nervous on that first contact, although I have found that having someone there to talk through the more difficult moments was a lifeline. The support and advice has always been practical and realistic.

If I could change anything it would be people's perceptions of mental illness. Mental health is still a taboo subject. People seem to have this (unfounded) fear of mental illness because of badly made films and no experience on a personal basis.

Mental illness is no scarier than any physical illness. If you break a bone for example you see a specialist who puts on a cast to allow it to repair. If you have a breakdown you see a specialist who identifies the cause and provides medication to help the mind repair itself.

My partner has always wanted to be a teaching assistant. Since she has had her medication changed she has been much more focused on this and is attending courses to gain the necessary qualifications. My hopes for the future are that she will be able to realise that ambition; then all the sleepless nights would have been worthwhile.

Source: www.carers.org/johns-story

Conclusion

Despite greater recognition of the needs of carers, much remains to be done if carers generally (and the carers of people with mental health problems in particular) are to receive sufficient support to be able to continue in their role. Caring has a substantial impact on the lives of many people in the UK and, although we have only begun to acknowledge it relatively recently, it is the contribution of carers that makes the work of statutory health and social services possible. While caring can be a positive experience, it can also bring a series of negative consequences (both for the carer and for the person being cared for). As a result, statutory services have a duty to provide much better and more responsive support than they currently do in order to give carers the help they deserve and need. While there has been relatively little research in this area (compared to other chapters in this book), it seems clear that the way forward must lie in providing a range of support (from accessible information and practical advice to specialist and crisis support). However, also significant seems to be the value base and interpersonal skills of individual workers, with a much greater need for human skills such as empathy and the ability to listen, and a much greater willingness to acknowledge the expertise of carers and value them as people with a key contribution to make. If we could achieve this, then the 'silent partners' of Hogman and Pearson's (1995) study could one day become genuine partners – valued, listened to and supported to continue in their role as the key providers of community care.

Above all, Glasby et al.'s (2010) work for Downing Street and the Department of Health suggests a fundamental tension in support services for carers – with three potentially overlapping rationales:

1. Do we support carers because this is a cost-effective way of supporting users (and indeed because the current system could not function if we didn't)?
2. Are we supporting carers because too many people leave the labour market to become full-time carers – and we would maximise people's social and economic contribution if they did not have so many caring responsibilities?
3. Are we supporting carers because they are citizens too and have the same right as anyone else to a good life?

All these are potentially legitimate approaches, but the danger is that we might be designing services with a mix of different motives in mind. Supporting carers only to support the end user is arguably very different to wanting to maximize people's economic contribution, which is different again to supporting people as citizens. Perhaps one of the reasons why policy and practice remain somewhat underdeveloped in this area compared to other chapters of this book is that we have not yet fully reconciled these potential tensions.

Reflection exercises

1. The impact of caring (*exercise for all readers*)

Imagine that someone you care about develops a mental health problem:

- Why did you become friends in the first place and what do you most like about the person?
- How would you respond to them developing a mental health problem – particularly if you work in mental health yourself?
- Would it change the nature of your relationship and, if so, how?
- If the person is a family member, what impact might it have on family life?
- How would your friends and family react if you developed a mental health problem?

2. Services for carers (*exercise for all practitioners*)

Reflect on someone you have worked with recently who the system would define as a 'carer':

- How might people find out about services for carers locally?
- Would this involve the person identifying themselves as a carer?
- Are some groups of carers more likely to recognise this label and apply it to themselves than others?
- How does your organisation identify and support carers?
- How much do you know about the experiences of carers locally and about what services are available?

If you work in a team setting, try to raise the issues identified in this chapter in a team meeting to explore as a group.

3. Working with carers (*exercise for all practitioners*)

- How does your agency/profession identify and support carers?
- How do other professions/agencies do this?

Discuss your findings with someone from a different organisational or professional background. Do you both have similar approaches and do you both know the range of services available locally? If not, how might it impact on a carer depending on where they first accessed the system?

Further resources

1. Tew, J. (2100) *Social Approaches to Mental Distress*. Basingstoke: Palgrave.

   Chapter 6 provides an overview of practice issues in relation to families and carers.

2. Repper, J. *et al.* (2008) 'Carers' experiences of mental health services and views about assessments', in Stickley, T. and Basset, T. (eds) *Learning about Mental Health Practice*. Chichester: Wiley; and Parr, H. (2009) *Carers and Supporting Recovery*. Scottish Recovery Network (www.scottishrecovery.net) provide vivid summaries of research interviews with carers on their experiences.

3. There are a number of research reports and briefing papers on supporting families and children where parents have mental health difficulties. These include:

   Evans, J. and Fowler, R. (2008) *Family Minded: Supporting Children in Families Affected by Mental Illness*. Ilford: Barnardo's.
   Aldridge, J. and Becker, S. (2003) *Children caring for parents with mental illness.* Bristol: The Policy Press.

4. The Royal College of Psychiatrists (2011) has published guidance on working with parents and their children. Further resources and information is also available from the Children's Society (www.youngcarer.com), YCNet (an online information and discussion forum for young carers) (www.youngcarers.net) and the NHS Choices Young Carers website (www.nhs.uk/CarersDirect/young/Pages/Youngcarershome.aspx).

5. Arksey *et al.*'s (2002) report *Services to Support Carers of People with Mental Health Problems* summarises a review of the literature (1985–2001) and consultation with national statutory and voluntary agencies, local managers and practitioners and carers. A second report by the same funder on sharing information with carers offers a helpful guide to good practice (Pinfold *et al.*, 2004).

6. Carers UK is a national voluntary organisation which campaigns for the rights of carers, conducts research, produces policy briefings and develops good practice guides based on the experiences of carers (see www.carersuk.org). Additional information is also available from the former Princess Royal Trust for Carers, who have worked with the Royal College of Psychiatrists to campaign for the carers of people with mental health problems and people with learning disabilities (see www.partnersincare.co.uk).

7. The Mental Health Care website (www.mentalhealthcare.org.uk) contains information for carers about mental health and research from the Institute of Psychiatry and the South London and Maudsley NHS Foundation Trust. It is supported by the mental health charity, Rethink.

8. For overall policy, see the government's 2008 carers' strategy (HM Government, 2008) and a subsequent 2010 update (HM Government, 2010). The DH (2002f) has also published guidance (*Developing Services for Carers and Families of People with Mental Illness*).

10 Conclusion

Although mental health policy and practice across the four countries of the UK has moved forward very significantly over the last 15 years, mental health services still seem some way away from a clear and consistent vision as to the way forward – and a series of long-standing and complex problems remain. Arguably still underfunded compared to other parts of the NHS, mental health too often seems to be seen as a stand-alone and poorly understood area of policy and practice. From a recent period in which there was a stronger political will to improve mental health services, and a commitment of additional resources by which to achieve this, service developments in the coming years will have to be conceived and introduced within a challenging financial climate where total available funding across health and social care sectors may remain static or actually reduce in real terms.

The formulation of policy is still far from evidence based; nor does it often promote the sort of service provision that many service users (or family members) say would be most helpful for them. If any of the countries of the UK were to start from scratch, with a brief to establish mental health services that were truly fit for purpose, it is unlikely that the resulting configuration would remotely resemble what is now provided. In particular, it is unlikely that such a large proportion of resources would be put into inpatient services that are often not evaluated positively by service users or families, and which tend not to be effective in terms of addressing the full range of medical, psychological and social issues that may need to be dealt with, if people are to be enabled to move forward on a path to longer-term recovery.

However, policy makers and practitioners do not start from a blank sheet – and current policies and practices may be seen as resulting from particular histories of evolving service provision. Changes in policy and practice have been influenced in part by genuine concern and compassion on the part of those charged with organising the delivery of services, but also by popular attitudes, media constructions, political discourses, professional self-advancement and a range of other factors which may not necessarily put what is best for the service user at the centre. In this book, we have sought to explore and analyse these processes in the hope that greater clarity as to where policy has come from may, in turn, open up a more informed debate as to where policy should be going.

Looking back to the Enlightenment and forward to the present day, it may be surprising that we seem little closer to developing shared answers to some of the key questions that relate to mental health. For example:

- What is mental ill-health and what causes it?
- What is the best way of responding?
- What are the factors that really make a difference in enabling people to recover?
- How should society deal with behaviour it finds difficult to comprehend?
- How do we balance individual rights and well-being with the safety of others?

However, it is perhaps this very lack of certainty – and the need to remain open-minded – that can make it so fascinating to work within this field.

We have some indications of what may be at the forefront of policy development over the coming years. There is now a broad political consensus across all the countries of the UK that making real improvements to people's mental health requires concerted action across government and not just within the health and social care sector – although there is less clarity as to how to deliver this in practice. Alongside this, the concept of well-being is potentially helpful in focusing attention on policy outcomes that go beyond economic growth – and there is a rekindling of interest in issues such as community cohesion that, if approached in the right way, could benefit both the general population and those suffering mental ill-health. The roll-out of different strategies and approaches across the four countries of the UK will provide interesting opportunities for learning and comparison in terms of what may be most effective.

There is also an emerging consensus that, as for people with other health conditions or care needs, people with mental health difficulties should be enabled to have more choice and control in relation to the services that they receive – and be invited to self-manage and co-produce solutions that work for them, rather than be expected to wait passively while 'experts' make them better. This has major implications for practitioners from all professions – and delivering this in practice will be challenging to established attitudes and ways of working. It will be interesting to see whether opening up personal health budgets for mental health service users may act as a catalyst for change in this area.

Although the more technical debates in this book are important (for example, the best way of providing community mental health services), the broader issues seem to be moral and political. What kind of life do we want to have as a society, how do we best achieve this and how do we support people experiencing mental distress to live a full and satisfying life? No matter how difficult these questions are to answer, it is our contention that a solution will never be forthcoming unless the voices of mental health service users, their families and mental health workers are heard more fully than has been the case in the past.

References

11 Million (Office of the Children's Commissioner for England) (2007) *Pushed into the Shadows: Young People's Experiences of Adult Mental Health Facilities*. London: 11 Million.

Abel-Smith, B. (1964) *The Hospitals 1800–1948: A Study in Social Administration in England and Wales*. London: Heinemann.

Addis, S. *et al.* (2009) 'The health, social care and housing needs of lesbians, gay, bisexual and transgender older people: A review of the literature', *Health and Social Care in the Community*, 17(6): 647–58.

Age Concern (2007) *Improving Services and Support for Older People with Mental Health Problems*. London: Age Concern.

Alakeson, V. (2007) *The Contribution of Self-Direction to Improving the Quality of Mental Health Services*. US Department of Health and Human Services (available online via http://aspe. hhs.gov/daltcp/reports/2007/Mhslfdir.htm).

Alakeson, V. (2014) *Delivering Personal Health Budgets: A Guide to Policy and Practice*. Bristol: The Policy Press.

Aldridge, J. and Becker, S. (2003) *Children Caring for Parents with Mental Illness: Perspectives of Young Carers, Parents and Professionals*. Bristol: The Policy Press.

Allen, C. (1997) 'Somebody cares', *Health Service Journal*, 107(5558): 34–5.

Anthony, W. A. (1993) 'Recovery from mental illness: The guiding vision of the mental health service system in the 1990s', *Psychological Rehabilitation Journal*, 16, 11–24.

Appleby, J., Harrison, A. and Devlin, N. (2003) *What Is the Real Cost of More Patient Choice?* London: King's Fund.

Appleby, L. (2008) *Policies and Practice for Europe*, DH / WHO Europe, 10 October.

Arksey, H. *et al.* (2002) *Services to Support Carers of People with Mental Health Problems: Overview Report*. York: Social Policy Research Unit, University of York.

Armstrong, E. (2002) *The Guide to Mental Health for Nurses in Primary Care*. Abingdon: Radcliffe Medical Press.

Armstrong, L. (1997) 'Do practice nurses want to learn about depression?', *Practice Nursing*, 8, 21–6.

Arnstein, S. R. (1969) 'A ladder of citizen participation', *American Institute of Planning Journal*, July, 216–24.

Arshad, J. and Johal, B. (1999) 'Culture club', *Nursing Times*, 95(9): 66–7.

Audit Commission (1986) *Making a Reality of Community Care*. London: HMSO.

Audit Commission (1997) *The Coming of Age: Improving Care Services for Older People*. London: Audit Commission.

Audit Commission (2000a) *The Way to Go Home: Rehabilitation and Remedial Services for Older People*. London: Audit Commission.

Audit Commission (2000b) *Forget Me Not: Mental Health Services for Older People*. London: Audit Commission.

Audit Commission (2002) *Integrated Services for Older People: Building a Whole Systems Approach in England*. London: Audit Commission.

Audit Commission (2004) *Transforming Primary Care*. London: Audit Commission.

Badger, D. *et al.* (1999) 'Planning to meet the needs of offenders with mental disorders in the United Kingdom', *Psychiatric Services*, 50(12): 1624–7.

Baguley, C., Rushforth, D. and Whyte, M. (2006) *The Graduate Primary Care Mental Health Worker Programme: A View from Higher Education Training Providers*. HEA Psychology Network, University of York.

Bahl, V. (1999) 'Mental illness: A national perspective', in D. Bhugra and V. Bahl (eds), *Ethnicity: An Agenda for Mental Health*. London: Gaskell.

Baker, S. (2000) *Environmentally Friendly? Patients' Views of Conditions on Psychiatric Wards*. London: Mind.

Baldwin, S. and Twigg, J. (1990) 'Women and community care: Reflections on a debate', in M. Maclean and D. Groves (eds), *Women's Issues in Social Policy*. London: Routledge.

Barnado's (n. d.) *Keeping the Family in Mind: A Briefing on Young Carers Whose Parents Have Mental Health Problems*. Ilford, Barnado's.

Barnes, M. and Bowl, R. (2001) *Taking over the Asylum: Empowerment and Mental Health*. Basingstoke: Palgrave.

Barnes, M. and Walker, A. (1996) 'Consumerism versus empowerment: A principled approach to the involvement of older service users', *Policy and Politics*, 24(4): 375–93.

Bartlett, C. *et al.* (1999) 'Projection of alternatives to acute psychiatric beds: Review of an emerging service assessment method', *Journal of Mental Health*, 8(6): 555–68.

Bates, S. and Coren, E. (2006) *The Extent and Impact of Parental Mental Health Problems on Families and the Acceptability, Accessibility and Effectiveness of Interventions*. London: SCIE.

Bean, P. and Mounser, P. (1993) *Discharged from Mental Hospitals*. Basingstoke: Macmillan.

Bebbington, P. *et al.* (2004) 'Psychosis, victimisation and childhood disadvantage: Evidence from the second British National Survey of Psychiatric Morbidity', *British Journal of Psychiatry*, 185: 220–6.

Beck, A. *et al.* (1997) 'The Nottingham Acute Bed Study: Alternatives to acute psychiatric care', *British Journal of Psychiatry*, 170, 247–52.

Beer, D. *et al.* (2005) 'Low secure units: factors predicting delayed discharge', *Journal of Forensic Psychiatry and Psychology*, 16(4): 621–37.

Bennet, C. (1989) 'The Worcester Development Project: General practitioner satisfaction with a new community psychiatry service', *Journal of the Royal College of General Practitioners*, 39(320): 106–9.

Bennett, J., Kalathil, J. and Keating, F. (2007) *Race Equality Training in Mental Health Services in England: Does One Size Fit All?* London: Sainsbury Centre for Mental Health.

Bentall, R. (2003) *Madness Explained: Psychosis and Human Nature*. London: Allen Lane.

Beresford, P. (2000) 'What have madness and psychiatric system survivors got to do with disability studies?', *Disability and Society*, 15(1): 167–72.

Beresford, P. (2002) 'Thinking about mental health: Towards a social model', *Journal of Mental Health*, 11(6): 581–4.

Beresford, P. (2003) *It's Our Lives: A Short Theory of Knowledge, Distance and Experience*. London: Citizen Press/Shaping Our Lives.

Bevan, A. (1948) 'A message to the medical profession', *British Medical Journal*, ii, 1.

Bevan, G. *et al.* (2014) *The Four Health Systems of the UK: How Do They Compare*. London: Health Foundation/Nuffield Trust.

Beveridge, W. (1942) *Social Insurance and Allied Services*. London: HMSO.

Bhui, K. and Bhugra, D. (1999) 'Service provision for ethnic minorities', in D. Bhugra and V. Bahl (eds), *Ethnicity: An Agenda for Mental Health*. London: Gaskell.

Bhui, K., Bhugra, D. and McKenzie, K. (2000) *Specialist Services for Minority Ethnic Groups?* (Maudsley discussion paper no. 8). London: Institute of Psychiatry.

Birchwood, M. *et al.* (eds) (2002) *Early Intervention in Psychosis.* Chichester: Wiley.

Birchwood, M., Todd, P. and Jackson, C. (1998) 'Early intervention in psychosis: The critical period hypothesis', *British Journal of Psychiatry*, supplement, 172, 53–9.

Black, K. and Shillitoe, R. (1997) 'Developing mental health services sensitive to women's needs', *British Journal of Health Care Management*, 3(1): 27–9.

Bloor, K. and Maynard, A. (1994) 'An outsider's view of the NHS reforms', *British Medical Journal*, 309, 352–3.

Blount, A. (1998) *Integrated Primary Care: The Future of Medical and Mental Health Collaboration.* London: Norton.

BMA/NHS Confederation (2003) *Investing in General Practice: The New General Medical Services Contract.* London: BMA.

Boardman, R. E. and Hodgson, A. P. (2000) 'Community in-patient units and halfway hospitals', *Advances in Psychiatric Treatment*, 6, 120–7.

Bochel, H. (ed.) (2011) *The Conservative Party and Social Policy.* Bristol: The Policy Press.

Borrill, J. (2000) *Developments in Treatment for People with Psychotic Experiences* (updates, vol. 2, issue 9). London: Mental Health Foundation.

Bower, P. and Sibbald, B. (2003) 'On-site mental health workers in primary care: Effects on professional practice' (Cochrane Review): *Cochrane Library*, 1, Oxford: Update Software.

Bower, P., Jerrim, S. and Gask, L. (2004) 'Primary care mental health workers: Role expectations, conflict and ambiguity', *Health and Social Care in the Community*, 12(4): 336–45.

Bowl, R. (2007) 'The need for change in UK mental health services: South Asian service users' views', *Ethnicity and Health*, 12(1): 1–19.

Boydell, J. *et al.* (2001) 'Incidence of schizophrenia in ethnic minorities in London: Ecological study into interactions with environment', *British Medical Journal*, 323, 1–4.

Boyle, M. (2002) *Schizophrenia: A Scientific Delusion?* London: Routledge.

Bracken, P. *et al.* (1998) 'Mental health and ethnicity: An Irish dimension', *British Journal of Psychiatry*, 172, 103–5.

Bracken, P. *et al.* (2012) 'Psychiatry beyond the current paradigm', *British Journal of Psychiatry*, 201, 430–4.

Bradby, H. *et al.* (2007) 'British Asian families and the use of child and adolescent mental health services: A qualitative study of a hard to reach group', *Social Science and Medicine*, 65, 2413–24.

Bradley, K. (2009) *The Bradley Report.* London: DH.

Braye, S. (2000) 'Participation and involvement in social care: An overview', in H. Kemshall and R. Littlechild (eds), *User Involvement and Participation in Social Care: Research Informing Practice.* London: Jessica Kingsley.

Breeze, J. and Repper, J. (1998) 'Struggling for control: The care experiences of "difficult" patients in mental health services', *Journal of Advanced Nursing*, 28(6): 1301–11.

British Medical Association (BMA) (1992) *Priorities for Community Care.* London: British Medical Association.

Brodie, D. (2003) 'Partnership working: A service user perspective', in J. Glasby and E. Peck (eds), *Care Trusts: Partnership Working in Action.* Abingdon: Radcliffe Medical Press.

Brooker, C. and Curran, J. (2006) 'The national continuous quality improvement tool for mental health education: Results of targeted and supported implementation in England', *Journal of Interprofessional Care*, 20(3): 276–89.

Brooker, C. and Repper, J. (2009) *Mental Health: From Policy to Practice.* Edinburgh: Elsevier.

Brooker, C. *et al.* (2009) 'Review of service delivery and organisational research focused on prisoners with mental disorders', *Journal of Forensic Psychiatry and Psychology*, 20(S1): S102–S123.

Brown, G.W. and Harris,T. (1978) *The Social Origins of Depression*. London:Tavistock Press.

Browne, D. (1997) *Black People and Sectioning: The Black Experience of Detention under the Civil Sections of the Mental Health Act*. London: Little Rock.

Buchanan, M. (2013) 'England's mental health services in crisis', London: BBC News, www.bbc.co.uk/news/health-2453704

Buchanan, M. (2014) 'Mental patients forced to travel miles for care', London: BBC News, www.bbc.co.uk/news/uk-27285555

Buckner, L. and Yeandle, S. (2011) *Valuing Carers 2011: Calculating the Value of Carers' Support*. London: Carers UK.

Burchadt,T. (2003) *Employment Retention and the Onset of Sickness or Disability: Evidence from the Labour Force Survey Longitudinal Datasets*. Department of Workforce and Pensions in-house report no. 109.

Burns, T. (2004) *Community Mental Health Teams: A Guide to Current Practices*. Oxford: Oxford University Press.

Burns, T. *et al.* (2007) 'Use of intensive case management to reduce time in hospital in people with severe mental illness: Systematic review and meta-regression', *British Medical Journal*, 335, 336–40.

Burns,T. *et al.* (2009) 'The impact of supported employment and working on clinical and social functioning', *Schizophrenia Bulletin*, 35(5): 949–58.

Burns,T. *et al.* (2013) 'Community treatment orders for patients with psychosis (OCTET): A randomised controlled trial', *The Lancet* (published online via http://dx.doi.org/10.1016).

Butterfield,W.J.A. H. (1964) *New Frontiers in Health*. London: Office of Health Economics.

Cabinet Office (1999) *Modernising Government*. London:TSO.

Cabinet Office (2007) *Reaching Out: Think Family*. London: Cabinet Office.

Calnan, M. and Gabe, J. (1991) 'Recent developments in general practice: A sociological analysis', in J. Gabe, M. Calnan and M. Bury (eds), *Sociology of the Health Service*. London: Routledge.

Camden and Islington Mental Health NHS Trust (2001) 'Drayton Park crisis project for women: An alternative to hospital admission for women in mental health crisis', unpublished leaflet, London: Camden and Islington Mental Health NHS Trust.

Campbell, J. and Oliver, M. (1996) *Disability Politics in Britain: Understanding Our Past, Changing Our Future*. London: Routledge.

Campbell, P. (1996) 'The history of the user movement in the United Kingdom', in T. Heller (eds), *Mental Health Matters*. Basingstoke: Macmillan.

Campbell, P. (2001) 'The role of users in psychiatric services in service development – Influence not power', *Psychiatric Bulletin*, 25, 87–8.

Campbell, P. (2008) 'Service user involvement', in T. Stickley and T. Basset (eds), *Learning about Mental Health Practice*. Chichester:Wiley.

Campbell, S. *et al.* (2007) 'Quality of primary care in England with the introduction of pay for performance', *New England Journal of Medicine*, 357, 181–90.

Canning, A. *et al.* (2009) 'A survey exploring the provision of carers' support in medium and high secure services in England and Wales', *Journal of Forensic Psychiatry and Psychology*, 20(6): 868–85.

Care Quality Commission (CQC) (2011) *Count Me in 2010: Results of the 2010 National Census of Inpatients and Patients on Supervised Community Treatment in Mental Health and Learning Disability Services in England and Wales*. London: CQC.

Carers UK (2003) *Missed Opportunities: The Impact of New Rights for Carers*. London: Carers UK.

Carers UK (2004) *In Poor Health: The Impact of Caring on Health*. London: Carers UK.

Carers UK (2006) *In the Know: The Importance of Information for Carers*. London: Carers UK.

Carpenter, J. and Sbaraini, S. (1997) *Choice, Information and Dignity: Involving Users and Carers in Mental Health Services*. Bristol: The Policy Press.

Carpenter, J. *et al.* (2004) 'Integration and targeting of community care for people with severe and enduring mental health problems: Users' experiences of the Care Programme Approach and care management', *British Journal of Social Work*, 34, 313–33.

Carr, S. (2004) *Has Service User Involvement Made a Difference to Social Care Services?* London: SCIE.

Carr, S. (2005) '"The sickness label infected everything we said" – Lesbian and gay perspectives on mental distress', in J. Tew (ed.), *Social Perspectives in Mental Health*. London: Jessica Kingsley.

Centre for Economic Performance's Mental Health Policy Group (2006) *The Depression Report: A New Deal for Depression and Anxiety Disorders*. London: London School of Economics.

Centre for Public Mental Health (2006) *Adult Mental Health Service Mapping: Report Autumn 2004 and Spring 2006*. Durham: University of Durham.

Chisholm, A. and Ford, R. (2004) *Transforming Mental Health Care: Assertive Outreach and Crisis Resolution in Practice*. London: Sainsbury Centre for Mental Health.

Churchill, R. *et al.* (2007) *International Experiences of Using Community Treatment Orders*. London: DH.

Clark, M. (2003) 'First of the few', *Community Care*, 2–8 October, 30–1.

Clark, M., Glasby, J. and Lester, H. E. (2004) 'Cases for change: User involvement in mental health services and research', *Research Policy and Planning*, 22(2): 31–8.

Clarke, S. (2004) *Acute Inpatient Mental Health Care: Education, Training and Continuing Professional Development for All*. Leeds: NIMHE.

Clement, S. *et al.* (2011) 'Disability hate crime and targeted violence and hostility: A mental health and discrimination perspective', *Journal of Mental Health*, 20(3): 219–25.

Coast, J. *et al.* (2005) 'Economic evaluation of a general practitioner with special interests led dermatology service in primary care', *British Medical Journal*, 33, 1444–9.

Cohen, A. (2008) *Delivering Mental Health in Primary Care*. London: RCGP.

Coid, J. and Dunn, W. (2004) 'Forensic psychiatry assessments and admissions from East London: 1987–1994', *Journal of Forensic Psychiatry and Psychology*, 15(1): 76–95.

Coid, J. *et al.* (2001) 'Medium secure forensic psychiatry services: Comparison of seven English health region', *British Journal of Psychiatry*, 178, 55–61.

Coid, J. and Kahtan, N. (2000) 'Are special hospitals needed?', *Journal of Forensic Psychiatry*, 11(1): 17–35.

Coldham, T. (2007) Direct payments and individual budgets: keys to independence, in A. Bell and P. Lindley (eds), *Beyond the Water Towers: The Unfinished Revolution in Mental Health Services 1985–2005*. London: Sainsbury Centre for Mental Health.

Coleman, R. (1999) *Recovery? An Alien Concept*. Gloucester: Handsell.

Commission for Health Improvement (CHI (2003) *What CHI Has Found in Mental Health Trusts*. London: CHI.

Commission for Racial Equality (CRE) (2007) *Report of Formal Investigation into the Department of Health*. London: CRE.

Community Care (2001) 'Father given suspended sentence for killing depressed daughter', *Community Care*, 11 June. Available online via www.communitycare.co.uk (accessed 8 April 2004).

Community Care (2004) 'Government rejects Bennett proposals', *Community Care*, 19 February. Available online via www.communitycare.co.uk (accessed 28 May 2004).

Community Care (2014) 'Queen's speech announces adult social care overhaul as cuts deepen'. Available online via www.communitycare.co.uk (accessed 17 April 2014).

Connolly, M. A. and Ritchie, S. (1997) 'An audit of in-patients aged 18–65 in acute psychiatric wards who are inappropriately placed three months after admission', *Health Bulletin*, 55(3): 156–61

Copperman, J. and Knowles, K. (2006) 'Developing women-only and gender sensitive practices in inpatient wards – Current issues and challenges', *Journal of Adult Protection*, 8(2): 15–30.

Coppock, V. and Hopton, J. (2000) *Critical Perspectives on Mental Health*. London: Routledge.

Copsey, N. (1997a) *Keeping Faith: The Provision of Community Mental Health Services Within a Multi-Faith Context*. London: Sainsbury Centre for Mental Health.

Copsey, N. (1997b) *Forward in Faith: An Experiment in Building Bridges Between Ethnic Communities and Mental Health Services in East London*. London: Sainsbury Centre for Mental Health.

Corney, R. (1999) 'Mental health services in primary care: The overlap in professional roles', *Journal of Mental Health*, 8, 187–94.

Corrigan, P. (2004) 'Target-specific stigma change: A strategy for impacting mental illness stigma', *Psychiatric Rehabilitation Journal*, 28, 113–121.

Craddock, N. *et al.* (2008) 'Wake-up call for British psychiatry', *British Journal of Psychiatry*, 193: 6–9.

Craig, T. K. J. *et al.* (2004) 'The Lambeth Early Onset Community Team: A randomized controlled trial of assertive outreach for psychosis', *British Medical Journal*, 329: 1067–73.

Crane, H. (2003) 'Doctor's diagnosis: depression', *British Medical Journal*, 326(7402): 1324.

Crawford, M. J. *et al.* (2002) 'Systematic review of involving patients in the planning and development of health care', *British Medical Journal*, 325, 1263–5.

Creed, F. *et al.* (1990) 'Randomised controlled trial of day patients versus in-patient psychiatric treatment', *British Medical Journal*, 300, 1033–7.

Creed, F. *et al.* (1997) 'Cost effectiveness of day and inpatient psychiatric treatment', *British Medical Journal*, 314, 1381–5.

Crosland, A. and Kai, J. (1998) 'They think they can talk to nurses: practice nurses' views of their roles in caring for mental health problems', *British Journal of General Practice*, 48, 1383–6.

Crowther, R. *et al.* (2001) 'Helping people with severe mental illness to obtain work: Systematic review', *British Medical Journal*, 322, 204–8.

CSIP (Care Services Improvement Partnership) (2006) *Women at Risk: The Mental Health of Women in Contact with the Criminal Justice System*. London: CSIP.

CSIP, Royal College of Psychiatrists and SCIE (2007) *A Common Purpose: Recovery in Future Mental Health Services*. London: SCIE.

CSIP (2007) *A Positive Outlook: A Good Practice Toolkit to Improve Discharge from Inpatient Mental Health Care*. London: CSIP.

CSIP (2008) *Mental Health Digest*. London: CSIP.

CSIP/National Mental Health Partnership/DH (2006) *National Acute Inpatient Project Position Statement (December 2006)*. London: CSIP/National Mental Health Partnership/DH.

CSIP/NIMHE/Changing Workforce Programme/Royal College of Psychiatrists (2005) *New Ways of Working for Psychiatrists: Enhancing Effective, Person-centred Services through New Ways of Working in Multidisciplinary and Multi-Agency Contexts*. London: DH.

Davies, S. *et al.* (2007) 'Long-term outcomes after discharge from medium secure care: A cause for concern', *British Journal of Psychiatry*, 191, 70–4.

Dean, C. and Gadd, E. (1990) 'Home treatment for psychiatric illness', *British Medical Journal*, 301: 1021–3.

Deegan, P. (1988) 'Recovery: The lived experience of rehabilitation', *Psychosocial Rehabilitation Journal*, 11(4): 11–19.

Department for Constitutional Affairs (2007) *Mental Capacity Act 2005 Code of Practice*. London: TSO.

DH (Department of Health) (1989a) *Caring for People: Community Care in the Next Decade and Beyond*. London: HMSO.

DH (1989b) *Working for Patients*. London: HMSO.

DH (1990a) *The Care Programme Approach for People with a Mental Illness Referred to the Specialist Psychiatric Services*. London: DH.

DH (1990b) *Community Care in the Next Decade and Beyond: Policy Guidance*. London: HMSO.

DH (1991) *The Patient's Charter*. London: HMSO.

DH (1992) *The Health of the Nation*. London: TSO.

DH (1993) *Attitude to Mental Illness*. London: Taylor Nelson Sofres.

DH (1994) *Working in Partnership: A Collaborative Approach to Care – Report of the Mental Health Nursing Review*. London: HMSO.

DH (1995) *Building Bridges: A Guide to the Arrangements for Interagency Working for the Care and Protection of Severely Disabled People*. London: DH.

DH (1996a) *Carers (Recognition and Services) Act 1995: Policy Guidance and Practice Guidance*. London: DH.

DH (1996b) *Guidance on Supervised Discharge (After-Care under Supervision) and Related Provisions*. London: DH.

DH (1997a) *The New NHS: Modern, Dependable*. London: TSO.

DH (1997b) *Omnibus Survey of Public Attitudes to Mental Illness*. London: DH.

DH (1998) *Modernising Mental Health Services: Safe, Sound and Supportive*. London: DH.

DH (1999a) *National Service Framework for Mental Health: Modern Standards and Service Models*. London: DH.

DH (1999b) *Effective Care Coordination in Mental Health Services: Modernizing the Care Programme Approach – A Policy Booklet*. London: DH.

DH (1999c) *Still Building Bridges: The Report of a National Inspection of Arrangements for the Integration of Care Programme Approach with Care Management*. London: Social Services Inspectorate/DH

DH (2000a) *The NHS Plan: A Plan for Investment, a Plan for Reform*. London: DH.

DH (2000b) *Attitudes to Mental Illness*. London: Taylor, Nelson and Sofres

DH (2000c) *Caring About Carers: A National Strategy for Carers* (2nd edn, first published in 1998). London: DH.

DH (2001a) *Safety First: Five-Year Report of the National Confidential Inquiry into Suicide and Homicide by People with Mental Illness*. London: DH.

DH (2001b) *The Journey to Recovery: The Government's Vision for Mental Health Care*. London: DH.

DH (2001c) *Shifting the Balance of Power within the NHS: Securing Delivery*. London: DH.

DH (2001d) *Reforming the Mental Health Act – Part I: The New Legal Framework*. London: DH.

DH (2001e) *Reforming the Mental Health Act – Part II: High Risk Patients*. London: DH.

DH (2001f) *Mental Health National Service Framework (and the NHS Plan) Workforce Planning, Education and Training Underpinning Programme: Adult Mental Health Services: Final Report by the Workforce Action Team*. London: DH.

DH (2001g) *Mental Health Policy Implementation Guidance*. London: DH.

DH (2001h) *Valuing People: A New Strategy for Learning Disability for the 21st Century*. London: DH.

DH (2001i) *National Service Framework for Older People: Modern Standards and Service Models*. London: DH.

DH (2001j) *Carers and Disabled Children's Act 2000: Carers and People with Parental Responsibility for Disabled Children – Policy Guidance*. London: DH

DH (2001k) *The Mental Health Policy Implementation Guide: Crisis Resolution/Home Treatment Teams*. London: DH.

DH (2002a) *Adult Acute In-patient Care Provision*. London: DH.

DH (2002b) *National Suicide Prevention Strategy for England*. London: DH.

DH (2002c) *Shifting the Balance of Power: The Next Steps*. London: DH.

DH (2002d) *Mental Health Policy Implementation Guidance: Community Mental Health Teams*. London: DH.

DH (2002e) *Women's Mental Health: Into the Mainstream*. London: DH.

DH (2002f) *Developing Services for Carers and Families of People with Mental Illness*. London: DH.

DH (2003a) *Practitioners with Special Interests in Primary Care: Implementing a Scheme for Nurses with Special Interests in Primary Care – Liberating the Talents*. London: DH.

DH (2003b) *Fast-Forwarding Primary Care Mental Health: Graduate Primary Care Mental Health Workers – Best Practice Guidance*. London: DH.

DH (2003c) *Guidelines for the Appointment of General Practitioners with Special Interests in the Delivery of Clinical Services: Mental Health*. London: DH.

DH (2003d) *National Statistics on Adults' Attitudes to Mental Illness in Great Britain*. London: DH.

DH (2003e) *Mental Health Policy Implementation Guide: Support, Time and Recovery Workers*. London: DH.

DH (2003f) *Building on the Best: Choice, Responsiveness and Equity in the NHS*. London: TSO.

DH (2003g) *Mainstreaming Gender and Women's Mental Health*. London: DH.

DH (2003h) *Delivering Race Equality: A Framework for Action – Mental Health Services – Consultation Document*. London: DH.

DH (2004a) *The National Service Framework for Mental Health – Five Years on*. London: DH.

DH (2004b) *The NHS Improvement Plan*. London: DH.

DH (2004c) *Practice-Based Commissioning: Engaging Practices in Commissioning*. London: DH.

DH (2004d) *The Ten Essential Shared Capabilities: A Framework for the Whole of the Mental Health Workforce*. London: DH (www.iapt.nhs.uk/silo/files/10-essential-shared-capabilities.pdf).

DH (2005a) *Community Development Workers for Black and Minority Ethnic Communities*. London: DH.

DH (2005b) *Delivering Race Equality in Mental Health Care: An Action Plan for Reform Inside and Outside Services and the Government's Response to the Independent Inquiry into the Death of David Bennett*. London: DH.

DH (2006a) *Mental Health Bill: Regulatory Impact Assessment*. London: DH.

DH (2006b) *Crisis Resolution and Home Treatment Guidance Statement*. London: DH.

DH (2006c) *Direct Payments for People with Mental Health Problems: A Guide to Action*. London: DH.

DH (2007a) *Our NHS, Our Future: NHS Next Stage Review – Interim Report*. London: DH.

DH (2007b) *Improving Access to Psychological Therapies Programme: Computerized Cognitive Behavioural Therapy Implementation Guidance*. London: DH.

DH (2007c) *Valuing People Now: From Progress to Transformation*. London: DH.

DH (2008a) *High Quality Care for All: NHS Next Stage Review – Final Report*. London: DH.

DH (2008b) *Refocusing the Care Programme Approach: Policy and Positive Practice Guidance*. London: DH.

DH (2008c) *Support, Time and Recovery Workers: A Competence Framework*. London: DH.

DH (2009a) *Living Well with Dementia: A National Dementia Strategy*. London: DH.

DH (2009b) *Improving Access to Psychological Therapies: Offenders – Positive Practice*. London: DH.

DH (2009c) *New Horizons: A Shared Vision for Mental Health*. London: DH.

DH (2011) *Statement of Government Policy on Adult Safeguarding*. London: DH.

DH (2013) *Mental Health Dashboard*. London: DH.

DH (2014) *Making Mental Health Services More Effective and Accessible*. London: DH.

DH/HM Prison Service/National Assembly for Wales (2001) *Changing the Outlook: A Strategy for Developing and Modernising Mental Health Services in Prisons*. London: DH.

DH/Home Office (1992) *Review of Services for Mentally Disordered Offenders and Others Requiring Similar Services: Final Summary Report* (the Reed Report). London: HMSO.

DH/National Schizophrenia Fellowship (2001) *A Commitment to Carers*. London: National Schizophrenia Fellowship.

DH/NIMHE (2005) *Offender Mental Health Care Pathway*. London: DH.

DHSS (Department of Health and Social Security) (1975) *Better Services for the Mentally Ill*. London: HMSO.

DHSS (1983) *NHS Management Inquiry*. London: DHSS.

DHSSPS (2005) *The Bamford Review of Mental Health and Learning Disability (Northern Ireland): A Strategic Framework for Adult Mental Health Services*. Belfast: DHSSPS.

DHSSPS (2007) *The Bamford Review of Mental Health and Learning Disability (Northern Ireland): Comprehensive Legislative Framework Report*. Belfast: DHSSPS.

DHSSPS (2009a) *Delivering the Bamford Vision. Action Plan 2009–11*. Belfast: DHSSPS

DHSSPS (2009b) *Legislative Framework for Mental Capacity and Mental Health Legislation in Northern Ireland*. Belfast: DHSSPS.

DHSSPS (2011) *Service Framework for Mental Health and Wellbeing*. Belfast: DHSSPS

Dillon, J. (2010) 'The tale of an ordinary little girl', *Psychosis*, 2(1): 79–83.

Disability Rights Commission (DRC) (2006) *Equal Treatment: Closing the Gap. A Formal Investigation into Physical Health Inequalities Experienced by People with Learning Disabilities/and or Mental Health Problems*. London: DRC.

Dixon, M. (2005) 'Risk assessment for compulsory detention under the Mental Health Act (1983): A grounded analysis of psychiatrists' perspectives', Ph.D. thesis, University of Central England, Birmingham.

Docherty, J. D. (1997) 'Barriers to the diagnosis of depression in primary care', *Journal of Clinical Psychology*, 58, 5–10.

Dohrenwend, B. P. (2000) 'The role of adversity and stress in psychopathology: Some evidence and its implication for theory and research', *Journal of Health and Social Behavior*, 41(1): 1–19.

Dolan, M. and Lawson, A. (2001) 'Characteristics and outcomes of patients admitted to a psychiatric intensive care unit in a medium secure unit', *Psychiatric Bulletin*, 25(8): 296–9.

Doran, T. *et al.* (2008) 'Effect of financial incentives on inequalities in the delivery of primary clinical care in England: Analysis of clinical activity indicators for the quality and outcomes framework', *The Lancet*, 372, 728–36.

Durcan, G. (2008) *From the Inside: Experiences of Prison Mental Health Care*. London: Sainsbury Centre for Mental Health.

Durkheim, É. (1897) *Le Suicide*. Paris: Alcan.

Edgar, K. and Rickford, D. (2009) *Too Little Too Late: An Independent Review of Unmet Mental Health Need in Prison*. London: Prison Reform Trust.

Edwards, N. (2013) 'Implementation of the Health and Social Care Act', *British Medical Journal*, 346: 2090.

Elder, A. and Holmes, J. (2002) *Mental Health in Primary Care*. Oxford: Oxford University Press.

Engel, G. (1980) 'The clinical application of the biospychosocial model', *American Journal of Psychiatry*, 137, 535–44.

England, E. and Lester, H. E. (2007) 'Implementing the role of the graduate primary care mental health worker: A qualitative study', *British Journal of General Practice*, 57, 204–11.

Enthoven, A. (1985) *Reflections in the Management of the NHS*. London: Nuffield Provincial Hospitals Trust.

Evans, J. and Fowler, R. (2008) *Family Minded: Supporting Children in Families Affected by Mental Illness*. Ilford, Barnardo's.

Evans, P. (2003) 'Silent fight', *Guardian*, 20 August. Available online via www.society.guardian.co.uk (accessed 20 August 2003).

Fadden, G. (2006b) 'Training and disseminating family interventions for schizophrenia: Developing family intervention skills with multi-disciplinary groups', *Journal of Family Therapy*, 28, 23–38.

Fadden, G. (2006a) 'Family interventions', in G. Roberts *et al.* (eds), *Enabling Recovery*. London: Gaskell.

Falloon, I. and Fadden, G. (1993) *Integrated Mental Health Care*. Cambridge: Cambridge University Press.

Faulkner, A. and Layzell, S. (2000) *Strategies for Living: A Report of User-Led Research into People's Strategies for Living with Mental Distress*. London: Mental Health Foundation.

Fawcett, B. and Karban, K. (2005) *Contemporary Mental Health: Theory, Policy and Practice*. Abingdon: Routledge.

Fearon, P. *et al.* (2006) 'Incidence of schizophrenia and other psychoses in ethnic minority groups: Results from the MRC AESOP Study', *Psychological Medicine*, 26, 1–10.

Ferns, P. (2005) 'Finding a way forward: A black perspective on social approaches to mental health', in J. Tew (ed.), *Social Perspectives in Mental Health*. London: Jessica Kingsley.

Finch, J. and Groves, D. (eds) (1983) *A Labour of Love: Women, Work and Caring*. London: Routledge.

Fletcher, J. *et al.* (2008) 'A collaborative approach to embedding graduate primary care mental health workers in the UK National Health Service', *Health and Social Care in the Community*, 16, 5, 451–9.

Ford, R. *et al.* (1993) 'Developing case management for the long-term mentally ill', *Psychiatric Bulletin*, 17(7): 409–11.

Forder, J. *et al.* (2012) *Evaluation of the Personal Health Budget Pilot Programme*. Canterbury: PSSRU.

Foresight Programme (2008) *Mental Capital and Wellbeing: Final Project Report*. London: Government Office for Science.

Foucault, M. (1967) *Madness and Civilisation*. London: Tavistock.

Franklin, D. *et al.* (2000) 'Consultant psychiatrists' experiences of using supervised discharge: Results of a national survey', *Psychiatrist*, 24, 412–15.

Freeman, G. *et al.* (2002) *Promoting Continuity of Care for People with Severe Mental Illness Whose Needs Span Primary, Secondary and Social Care*. London: SDO.

Friedli, L. and Parsonage, M. (2007) *Mental Health Promotion: Building an Economic Case*. Belfast: Northern Ireland Association for Mental Health.

Fulop, N., Koffman, J. and Hudson, M. (1992) 'Challenging bed behaviours: The use of acute psychiatric beds in an inner-London District Health Authority', *Journal of Mental Health*, 1, 335–41.

Fulop, N. J. *et al.* (1996) 'Use of psychiatric beds: A point prevalence study in North and South Thames regions', *Journal of Public Health Medicine*, 18(2): 207–16.

Gask, L. *et al.* (2003) 'Qualitative study of patients' perceptions of the quality of care for depression in general practice', *British Journal of General Practice*, 53, 278–83.

Gask, L. *et al.* (eds) (2009) *Primary Care Mental Health*. London: Royal College of Psychiatrists.

Gask, L., Sibbald, B. and Creed, F. (1997) 'Evaluating models of working between mental health and primary care', *British Journal of Psychiatry*, 70, 6–11.

Gater, R. *et al.* (1997) 'The care of patients with chronic schizophrenia: A comparison between two services', *Psychological Medicine*, 27(6): 1325–36.

Gentleman, A. (2014) 'Vulnerable man starved to death after cut to benefits', *Guardian*, 1 March, 11.

Georgiades, N. J. and Phillimore, L. (1975) *The Myth of the Hero-Innovator and Alternative Strategies for Organisational Change*. New York: Associated Scientific.

Gibbons, J. (1988) 'Residential care for mentally ill adults', in I. Sinclair (ed.), *Residential Care: The Research Reviewed*. London: HMSO.

Giddens, A. (1998) *The Third Way: The Renewal of Social Democracy*. Cambridge, Polity Press.

Gilburt, H. *et al.* (2014) *Service Transformation: Lessons from Mental Health*. London: King's Fund.

Gillen, S. (2005) 'Campaigners furious as government "ducks" key Bennett inquiry findings, *Community Care*, 13–19 January, 6.

Glasby, J. (2012) *Understanding Health and Social Care* (2nd edn). Bristol: The Policy Press.

Glasby, J. and Beresford, P. (2006) 'Who knows best? Evidence-based practice and the service user contribution', *Critical Social Policy*, 26(1): 268–84.

Glasby, J. and Dickinson, H. (2014) *Partnership Working in Health and Social Care: What Is Integrated Care and How Can We Deliver It?* (2nd edn). Bristol: The Policy Press.

Glasby, J. and Lester, H. (2004) 'Delayed hospital discharge and mental health: The policy implications of recent research', *Social Policy and Administration*, 38(7): 744–57.

Glasby, J. and Littlechild, R. (2004) *The Health and Social Care Divide: The Experiences of Older People* (2nd edn). Bristol: The Policy Press.

Glasby, J. and Littlechild, R. (2009) *Direct Payments and Personal Budgets: Putting Personalisation into Practice* (2nd edn). Bristol: The Policy Press.

Glasby, J. *et al.* (2010) *The Case for Social Care Reform – The Wider Economic and Social Benefits*. Birmingham: Health Services Management Centre/Institute of Applied Social Studies (on behalf of Downing Street/DH).

Glendinning, C. *et al.* (2008) *Evaluation of the Individual Budgets Pilot Programme*. York: Social Policy Research Unit.

Glover, G., Arts, G. and Babu, K. (2006) 'Crisis resolution/home treatment teams and psychiatric admission rates in England', *British Journal of Psychiatry*, 189, 441–5.

Gofal Cymru (2008) 'The community crisis house model: Evaluation of Wales' first crisis house'. Cardiff: Gofal Cymru www.gofal.org.uk/uploads/Policy_documents/Gofal_reports/crisis-house-english. pdf

Goffman, E. (1961) *Asylums: Essays on the Social Situation of Mental Patients and Other Inmates*. Harmondsworth: Penguin.

Goldberg, D. (2008) 'Improved investment in mental health services: Value for money?', *British Journal of Psychiatry*, 192, 88–91.

Goldberg, D. and Morrison, S. (1963) Schizophrenia and social class, *British Journal of Psychiatry*, 109, 785–802.

Golding, J. (1997) *Without Prejudice: Mind Lesbian, Gay, Bisexual Mental Health Awareness Research*. London: Mind.

Goodwin, I. *et al.* (1999) 'A qualitative analysis of the views of in-patient mental health service users', *Journal of Mental Health*, 8(1): 43–54.

Goodwin, S. (1990) *Community Care and the Future of Mental Health Service Provision.* Aldershot: Avebury.

Goodwin, S. (1997) *Comparative Mental Health Policy: From Institutional to Community Care.* London: Sage.

Gopfort, M., Webster, J. and Seeman, M. (eds) (2004) *Parental Psychiatric Disorder: Distressed Parents and Their Families.* Cambridge: Cambridge University Press.

Gournay, K. and Brooking, J. (1994) 'The CPN in primary care: An outcome study', *British Journal of Psychiatry*, 165, 231–8.

Gournay, K. and Brooking, J. (1995) 'The CPN in primary care: An economic analysis', *Journal of Advanced Nursing*, 22, 769–78.

Grant, S. (2004) *National Mental Health Service Assessment: Towards the Implementation of the NHS (Care and Treatment) (Scotland) Act 2003. Final Report.* Edinburgh: Scottish Government. www.scotland.gov.uk/Publications/2004/03/19084/34431

Grant-Pearce, C. M. and Deane, J. (1999) 'Joint working between the public and purchasing authorities to determine mental health information needs', in D. Bhugra and V. Bahl (eds), *Ethnicity: An Agenda for Mental Health.* London: Gaskell.

Gray, R. *et al.* (1999) 'A national survey of practice nurse involvement in mental health interventions', *Journal of Advanced Nursing*, 30, 901–6.

Gray, B. *et al.* (2008) ' "Confidentiality smokescreens" and carers for people with mental health problems: The perspectives of professionals', *Health and Social Care in the Community*, 16(4): 378–87.

Gregory, N. *et al.* (2006) 'Identifying the needs of carers in mental health services', *Nursing Times*, 102(17): 32–5.

Griffiths, R. (1988) *Community Care: An Agenda for Action.* London: HSMO.

Grounds, A. (2001) 'Reforming the Mental Health Act', *British Journal of Psychiatry*, 178, 387–9.

Grove, B. (1994) 'Reform of mental health care in Europe', *British Journal of Psychiatry*, 165, 431–3.

Grove, B. and Drurie, S. (1999) *Social Firms: An Instrument for Social and Economic Inclusion.* Redhill: Social Firms UK.

Grove, B., Freudenberg, G. M. and Harding, A. (1997) *The Social Firm Handbook.* Brighton: Pavilion.

Hacking, S. and Bates, P. (2008) 'The inclusion web: A tool for person-centred planning and service evaluation', *Mental Health Review Journal*, 13, 4–15.

Hall, S. (2001) 'Argument rages over Sarah's law', *Guardian*, 13 December. Available online via www.guardian.co.uk (accessed 9 February 2004).

Halliday, P. (2005) 'What sort of mental health problems are experienced by women in contemporary British society? What do different feminist perspectives offer as alleviation?', *Journal of International Women's Studies*, 6(3): 40–9.

Ham, C. (2009) *Health Policy in Britain: The Politics and Organisation of the National Health Service* (6th edn). Basingstoke: Palgrave Macmillan.

Hammersley, P. and McLaughlin, T. (2006) 'Campaign for the abolition of the Schizophrenia label', asylum online www.asylumonline.net/resources/campaign-for-the-abolition-of-schizophrenia-label

Hannigan, B. (2003) 'The policy and legal context', in B. Hannigan and M. Coffey (eds), *The Handbook of Community Mental Health Nursing.* London: Routledge.

Hannigan, B. and Coffey, M. (eds) (2003) *The Handbook of Community Mental Health Nursing.* London: Routledge.

Hardcastle, M. *et al.* (eds) (2007) *Experiences of Mental Health in-Patient Care: Narratives from Service Users, Carers and Professionals*. London: Routledge.

Harding, C. M. and Zahniser, J. H. (1994) 'Empirical correction of seven myths about schizophrenia with implications for treatment', *Acta Psychiatrica Scandinavica*, 3(1): 140–6.

Harrison, G. *et al.* (2001) 'Association between schizophrenia and social inequality at birth: case-control study', *British Journal of Psychiatry*, 179, 346–50.

Harrison, P. (1973) 'Careless community', *New Society*, 28 June.

Hatton, C. *et al.* (2008) *A Report on in Control's Second Phase: Evaluation and Learning 2005–2007*. London: in Control.

Health and Social Care Information Centre (2012) *Inpatients Formally Detained in Hospitals under the Mental Health Act 1983 and Patients Subject to Supervised Community Treatment – England, 2011–2012, Annual Figures*. London: Health and Social Care Information Centre.

Healthcare Commission (2004) *Patient Survey Report 2004 – Mental Health*. London: Healthcare Commission.

Healthcare Commission (2005) *The National Audit of Violence (2003–2005): Final Report*. London: Royal College of Psychiatrists' Research Unit/Healthcare Commission.

Healthcare Commission (2008) *The Path to Recovery: A Review NHS Acute Inpatient Mental Health Services*. London: Healthcare Commission.

Hean, S. *et al.* (2011) 'Exploring the potential for joint training between legal professionals in the criminal justice system and health and social care professionals in the mental-health services', *Journal of Interprofessional Care*, 25(3): 196–202.

Heater, D. (1990) *Citizenship: The Civic Ideal in World History, Politics and Education*. London: Longman.

Heath, I. (1999) 'Uncertain clarity: contradiction, meaning and hope', *British Journal of General Practice*, 49, 651–7.

Heath, I., Hippisley-Cox, J. and Smeeth, L. (2007) 'Measuring performance and missing the point?', *British Medical Journal*, 335, 1075–6.

Heenan, D. (2009) 'Mental health policy in Northern Ireland: The nature and extent of user involvement', *Social Policy and Society*, 8(4): 451–62.

Heenan, D. and Birrell, D. (2006) 'The integration of health and social care: The lessons from Northern Ireland', *Social Policy and Administration*, 40, 47–66.

Heenan, D. and Birrell, D. (2009) 'Organisational integration in health and social care: Some reflections on the Northern Ireland experience', *Journal of Integrated Care*, 17(5): 3–12.

Hiday, V. A. (2006) 'Putting community risk in perspective: A look at correlations, causes and controls', *International Journal of Law and Psychiatry*, 29, 316 –331.

Higgins, R., Hurst, K. and Wistow, G. (1999) 'Nursing acute psychiatric patients: A quantitative and qualitative study', *Journal of Advanced Nursing*, 29(1): 52–63.

Higgitt, A, and Fonagy, P. (2002) 'Clinical effectiveness', *British Journal of Psychiatry*, 181, 170–4.

Hill, M. and Hupe, P. (2002) *Implementing Public Policy*. London: Sage.

Hill, R. G., Shepherd, G. and Hardy, P. (1998) 'In sickness and in health: The experiences of friends and relatives caring for people with manic depression', *Journal of Mental Health*, 7(6): 611–20.

Hill, S., Mather, G. and Laugharne, R. (2007) 'Attitudes of psychiatrists towards forensic psychiatry: A survey', *Medicine, Science and the Law*, 47(3): 220–4.

HM Government (2007) *Putting People First: A Shared Vision and Commitment to the Transformation of Adult Social Care*. London: DH.

HM Government (2008) *Carers at the Heart of 21st-Century Families and Communities.* London: DH.

HM Government (2010) *Recognised, Valued and Supported: Next Steps for the Carers Strategy.* London: DH.

HM Government (2011) *No Health without Mental Health: A Cross-government Mental Health Outcomes Strategy for People of All Ages.* London: DH.

HMI Probation *et al.* (2009) *A Joint Inspection on Work Prior to Sentence with Offenders with Mental Disorders.* London: HMI Probation.

Hoggett, P. (1992) 'The politics of empowerment', *Going Local*, 19, 18–19.

Hogman, G. and Pearson, G. (1995) *The Silent Partners: The Needs and Experiences of People Who Provide Informal Care to People with a Severe Mental Illness.* Kingston upon Thames: National Schizophrenia Fellowship. [now Rethink]

Hogman, G. and Sandamas, G. (2001) 'Mental patients are at last asked about the drugs they are given', *Health Summary*, January, 8–11.

Holloway, F. (1996) 'Community psychiatric care: from libertarianism to coercion – "Moral panic" and mental health policy in Britain', *Health Care Analysis*, 4, 235–43.

Home Office (1990) *Provision for Mentally Disordered Offenders.* Circular 66/90.

Hopper, K. (2007) 'Rethinking social recovery in schizophrenia: What a capabilities approach might offer', *Social Science and Medicine*, 65, 868–79.

Hoult, J. (1986) 'Community care of the acutely mentally ill', *British Journal of Psychiatry*, 149, 137–44.

House of Commons (1948) *Hansard*, vol. 447, col. 50, 9 February.

House of Commons and the House of Lords (2005) *Report of the Joint Scrutiny Committee on the Mental Health Bill.* PP HL (2004–5), 79/HC (2004–5), 95.

House of Commons Work and Pensions Committee (2008) *Valuing and Supporting Carers.* London: TSO.

Huang, M. C. and Slevin, E. (1999) 'The experiences of carers who live with someone who has schizophrenia: A review of the literature', *Mental Health and Learning Disabilities Care*, 3(3): 89–93.

Hughes, H. *et al.* (2011) 'Carers' experiences of assertive outreach services: An exploratory study', *Journal of Mental Health*, 20(1): 70–78.

Hutchinson, M. (2000) 'Issues around empowerment', in T. Basset (ed.), *Looking to the Future: Key Issues for Contemporary Mental Health Services.* Brighton: Pavilion.

Huxley, P. and Thornicroft, G. (2003) 'Social inclusion, social quality and mental illness', *British Journal of Psychiatry*, 182, 289–90.

Independent Police Complaints Commission (2008) *Police Custody as a 'Place of Safety': Examining the Use of Section 136 of the Mental Health Act 1983.* London: IPCC.

Information Centre (2007) *General and Personal Medical Services, England, 1996–2006.* Leeds: Information Centre.

Information Centre (2008a) *National Quality and Outcomes Framework Statistics for England 2007/08.* Leeds: Information Centre.

Information Centre (2008b) *General and Personal Medical Services, England, 30 September 2007.* Leeds: Information Centre.

Janssen, I. *et al.* (2003) 'Discrimination and delusional ideation', *British Journal of Psychiatry*, 182, 71–6.

Jewesbury, I. (1998) *Risks and Rights: Mentally Disordered Offenders and Public Protection.* London: NACRO.

Johnson, S (2011) 'Has the closure of psychiatric beds gone too far? No', *British Medical Journal*, 343, 7410

Johnson, S. and Needle, J. (2008) 'Introduction and concepts', in S. Johnson *et al.* (eds), *Crisis Resolution and Home Treatment in Mental Health.* Cambridge: Cambridge University Press.

Johnson, S. and Thornicroft, G. (1993) 'The sectorisation of psychiatric services in England and Wales', *Social Psychiatry and Psychiatric Epidemiology*, 28 (1): 45–7.

Johnson, S. *et al.* (2004) 'Women's experiences of admission to a crisis house and to acute hospital wards: A qualitative study', *Journal of Mental Health*, 13(3): 247–62.

Johnson, S. *et al.* (2005) 'Randomised controlled trial of acute mental health care by crisis resolution teams: The North Islington CRISIS study', *British Medical Journal*, 331, 599–602.

Johnson, S. *et al.* (eds) (2008) *Crisis Resolution and Home Treatment in Mental Health.* Cambridge: Cambridge University Press.

Joint Commissioning Panel for Mental Health (2012) *Guidance for commissioners of primary mental health care services – volume 2.* Joint Commissioning Panel for Mental Health (www.rcpsych. ac.uk/pdf/JCP-MH%20primary%20care%20(March%202012).pdf).

Joint Commissioning Panel for Mental Health (2013) *Guidance for Commissioners of Forensic Mental Health Services.* Joint Commissioning Panel for Mental Health (www.jcpmh. info).

Judge, J., Harty, M. A. and Fahy, T. (2004) 'Survey of community forensic psychiatry services in England and Wales', *Journal of Forensic Psychiatry and Psychology*, 15(2): 244–53.

Kai, J. and Crosland, A. (2001) 'Perspectives of people with enduring mental ill health from a community-based qualitative study', *British Journal of General Practice*, 51, 730–3.

Karp, D. A. (1996) *Speaking of Sadness: Depression, Disconnection and the Meanings of Illness.* Oxford: Oxford University Press.

Katon, W. and Unutzer, J. (2006) 'Collaborative care models for depression: Time to move from evidence to practice', *Archives of Internal Medicine*, 66, 2304–6.

Katon, W. *et al.* (1996) 'A multifaceted intervention to improve treatment of depression in primary care', *Archives of General Psychiatry*, 53, 924–32.

Katon, W. *et al.* (1999) 'Stepped collaborative care for primary care patients with persistent symptoms of depression', *Archives of General Psychiatry*, 56, 1109–15.

Katon, W. J. *et al.* (2004) 'The Pathways Study: A randomised trial of collaborative care in patients with diabetes and depression', *Archives of General Psychiatry*, 61, 1042–9.

Keating, F. and Robertson, D. (2004) 'Fear, black people and mental illness: A vicious cycle', *Health and Social Care in the Community*, 12(5): 439–47.

Keating, F. *et al.* (2002) *Breaking the Circles of Fear.* London: Sainsbury Centre for Mental Health.

Kendrick, T. *et al.* (1998) 'Practice nurse involvement in giving depot neuroleptic injections: Development of patient assessment and monitoring checklist', *Primary Care Psychiatry*, 4, 149–54.

Kennedy, P. (2008) 'We need to monitor implementation: Commentary on new ways of working', *Psychiatric Bulletin*, 32, 46.

Killaspy, H. (2007) 'Assertive community treatment in psychiatry', *British Medical Journal*, 335, 311–12.

Killaspy, H. *et al.* (1999) 'Non-attendance at psychiatric outpatient clinics: Communication and implications for primary care', *British Journal of General Practice*, 49, 880–3.

Killaspy, H. *et al.* (2000a) 'Prospective controlled study of psychiatric outpatient non attendance', *British Journal of Psychiatry*, 176, 160–5.

Killaspy, H. *et al.* (2000b) 'Drayton Park: An alternative to hospital admission for women in acute mental health crisis', *Psychiatric Bulletin*, 24(3): 101–4.

Killaspy, H. *et al.* (2006) 'REACT: A randomised evaluation of assertive community treatment in north London', *British Medical Journal*, 332, 815–19.

Kinderman, P., Sellwood, W. and Tai, S. (2008) 'Policy implications of a psychological model of mental disorder', *Journal of Mental Health*, 17(1): 93–103.

King, M. *et al.* (2003) *Mental Health and Social Wellbeing of Gay Men, Lesbians and Bisexuals in England and Wales: A Summary of Findings*. London: Mind.

King, M. *et al.* (2007) *Mental Disorders, Suicide, and Deliberate Self Harm in Lesbian, Gay and Bisexual People: A Systematic Review*. London: NIMHE.

Kingdon, J. W. (1995) *Agenda, Alternatives and Public Policies* (2nd edn). New York: HarperCollins.

King's Fund Institute (1988) *Health Finance: Assessing the Options*. London: King's Fund Institute.

Koffman, J. *et al.* (1996) 'No way out: The delayed discharge of elderly mentally ill acute and assessment patients in North and South Thames regions', *Age and Ageing*, 25(4): 268–72.

Koffman, J. *et al.* (1997) 'Ethnicity and use of acute psychiatric beds: One-day survey in North and South Thames regions', *British Journal of Psychiatry*, 171, 238–41.

Kosa, J. and Zola, I. K. (1975) (eds), *Poverty and Health: A Sociological Analysis*. Cambridge, MA/London: Harvard University Press.

Kumar, S., Guite, H. and Thornicroft, G. (2001) 'Service users' experience of violence within a mental health system: A study using a grounded theory approach', *Journal of Mental Health*, 10(6): 597–611.

Kupshik, G. and Fisher, C. (1999) 'Assisted bibliotherapy: Effective, efficient treatment for moderate anxiety problems', *British Journal of General Practice*, 49, 47–8.

La Grenade, J. (1999) 'The National Health Service and ethnicity: Services for black patients', in D. Bhugra and V. Bahl (eds), *Ethnicity: An Agenda for Mental Health*. London: Gaskell.

Laing, R. D. (1960) *The Divided Self*. London: Tavistock Press.

Laing, R. D. (1961) *The Self and Others*. London: Tavistock Press.

Larkin, W. and Morrison, A. (2006) *Trauma and Psychosis: New Directions for Theory and Therapy*. Hove: Routledge.

Larsen, J. *et al.* (2013) 'Implementing personalisation for people with mental health problems: A comparative case study of four local authorities in England', *Journal of Mental Health*, 22(2): 174–82.

Laurance, J. (2003) *Pure Madness: How Fear Drives the Mental Health System*. London: Routledge.

Lawton-Smith, S., Dawson, J., Burns, T. (2008) 'Community treatment orders are not a good thing', *British Journal of Psychiatry*, 193, 96–100.

Layard, R. (2006) *Happiness: Lessons from a New Science*. London: Penguin.

Layard, R. *et al.* (2006). *The Depression Report: A New Deal for Depression and Anxiety Disorders*. London: Centre for Economic Performance's Mental Health Policy Group, LSE.

Layard, R. *et al.* (2007) 'Cost–benefit analysis of psychological therapy', *National Institute Economic Review*, 202, 90–8.

Leason, K. (2003a) 'Mental health "tsar" admits services suffer from institutional racism', *Community Care*, 17–23 July, 18–19.

Leason, K. (2003b) 'Bennett case typical of way NHS treats black people, inquiry told', *Community Care*, 7–13 August, 12.

Leason, K. (2003c) 'Author of mental health report says government diluted racism findings', *Community Care*, 17–23 July, 8.

Leavey, G., Healy, H. and Brennan, G. (1998) 'Providing information to carers of people admitted to psychiatric hospital', *Mental Health Care*, 1(8): 260–2.

Leff, J. (1997) *Care in the Community: Illusion or Reality?* Chichester: Wiley.

Leff, J. *et al.* (2000) 'The TAPS Project: A report on 13 years of research 1985–1998', *Psychiatric Bulletin*, 24, 165–8.

Lelliott, P. (2008) 'Time for honest debate and critical friends: Commentary on new ways of working', *Psychiatric Bulletin*, 32: 47–8.

Lelliott, P., Audini, B. and Duffett, R. (2001) 'Survey of patients from an inner-London health authority in medium secure psychiatric care', *British Journal of Psychiatry*, 179, 62–6.

Lelliott, P. and Wing, J. (1994) 'A national audit of new long-stay psychiatric patients II: Impact on services', *British Journal of Psychiatry*, 165: 170–8.

Lester H. E. *et al.* (2007) 'Cluster randomized controlled trial of the effectiveness of graduate primary care mental health workers', *British Journal of General Practice*, 57, 196–203.

Lester, H. E. *et al.* (2009) Development and implementation of early intervention services for young people with psychosis: A case study, *British Journal of Psychiatry*, 194, 446–50.

Lester, H. E. and Tritter, J. Q. (2005) 'Listen to my madness: exploring the views of people with serious mental illness using a disability framework', *Sociology of Health and Illness*, 27(5): 649–69.

Lester, H. E., Tritter, J. and England, E. (2003) 'Satisfaction with primary care: The perspectives of people with schizophrenia', *Family Practice*, 20, 508–13.

Lester, H. E., Tritter, J. Q. and Sorohan, H. (2004) 'Managing crisis: The role of primary care for people with serious mental illness', *Family Medicine*, 36(1): 28–34.

Lester, H. E., Tritter, J. Q. and Sorohan, H. (2005) 'Providing "good enough" primary care: A focus group study', *British Medical Journal*, 330, 1122–8.

Lewis, R. and Glasby, J. (2006) 'Delayed discharge from mental health hospitals: Results of a postal survey', *Health and Social Care in the Community*, 14(3): 225–30.

Lewis, R. L., Curry, N. and Dixon, M. (2007) *Practice-based Commissioning: From Good Idea to Effective Practice*. London: King's Fund.

Li, P. L. *et al.* (1999) 'Barriers to meeting the mental health needs of the Chinese community', *Journal of Public Health Medicine*, 21(1): 74–80.

Lindow, V. (1999) 'Power, lies and injustice: The exclusion of service users' voices', in M. Parker (eds), *Ethics and Community in the Health Care Professions*. London: Routledge.

Link, B. J. and Phelan, J. C. (2001) 'Conceptualising stigma', *Annual Review of Sociology*, 27, 363–85.

Lintern, S. (2014) 'Mental health trust threatens legal challenge over tariff', *Health Service Journal*, 18 February, available online via www.hsj.co.uk (accessed 27 February 2014).

McCabe, A. and Ford, C. (2001) *Redressing the Balance: Crime and Mental Health*. Manchester: UK Public Health Association.

McCann, G. (1999) 'Care of mentally disordered offenders', *Mental Health Care*, 3(2): 65–7.

McClean, R. (2010) 'Assessing the security needs of patients in medium secure psychiatric care in Northern Ireland', *Psychiatrist*, 34, 432–436.

McCrone, P., Dhanasiri, S. and Patel, A. (2008) *Paying the Price: The Cost of Mental Health Care in England to 2026*. London: King's Fund.

McDonagh, M. S., Smith, D. H. and Goddard, M. (2000) 'Measuring appropriate use of acute beds: A systematic review of methods and results', *Health Policy*, 53(3): 157–84.

McFadyen, J. A. (1999) 'Safe, sound and supportive: forensic mental health services', *British Journal of Nursing*, 8(21): 1436–40.

McFarlane, L. (1998) *Diagnosis: Homophobic – The Experiences of Lesbians, Gay Men and Bisexuals in Mental Health Services*. London: PACE.

McGlynn, P. (ed.) (2006) *Crisis Resolution and Home Treatment Teams: A Practical Guide*. London: Sainsbury Centre for Mental Health.

McGovern, D. and Cope, R. (1987) 'First psychiatric admission rates of first and second generation Afro-Caribbeans', *Social Psychiatry*, 122, 139–40.

MacInnes, D. (2000) 'Interventions in forensic psychiatry: The caregiver's perspective', *British Journal of Nursing*, 9(15): 992–7.

McIntyre, B. (1999) 'Placement and community support needs of patients in a medium secure unit', *Mental Health Care*, 2(11): 379–82.

McKenna, J. et al. (1999) '"Long stay medium secure" patients in special hospital', *Journal of Forensic Psychiatry*, 10(2): 333–42.

McKenzie, K. and Bhui, K. (2007a) 'Better mental healthcare for minority ethnic groups – Moving away from the blame-game and putting patients first ...', *Psychiatric Bulletin*, 31, 368–9.

McKenzie, K. and Bhui, K. (2007b) 'Institutional racism in mental health care', *British Medical Journal*, 334, 649–50.

McMillan, I. (1997) 'Refuge reaching out', *Nursing Standard*, 11(39): 26–7.

Maden, A. et al. (1999a) 'Outcome of admission to a medium secure psychiatric unit 1: Short- and long-term outcome', *British Journal of Psychiatry*, 175, 313–16.

Maden, A. et al. (1999b) 'Outcome of admission to a medium secure psychiatric unit: 2 – role of ethnic origin', *British Journal of Psychiatry*, 175, 317–21.

Maguire, N. (1999) 'Models of imperfection', *Health Service Journal*, 109(5654): 20–2.

Malone, D. et al. (2000) 'Community mental health teams (CMHTs) for people with severe mental illnesses and disordered personality' (Cochrane Review): *Cochrane Library*, 3, Oxford: Update Software.

Mandelstam, M. (1998) *An A–Z of Community Care Law*. London: Jessica Kingsley.

Mannion, R., Davies, H.T.O. and Marshall, M. N. (2003) *Cultures for Performance in Health Care: Evidence on the Relationships between Organisational Culture and Organisational Performance*. York: Centre for Health Economics.

Markham, G. (2000) 'Policy and service development trends: Forensic mental health and social care services', *Tizard Learning Disability Review*, 5(2): 26–31.

Marmot, M. (2004) 'Evidence based policy or policy based evidence?', *British Medical Journal*, 328, 906–7.

Marshall, M. and Lockwood, A. (1998) 'Assertive community treatment for people with severe mental disorders' (Cochrane Review): *Cochrane Library*, 3, Oxford: Update Software.

Marshall, M. et al. (2001) 'Systematic reviews of the effectiveness of day care for people with severe mental disorders: (1) acute day hospital versus admission; (2) vocational rehabilitation; (3) day hospital versus outpatient care', *Health Technology Assessment*, 5, 1–75.

Marshall, M., Lockwood, A., and Green, R. (1998) 'Case management for people with severe mental disorders' (Cochrane Review): *Cochrane Library*, 1 Oxford: Update Software.

Marshall, R. (1990) 'The genetics of schizophrenia: Axiom or hypothesis?', in R. P. Bentall (ed.), *Reconstructing Schizophrenia*. London: Routledge.

Marshall, T. H. (1950) *Citizenship and Social Class and Other Essays*. Cambridge: Cambridge University Press.

Martin, J. P. (1984) *Hospitals in Trouble*. Oxford: Basil Blackwell.

Mauksch, L. B. and Leahy, D. (1993) 'Collaboration between primary care medicine and mental health in an HMO', *Family Systems Medicine*, 11, 121–35.

May, R. (2001) 'Crossing the "them and us" barriers: An insider perspective on user involvement in clinical psychology', *Clinical Psychology Forum*, 150, 14–17.

Maynard, A. and Tingle, R. (1975) 'The objectives and performance of the mental health services in England and Wales in the 1960s', *Journal of Social Policy*, 4(2): 151–68.

Mays, N. *et al.* (1998) *Total purchasing: A Step towards Primary Care Groups*. London: King's Fund.

Means, R. and Smith, R. (1998) *Community Care: Policy and Practice* (2nd edn). Basingstoke: Palgrave Macmillan.

Means, R., Richards, S. and Smith, R. (2008) *Community Care: Policy and Practice* (4th edn). Basingstoke: Palgrave Macmillan.

Medawar, C. *et al.* (2002) 'Paroxetine, *Panorama* and user reporting of ATDRs: Consumer intelligence matters in clinical practice and post-marketing drug surveillance', *International Journal of Risk and Safety in Medicine*, 15, 161–9.

Meehan, E. (1993) 'Citizenship and the European Community', *Political Quarterly*, 64(2): 172–86.

Meltzer, H. *et al.* (2002) *The Social and Economic Circumstances of Adults with Mental Disorders*. London: ONS.

Mental Health After Care Association (1999) *First National GP Survey of Mental Health in Primary Care*. London: MACA.

Mental Health Foundation (2001) *'Is Anybody There?' A Survey of Friendship and Mental Health* (Mental Health Foundation Updates, vol. 2, issue 16). London: Mental Health Foundation.

Mental Health Foundation (2003) *Black Spaces Project*. London: Mental Health Foundation.

Mental Health Foundation (2007) *Keeping the Faith: Spirituality and Recovery from Mental Health Problems*. London: Mental Health Foundation.

Mind (1996) *Lesbians, Gay Men, Bisexuals and Mental Health*. Mind factsheet (updated 2002). Available online via www.mind.org.uk (accessed 4 February 2004)

Mind (2003a) *Developing a visual impairment and mental health*. Mind factsheet, available online via www.mind.org.uk (accessed 4 February 2004).

Mind (2003b) *Deafness and Mental Health*. Mind factsheet, available online via www.mind.org.uk (accessed 4 February 2004).

Mind (2004) *Ward Watch*. London: Mind.

Mind (n. d.) *Mind: The Mental Health Charity*. Available online via www.mind.org.uk (accessed 4 February 2004).

Minghella, E. and Ford, R. (1997) 'Focal points?', *Health Service Journal*, 107(5583): 36–7.

Minghella, E. *et al.* (1998) *Open All Hours: 24-Hour Response for People with Mental Health Emergencies*. London: Sainsbury Centre for Mental Health.

Ministry of Health (1962) *A Hospital Plan for England and Wales*. London: HMSO.

Ministry of Justice (2009) *Access to Justice: A Review of the Existing Evidence of the Experiences of Adults with Mental Health Problems*. London: Ministry of Justice

Ministry of Justice/DH (2009) *A Guide for the Management of Dual Diagnosis for Prisons*. London: DH.

Ministry of Justice/DH (2011) *Working with Personality Disordered Offenders: A Practitioner's Guide*. London: Ministry of Justice.

Mohan, R. and Fahy, T. (2006) 'Is there a need for community forensic mental health services?', *Journal of Forensic Psychiatry and Psychology*, 17(3): 365–71.

Mohan, R., Slade, M. and Fahy, T. A. (2004) 'Clinical characteristics of community forensic mental health services', *Psychiatric Services*, 55(11): 1294–8.

Monahan, J. (1993) 'Dangerousness: An American perspective', in J. Gunn and P. Taylor (eds), *Forensic Psychiatry*. London: Butterworth-Heinemann.

Morgan, C. *et al.* (2007) 'Social exclusion and mental health: Conceptual and methodological review', *British Journal of Psychiatry*, 191, 477–83.

Morgan, H. (1998) 'A potential for partnership? Consulting with users of mental health services', in A. Foster and V. Z. Roberts (eds), *Managing Mental Health in the Community: Chaos and Containment*. London: Routledge.

Morgan, R. D., Rozycki, A. T. and Wilson, S. (2004) 'Inmate perceptions of mental health services', *Professional Psychology: Research and Practice*, 35, 389–96.

Morris, J. (2004a) *'One Town for My Body, Another for My Mind': Services for People with Physical Impairments and Mental Health Support Needs.* York: Joseph Rowntree Foundation.

Morris, J. (2004b) *Services for People with Physical Impairments and Mental Health Support Needs* (Joseph Rowntree Foundation Findings 574). York: Joseph Rowntree Foundation.

Morris, K. *et al.* (2008) *Think Family: A Literature Review of Whole Family Approaches.* London: Cabinet Office Social Exclusion Task Force.

Morrissey, M. (1998) 'Improving information for clients in mental health care', *Mental Health Nursing*, 18(2): 25–7.

Mulvany, J. (2000) 'Disability, impairment or illness? The relevance of the social model of disability to the study of mental disorder', *Sociology of Health and Illness*, 22(5): 582–681.

Munro, E. and Rumgay, J. (2000) 'Role of risk assessment in reducing homicides by people with mental illness', *British Journal of Psychiatry*, 176, 116–120.

Murphy, E. (1991) *After the Asylums: Community Care for People with Mental Illness.* London: Faber and Faber.

Murray, S. (1998) 'Evaluation of shifted out-patient clinics', *Psychiatry Audit Trends*, 6, 64–7.

Mynors-Wallis, L. M. *et al.* (2000) 'Randomised controlled trial of problem solving treatment, antidepressant medication, and combined treatment for depression in primary care', *British Medical Journal*, 320, 26–30.

NACRO (2005) *Findings of the 2004 Survey of Court Diversion/Criminal Justice Mental Health Liaison Schemes for Mentally Disordered Offenders in England and Wales.* London: NACRO.

NACRO (2009) *Liaison and Diversion for BME Service Users: A Good Practice Guide.* London: NACRO.

National Assembly for Wales (2002) *National Service Framework for Adult Mental Health Services in Wales.* Cardiff: National Assembly for Wales.

National Association of Psychiatric Intensive Care Units (2006) *Behind Closed Doors: Acute Mental Health in the UK.* London: NAPICU/Rethink/SANE/Zito Trust.

National Audit Office (2007) *Helping People through Mental Health Crisis: The Role of Crisis Resolution and Home Treatment Services.* London: National Audit Office.

National Confidential Inquiry into Suicide and Homicide (2006) *Five Year Report of the National Confidential Inquiry into Suicide and Homicide by People with Mental Illness.* Manchester: University of Manchester.

National Institute for Clinical Excellence (2004) *Depression: Management of Depression in Primary and Secondary Care.* London: National Institute for Clinical Excellence.

National Mental Health Development Unit (2010) *Mental Well-being Checklist.* Available online via www.nmhdu. org

National Patient Safety Agency (NPSA) (2006) *With Safety in Mind: Mental Health Services and Patient Safety.* London: NPSA.

National Schizophrenia Fellowship (1997) *How to Involve Users and Carers in Planning, Running and Monitoring Care Services and Curriculum Development.* Kingston-upon-Thames: National Schizophrenia Fellowship. [now Rethink]

National Schizophrenia Fellowship (2000) *No Change?* London: National Schizophrenia Fellowship.

National Schizophrenia Fellowship (n. d) *Carers Facts and Figures.* Available online at www.nsf.org.uk (accessed 26 June 2001).

Needham, C. and Carr, S. (2009) *Co-production: An Emerging Evidence Base for Adult Social Care Transformation.* London: SCIE.

Neill, J. and Williams, J. (1992) *Leaving Hospital: Older People and Their Discharge to Community Care*. London: HMSO.

Newnes, C., Long, N. and MacLachlan, A. (2001) 'Recruits you, sir', *OpenMind*, 108, 12.

NHS Centre for Involvement (2008) *The Current State of Patient and Public Involvement in NHS Trusts across England*. Coventry, NHS Centre for Involvement.

NHS Choices (2013) *Community Treatment Orders 'Don't Reduce Psychiatric Readmissions'*. NHS Choices (www.nhs.uk/news/2013/04April/pages/community-treatment-orders-psychiatric-readmissions.aspx).

NHS Confederation (2003) *The Role of Nurses under the New GMS Contract*. London: NHS Confederation.

NHS Confederation (2009) *Key Facts and Trends around Mental Health*. London: NHS Confederation.

NHS Confederation (2014) *Key Facts and Trends in Mental Health*. London: NHS Confederation.

NHS Executive (1994) *Introduction of Supervision Registers for Mentally Ill People from 1 April 1994*. HSG(84)5.

NHS Executive (1996) *Workforce Planning for General Medical Services*. Leeds: NHS Executive.

NHS Executive (1998) *Signposts for Success in Commissioning and Providing Health Services for People with Learning Disabilities*. Leeds: NHS Executive.

NHS Management Executive (1992) *Local Voices: The Views of Local People in Purchasing for Health*. Leeds: NHS Management Executive.

Nielssen, O. *et al.* (2011) 'Homicide of strangers by people with a psychotic illness', *Schizophrenia Bulletin*, 37(3): 572–9.

NIMHE (2003a) *Inside Outside: Improving Mental Health Services for Black and Minority Ethnic Communities in England*. Leeds: NIMHE.

NIMHE (2003b) *Engaging and Changing: Developing Effective Policy for the Care and Treatment of Black and Minority Ethnic Detained Patients*. Leeds: NIMHE.

NIMHE (2004a) *Celebrating Our Cultures: Guidelines for Mental Health Promotion with Black and Minority Ethnic Communities*. Leeds: NIMHE.

NIMHE (2004b) *From Here to Equality: A Strategic Plan to Tackle Stigma and Discrimination on Mental Health Grounds, 2004–2009*. Leeds: NIMHE.

NIMHE (2008) *Mental Health Act 2007 New Roles: Guidance for Approving Authorities and Employers on Approved Mental Health Professionals and Approved Clinicians*. London: NIMHE.

Nolan, P., Bradley, E. and Brimblecombe, N. (2011) 'Disengaging from acute inpatient psychiatric care: A description of service users' experiences and views', *Journal of Psychiatric and Mental Health Nursing*, 18, 359–67.

Norfolk, Suffolk and Cambridgeshire Strategic Health Authority (2003) *Independent Inquiry into the Death of David Bennett*. Cambridge, Norfolk, Suffolk and Cambridgeshire Strategic Health Authority.

Norman, R. and Malla, A. (2001) 'Duration of untreated psychosis: A critical examination of the concept and its importance', *Psychological Medicine*, 31, 381–400.

Norman, R. M. G. and Townsend, L. A. (1999) 'Cognitive behavioural therapy for psychosis: A status report', *Canadian Journal of Psychiatry*, 44, 245–52.

Nurse, J., Woodcock, P. and Ormsby, J. (2003) 'Influence of environmental factors on mental health within prisons: Focus group study', *British Medical Journal*, 327, 480–5.

Office of the Deputy Prime Minister (2006) *Reaching Out: An Action Plan for Social Inclusion*. London: ODPM.

Office of the Deputy Prime Minister (ODPM) (2004) *Mental Health and Social Exclusion (Social Exclusion Unit Report)*. London: ODPM.

Okai, D. *et al.* (2007) 'Mental capacity in psychiatric patients: systematic review', *British Journal of Psychiatry*, 191, 291–7.

Oliver, M. (1983) *Social Work with Disabled People.* Basingstoke: Macmillan.

Oliver, M. (1990) *The Politics of Disablement.* Basingstoke: Macmillan.

Oliver, M. (1996) 'Defining impairment and disability: Issues at stake', in E. Barnes and G. Mercer (eds), *Exploring the Divide: Illness and Disability.* Leeds: Disability Press.

Oliver, M. and Sapey, B. (2006) *Social Work with Disabled People* (3rd edn). Basingstoke: Palgrave Macmillan.

Olumoroti, O. *et al.* (2009) 'Mentally ill prisoners in need of urgent hospital transfer: Appeal panels should resolve disputes to reduce delays', *Journal of Forensic Psychiatry and Psychology*, 20(S1): S5–10.

ONS (Office for National Statistics) (2000) *Carers 2000.* London: ONS.

ONS (2002) *Labour Force Survey.* London: ONS.

ONS (2003) *Labour Force Survey, Autumn 2003.* London: ONS.

ONS (2007) *Attitudes to Mental Illness 2007.* London: ONS.

Onyett, S., Standee, R. and Peck, E. (1997) 'The challenge of managing community mental health teams', *Health and Social Care in the Community*, 5(1): 40–7.

Onyett. S (1998) *Case Management in Mental Health.* Cheltenham: Nelson Thornes.

Organisation for Economic Co-operation and Development (OECD) (2001) *OECD Health Data.* Paris: OECD.

Otis, M. and Skinner, W (1996) 'The prevalence of victimisation and its effect on mental well-being among lesbian and gay people', *Journal of Homosexuality*, 30(3): 93–121.

Pakes, F. and Winstone, J. (2010) 'A site visit survey of 101 mental health liaison and diversion schemes in England', *Journal of Forensic Psychiatry and Psychology*, 21(6): 873–886.

Parkman, S. *et al.* (1997) 'Ethnic differences in satisfaction with mental health services among representative people with psychosis in south London', PRiSM study 4, *British Journal of Psychiatry*, 171, 260–4.

Parsonage, M. (2009) 'The NSF for mental health: costs of implementation', in C. Brooker and J. Repper (eds), *Mental Health: From Policy to Practice.* Edinburgh: Elsevier.

Patel, K. and Shaw, I. (2009) 'Mental health and the Gujarati community: Accounting for the low incidence rates of mental illness', *Mental Health Review*, 14(4): 12–24.

Patmore, C. and Weaver, T. (1991) *Community Mental Health Teams: Lessons for Planners and Managers.* London: Good Practice in Mental Health.

Paton, J. M., Fahy, M. A. and Livingston, G. A. (2004) 'Delayed discharge – A solvable problem? The place of intermediate care in mental health care of older people', *Aging and Mental Health*, 8(1): 34–9.

Payne, S. (1998) '"Hit and miss": The success and failure of psychiatric services for women', in L. Doyal (ed.), *Women and Health Services.* Buckingham: Open University Press.

Payne, S. (1999) 'Outside the walls of the asylum? Psychiatric treatment in the 1980s and 1990s', in P. Bartlett and D. Wright (eds), *Outside the Walls of the Asylum: The History of Care in the Community.* London: Athlone Press.

Peck, E. and Greatley, A. (1999) 'Developing the mental health agenda for primary care groups', *Managing Community Care*, 7, 3–6.

Peck, E., Gulliver, P., Towell, D. (2002) 'Information, consultation or control: User involvement in mental health services in England at the turn of the century', *Journal of Mental Health*, 11(4): 441–51.

Percy Commission (1957) *The Report of the Royal Commission on Mental Illness and Mental Deficiency.* London: HMSO.

Perkins, R., Repper, J., Rinaldi, M. and Brown, H. (2012) 'Recovery Colleges'. London: Centre for Mental Health/NHS Confederation (www.nhsconfed.org/Documents/ImROC%20Briefing%20Recovery%20Colleges.pdf).

Perring, C., Twigg, J. and Atkin, K. (1990) *Families Caring for People Diagnosed as Mentally Ill: The Literature Re-examined*. London: HMSO.

Petch, E. (2001) 'Risk management in UK mental health services – An overvalued idea?', *Psychiatric Bulletin*, 25, 203–5.

Peterson, L. *et al.* (2005) 'A randomised multi-centre trial of integrated versus standard treatment for patients with a first episode of psychotic illness', *British Medical Journal*, 331, 602–9.

Peveler, R. *et al.* (1999) 'Effect of antidepressant drug counselling and information leaflets on adherence to drug treatment in primary care: Randomised controlled trial', *British Medical Journal*, 319, 612–15.

Pierre, S. (1999) 'The experiences of African and Afro-Caribbean people in acute psychiatric hospital: A qualitative study', *Mental Health Care*, 3(2): 52–6.

Pilgrim, D. (2002) 'The biopsychosocial model in Anglo-American psychiatry: Past, present and future?', *Journal of Mental Health*, 11(6): 585–94.

Pilgrim, D. (2008) 'Recovery and current mental health policy', *Chronic Illness*, 4, 295–304.

Pilgrim, D. and Ramon, S. (2009) 'English mental health policy under New Labour', *Policy and Politics*, 37(2): 273–88.

Pilgrim, D. and Rogers, A. (2010) *A Sociology of Mental Health and Illness* (4th edn). Buckingham: Open University Press.

Pinfold, V. *et al.* (2001) 'Persuading the persuadable: Evaluating compulsory treatment in England using Supervised Discharge Orders', *Social Psychiatry & Psychiatric Epidemiology*, 36(5): 260–6.

Pinfold, V. *et al.* (2004) *Positive and Inclusive? Effective Ways for Professionals to Involve Carers in Information Sharing*. London: Rethink/Institute of Psychiatry/King's College London.

Pinfold, V. *et al.* (2005) 'Active ingredients in anti-stigma programmes in mental health', *International Review of Psychiatry*, 17(2): 123–131.

Pinfold, V., Smith, J. and Shiers, D. (2007) 'Audit of early intervention in psychosis service development in England in 2005', *Psychiatric Bulletin*, 31, 7–10.

Pinnock, H. *et al.* (2005) 'General practitioners with a special interest in respiratory medicine: National survey of UK primary care organisation', *BMC Health Services Research*, 5(1): 40.

Plumb, A. (1994) *Distress or Disability?* Manchester: Greater Manchester Coalition of Disabled People.

Plummer, S. E. *et al.* (2000) 'Detection of psychological distress by practice nurses in general practice', *Psychological Medicine*, 30, 1233–7.

Polczyk-Przybyla, M. and Gournay, K. (1999) 'Psychiatric nursing in prison: The state of the art?', *Journal of Advanced Nursing*, 30(4): 893–900.

Poll, C. *et al.* (2006) *A Report on in Control's First Phase, 2003–2005*. London: in Control.

Porter, R. (1987) *Mind Forged Manacles*. Harmondsworth: Penguin.

Porter, R. (1999) *A Social History of Madness: Stories of the Insane*. London: Phoenix.

Porter, R. (2002) *Madness: A Brief History*. Oxford: Oxford University Press.

Powell, E. (1961) Speech to the Annual Conference of the National Association of Mental Health. [now Mind]

Pressman, J. and Wildavsky, A. (1973) *Implementation*. Berkeley, CA: University of California Press.

Price, J. (1997) *Queer in the Head: An Examination of the Response of Social Work Mental Health Services to the Needs and Experiences of Lesbians and Gay Men*. Surbiton: Social Care Association.

Priebe, S. *et al.* (2005) 'Reinstitutionalisation in mental health care: Comparison in data in service provision from six European countries', *British Medical Journal*, 33, 123–6.

Priebe, S., Burns, T. and Craig, T. (2013) 'The future of academic research may be social', *British Journal of Psychiatry*, 202, 319–320.

Quirk, A. and Lelliott, P. (2001) 'What do we know about life on acute psychiatric wards in the UK? A review of the research evidence', *Social Science and Medicine*, 53(12): 1565–74.

Quirk, A., Lelliott, P. and Seale, C. (2004) 'Service users' strategies for managing risk in the volatile environment of an acute psychiatric ward', *Social Science and Medicine*, 59, 2573–83.

Quirk, A., Lelliott, P. and Seale, C. (2006) 'The permeable institution: An ethnographic study of three acute psychiatric wards in London', *Social Science and Medicine*, 63, 2105–17.

Race, D., Boxall, K. and Carson, I. (2005) 'Towards a dialogue for practice: Reconciling social role valorization and the social model of disability', *Disability & Society*, 20(5): 507–521.

Ramon, S. (1996) *Mental Health in Europe*. Basingstoke: Macmillan.

Ramsay, R., Weich, S. and Youard, E. (2001) 'Needs of women patients with mental illness', *Advances in Psychiatric Treatment*, 7, 85–92.

Rapaport, J. *et al.* (2006) 'Carers and confidentiality in mental health care: Considering the role of the carer's assessment: A study of service users', carers' and practitioners' views', *Health and Social Care in the Community*, 14(4): 357–65.

RCGP (2003) *RCGP Information Sheet Number 21: The Primary Health Care Team*. London: RCGP.

RCGP (2006) *RCGP Information Sheet: General Practitioners with Special Interests*. London: RCGP.

RCP (2009) *Standards for Safe and Appropriate Care for Young People on Adult Mental Health Wards*. London: RCP.

RCP (2011) *Parents as Patients: Supporting the Needs of Patients Who Are Parents and Their Children*. London: RCP.

Read, J. and Baker, S. (1996) *Not Just Sticks and Stones: A Survey of the Discrimination Experienced by People with Mental Health Problems*. London: Mind.

Read, J. *et al.* (2004) 'Childhood trauma, loss and stress', in J. Read, L. Mosher and R. Bentnall (eds), *Models of Madness*. Hove: Brunner-Routledge.

Read, J. *et al.* (2005) 'Childhood trauma, psychosis and schizophrenia: A literature review with theoretical and clinical implications', *Acta Psychiatrica Scandanavica*, 112(5): 330–350.

Read, J. *et al.* (2006) 'Prejudice and schizophrenia: A review of the "mental illness is an illness like any other" approach', *Acta Psychiatrica Scandanavica*, 114, 303–18.

Regen, E., Smith, J. and Shapiro, J. (1999) *First off the Starting Blocks: Lessons from GP Commissioning Pilots for PCGs*. Birmingham: HSMC, University of Birmingham.

Regier, D. A. *et al.* (1988) The NIMH depression awareness, recognition, and treatment program: structure, aims, and scientific basis, *American Journal of Psychiatry*, 145: 1351–7.

Repper, J. and Breeze, J. (2006) 'User and carer involvement in the training and education of health professionals: A review of the literature', *International Journal of Nursing Studies*, 44(3): 511–19.

Rethink (2003a) *Reaching People Early: A Status Report on the Early Support Received by People with Severe Mental Illness and Their Informal Carers*. London: Rethink.

Rethink (2003b) *Who Cares? The Experiences of Mental Health Carers Accessing Services and Information*. London: Rethink.

Rethink (2003c) *Under Pressure*. London: Rethink.

Rethink (2005) *Future Perfect*. London: Rethink.

Rethink (2007) *Our Voice: The Pakistani Community's View of Mental Health Services in Birmingham*. London: Rethink.

Rethink/CSIP (2007) *Involving Carers in Out of Area Treatments: A Good Practice Guide*. London: Rethink/CSIP.

Rethink/Sane/Zito Trust/NAPICU (2006) *Behind Closed Doors: Acute Mental Health Care in the UK*. London: Rethink.

Reynolds, J. *et al.* (eds) (2009) *Mental Health Still Matters*. Basingstoke: Palgrave Macmillan.

Rickford, D. and Edgar, K. (2005) *Troubled Inside: Responding to the Mental Health Needs of Men in Prison*. London: Prison Reform Trust.

Rimington, L. D., Davies, D. H. and Pearson, M. G. (2001) 'Relationship between anxiety, depression and morbidity in adult asthma patients', *Thorax*, 56, 266–71.

Ritchie Report (1994) *Report of the Inquiry into the Care and Treatment of Christopher Clunis*. London: HMSO.

Robert, G. *et al.* (2003) 'Redesigning mental health services: Lessons on user involvement from the Mental Health Collaborative', *Health Expectations*, 6, 60–71.

Robinson, G., Beaton, S. and White, P. (1993) 'Attitudes towards practice nurses', *British Journal of General Practice*, 43, 25–9.

Rogers, A. and Pilgrim, D. (2001) *Mental Health Policy in Britain* (2nd edn). Basingstoke: Palgrave.

Rogers, A. and Pilgrim, D. (2003) *Mental Health and Inequalities*. Basingstoke: Palgrave Macmillan.

Rogers, A. *et al.* (2002) 'Some national service frameworks are more equal than others: Implementing clinical governance for mental health in primary care groups and trusts', *Journal of Mental Health*, 11, 199–212.

Romme, M. and Escher, A. (1989) 'Hearing voices', *Schizophrenia Bulletin*, 15, 209–16.

Rooney, P. (2002) *Mental Health Policy Implementation Guide: Adult Acute Inpatient Care Provision*. London: DH.

Rose, D. (2001) *Users' Voices: The Perspectives of Mental Health Service Users on Community and Hospital Care*. London: Sainsbury Centre for Mental Health.

Royal College of General Practitioners (RCGP) (2002) *RCGP Information Sheet Number 4: General Practice in the UK*. London: RCGP.

Royal College of Nursing (RCN)/CSIP/NIMHE (2008) *Informed Gender Practice: Mental Health Acute Care that Works for Women*. London: CSIP/DH.

Royal College of Psychiatrists (RCP) (2002) 'Acute hospitals should be at the forefront of psychiatric services', press release, 1 March. London: RCP.

Rutherford, M. and Duggan, S. (2007) *Forensic Mental Health Services: Facts and Figures on Current Provision*. London: Sainsbury Centre for Mental Health.

Ryan, R. and Deci, E. (2001) 'On happiness and human potential: A review of research on hedonic and eudaimonic well-being', *Annual Review of Psychology*, 52, 141–66

Ryan, T. (2002) 'Exploring the risk management strategies of informal carers of mental health service users', *Journal of Mental Health*, 11(1): 17–25.

Ryan, T. and Bamber, C. (2002) 'A survey of policy and practice on expenses and other payments to mental health service users and carers participating in service development', *Journal of Mental Health*, 11(6): 635–44.

Ryan, T. *et al.* (2011) *In Sight and in Mind: A Toolkit to Reduce the Use of Out of Area Mental Health Services*. London: Royal College of Psychiatrists and partners.

Sainsbury Centre for Mental Health (1998a) *Keys to Engagement: Review of Care for People with Severe Mental Illness Who Are Hard to Engage with Services*. London: Sainsbury Centre for Mental Health.

Sainsbury Centre for Mental Health (1998b) *Acute Problems: A Survey of the Quality of Care in Acute Psychiatric Wards*. London: Sainsbury Centre for Mental Health.

Sainsbury Centre for Mental Health (1999) *The National Service Framework for Mental Health: An Executive Briefing*. London: Sainsbury Centre for Mental Health.

Sainsbury Centre for Mental Health (2001a) *Setting the Standard: The New Agenda for Primary Care Organisations Commissioning Mental Health Services*. London: Sainsbury Centre for Mental Health.

Sainsbury Centre for Mental Health (2001b) *Crisis Resolution*. London: Sainsbury Centre for Mental Health.

Sainsbury Centre for Mental Health (2002a) *Being There in a Crisis*. London: Mental Health Foundation/Sainsbury Centre for Mental Health.

Sainsbury Centre for Mental Health (2002b) *Breaking the Circles of Fear*. London: Sainsbury Centre for Mental Health.

Sainsbury Centre for Mental Health (2004) *Acute Care 2004: A National Survey of Adult Psychiatric Wards in England* (briefing 28). London: Sainsbury Centre for Mental Health.

Sainsbury Centre for Mental Health (2005) *Beyond the Water Towers: The Unfinished Revolution in Mental Health Services 1985–2005*. London: Sainsbury Centre for Mental Health.

Sainsbury Centre for Mental Health (2006a) *The Search for Acute Solutions: Improving the Quality of Care in Acute Psychiatric Wards*. London: Sainsbury Centre for Mental Health.

Sainsbury Centre for Mental Health (2006b) *London's Prison Mental Health Services: A Review*. London: Sainsbury Centre for Mental Health.

Sainsbury Centre for Mental Health (2006c) *First Steps to Work – A Study at Broadmoor Hospital*. London: Sainsbury Centre for Mental Health.

Sainsbury Centre for Mental Health (2006d) *The Costs of Race Inequality*. London: Sainsbury Centre for Mental Health.

Sainsbury Centre for Mental Health (2007a) *Work and Wellbeing: Developing Primary Mental Health Care Services*. London: Sainsbury Centre for Mental Health.

Sainsbury Centre for Mental Health (2007b) *Mental Health Care in Prisons*. London: Sainsbury Centre for Mental Health.

Sainsbury Centre for Mental Health (2007c) *Getting the Basics Right: Developing a Primary Care Mental Health Service in Prisons*. London: Sainsbury Centre for Mental Health.

Sainsbury Centre for Mental Health (2008) *Short-changed: Spending on Prison Mental Health Care*. London: Sainsbury Centre for Mental Health.

Sainsbury Centre for Mental Health (2009a) *Securing Employment for Offenders with Mental Health Problems: Towards a Better Way*. London: Sainsbury Centre for Mental Health.

Sainsbury Centre for Mental Health (2009b) *The Bradley Report and the Government's Response*. London: Sainsbury Centre for Mental Health.

Sainsbury Centre for Mental Health (2009c) *Mental Health Care and the Criminal Justice System*. London: Sainsbury Centre for Mental Health.

Salisbury, C. *et al.* (2005) 'Evaluation of a general practitioner with special interest service for dermatology: Randomised controlled trial', *British Medical Journal*, 331, 1441–6.

Sashidharan, S. P. (1999) 'Alternatives to institutional psychiatry', in D. Bhugra and V. Bahl (eds), *Ethnicity: An Agenda for Mental Health*. London: Gaskell

Saultz, J. W. (2003) 'Defining and measuring interpersonal care', *Annals of Family Medicine*, 3, 134–44.

Sayce, L. (1997) 'Stigma and social exclusion: Top priorities for mental health professionals', *Eurohealth*, 3(3): 5–7.

Sayce, L. (1999) 'High time for justice', *Nursing Times*, 95(9): 64–6.

Sayce, L. (2000) *from Psychiatric Patient to Citizen: Overcoming Discrimination and Social Exclusion*. Basingstoke: Palgrave.

Sayce, L., Craig, T. K. J. and Boardman, A. P. (1991) 'The development of community mental health centres in the UK', *Social Psychiatry and Psychiatric Epidemiology*, 26, 14–20.

Schon, D. (1983) *The Reflective Practitioner: How Professionals Think in Action*. London: Temple Smith.

Scottish Development Centre for Mental Health (2004) *A Crisis Centre for Edinburgh – Lessons from Other Areas*. Edinburgh: Scottish Development Centre for Mental Health (www.edinburghcrisiscentre.org.uk/wordpress/wp-content/uploads/2010/11/Crisis-Centre-Report.pdf).

Scottish Executive Health Department (1997) *The Framework for Mental Health Services in Scotland*. Edinburgh: Scottish Executive.

Scottish Government (2006) *Delivering for Mental Health*. Edinburgh: Scottish Government.

Scottish Government (2009) *Towards a Mentally Flourishing Scotland: Policy and Action Plan 2009–11*. Edinburgh: Scottish Government. www.scotland.gov.uk/Publications/2009/05/06154655/0

Scottish Government (2012) *Mental Health Strategy for Scotland 2012–15*. Edinburgh: Scottish Government.

Scull, A. (1977) *De-carceration: Community Treatment and the Deviant – A Radical View*. Englewood-Cliffs, NJ: Prentice-Hall.

Scull, A. (1979) *Museums of Madness*. Harmondsworth: Penguin.

Scull, A. (1993) *The Most Solitary of Afflictions: Madness in Society in Britain, 1700–1900*. New Haven, CT: Yale University Press.

SDO (2006) *Sharing Mental Health Information with Carers: Pointers to Good Practice for Service Providers* (SDO briefing paper). London: SDO.

Secker, J. *et al.* (2000) 'Mental health in the community: Roles, responsibilities and organisation of primary care and specialist services', *Journal of Interprofessional Care*, 14(1): 49–58.

Seebohm, P. and Gilchrist, A. (2008) *Connect and Include: An Exploratory Study of Community Development and Mental Health*. London: Community Development Foundation.

Seikkula, J. *et al.* (2003) 'Open dialogue approach: Treatment principles and preliminary results of a two-year follow-up on first episode schizophrenia', *Ethical Human Sciences and Services*, 5, 163–182.

Seikkula, J., Alakare, B. and Aaltonen, J. (2011) 'The comprehensive open-dialogue approach in Western Lapland: II – Long-term stability of acute psychosis outcomes in advanced community care, *Psychosis*, 3(3): 192–204.

Selbie, D. (2006) *Local Delivery Plans – Mental Health Early Intervention Services: Letter to SHA Chief Executives, SHA Directors of Performance and Directors of Social Services*. London: DH.

Seligman, M. (1991) *Learned Optimism*. New York: Pocket Books.

Seymour, L. *et al.* (2011) *Mental Health, Employment and the Social Care Workforce*. London: SCIE.

Shaw, J. *et al.* (2006) 'Rates of mental disorder in people convicted of homicide: National clinical survey', *British Journal of Psychiatry*, 188, 143–7.

Shaw, J., Appleby, L. and Baker, D. (2003) *Safer Prisons: A National Study of Prison Suicides, 1999–2000 by the National Confidential Inquiry into Suicides and Homicides by People with Services Mental Illness*. London: DH.

Shekelle, P. (2003) 'New contract for general practitioners', *British Medical Journal*, 326, 457–8.

Shelter (2003) *Housekeeping: Preventing Homelessness through Tackling Rent Arrears in Social Housing*. London: Shelter.

Shepherd, G. (1998) 'Models of community care', *Journal of Mental Health*, 7(2): 165–77.

Shepherd, G. *et al.* (1997) 'Relation between bed use, social deprivation, and overall bed availability in acute adult psychiatric units, and alternative residential options: A cross sectional survey, one day census data, and staff interviews', *British Medical Journal*, 314, 262–6.

Shepherd, M. (1966) *Psychiatric Illness in General Practice*. Oxford: Oxford University Press.

Shergill, S. and Szmukler, G. (1998) 'How predictable is violence and suicide in community psychiatric practice?', *Journal of Mental Health*, 7(4): 393–401.

Sibitz, I. *et al.* (2009) 'Stigma resistance in patients with schizophrenia', *Schizophrenia Bulletin*, 37(2): 316–23.

Sign (n. d.) *Mental Health Services for Deaf People: Are They Appropriate?* Beaconsfield: Sign.

Simonet, D (2013) 'The new public management theory in the British health care system: A critical review', *Administration and Society* doi: 10. 1177/0095399713485001

Simpson, A. *et al.* (2004) 'Homicide and mental illness in New Zealand, 1970–2000', *British Journal of Psychiatry*, 185, 394–8.

Sims, J. (2004) 'Sam's bill', *Care and Health*, 4–18 February, 25.

Singh, S. P. and Burns, T. (2006) 'Race and mental health: There is more to race than racism', *British Medical Journal*, 333, 648–51.

Singleton, N. *et al.* (2001) *Psychiatric Morbidity among Adults Living in Private Households, 2000*. London: TSO.

Singleton, N. *et al.* (2002) *Mental Health of Carers*. London: TSO.

Singleton, N., Meltzer, H. and Gatward, R. (1998) *Psychiatric Morbidity among Prisoners in England and Wales*. London: Office for National Statistics.

Smyth, M. and Hoult, J. (2000) 'The home treatment enigma', *British Medical Journal*, 320, 305–9.

Social Care Institute for Excellence (SCIE) (2012) *Think Child, Think Parent, Think Family: Final Evaluation Report*. London: SCIE.

Social Care Institute for Excellence (SCIE) (2003) *Users at the Heart: User Participation in the Governance and Operations of Social Care Regulatory Bodies*. London: SCIE.

Solomka, B. (2011) *Mental Health Payment by Results* (Royal College of Psychiatrists Specialist Advisor Update). Available online via www.rcpsych.ac.uk/pdf/Payment%by %Results%update%20Dec%202011.pdf

Sorohan, H. *et al.* (2002) 'The role of the practice nurses in primary care mental health: Challenges and opportunities', *Primary Care Psychiatry*, 8, 41–6

Spandler, H. (2007) 'From social exclusion to inclusion? A critique of the inclusion imperative in mental health', *Medical Sociology Online* V2, 2, November, 3–16.

Spandler, H., Anderson, J., and Sapey, B. (eds) (in press) *Distress or Disability? Mental Health and the Politics of Disablement*. Bristol: The Policy Press.

Spandler, H. and Vick, N. (2004) *Direct Payments, Independent Living and Mental Health: An Evaluation*. London: Health and Social Care Advisory Service.

Spiers, S., Harney, K. and Chilvers, C. (2005) 'Service user involvement in forensic mental health: Can it work?', *Journal of Forensic Psychiatry and Psychology*, 16(2): 211–20.

Spitzer, R. and First, M. (2005) 'Classification of psychiatric disorders', *Journal of the American Medical Association*, 294, 1898–9.

Spudic, T. J. (2003) 'Assessing inmate satisfaction with mental health services', *Behaviour Therapy in Correctional Settings*, 217–18.

Srole, L. *et al.* (1962) *Mental Health in the Metropolis*. New York: McGraw-Hill.

Steadman, H. J. *et al.* (1998) 'Violence by people discharged from acute psychiatric inpatient facilities and by others in the same neighbourhoods', *Archives of General Psychiatry*, 55, 1–9.

Stein, L. I. and Test, M. A. (1980) 'An alternative to mental hospital treatment', *Archives of General Psychiatry*, 37, 392–9.

Stickley, T. and Felton, A. (2006) 'Promoting recovery through therapeutic risk taking', *Mental Health Practice*, 9(8): 26–30.

Stone, M. (1985) 'Shellshock and the psychologists', in W. F. Bynum, R. Porter and M. Shepherd (eds), *The Anatomy of Madness: Volume 2*. London: Tavistock.

Stott, N. C. H. and Davis, R. H. (1979) 'The exceptional potential in each primary care consultation', *Journal of the Royal College of General Practice*, 29, 201–5.

Styron, W. (2001) *Darkness Visible*. London: Vintage.

Summers, A. (2003) 'Involving users in the development of mental health services: A study of psychiatrists' views', *Journal of Mental Health*, 12(2):161–74.

Swanson, J. *et al.* (1990) 'Violence and psychiatric disorder in the community: Evidence from the epidemiological catchment area surveys', *Hospital and Community Psychiatry*, 41, 761–70.

Symons, L., Tylee, A. and Mann, A. (2002) 'Nurse facilitated open access depression clinic in primary care – London pilot'. London: Institute of Psychiatry. Kings College London (unpublished).

Szasz, T. (1961) *The Myth of Mental Illness: Foundations of a Theory of Personal Conduct*. New York: Harper & Row.

Szasz, T. (1970) *Ideology and Insanity: Essays on the Psychiatric Dehumanisation of Man*. Garden City, NY: Double Day.

Szasz, T. (2003) 'The psychiatric protection order for the "battered mental patient"', *British Medical Journal*, 327, 1449–51.

Tabassum, R., Macaskill, A. and Ahmad, I. (2000) 'Attitudes towards mental health in an urban Pakistani community in the United Kingdom', *International Journal of Social Psychiatry*, 46(3): 170–81.

Taylor, P. J. and Gunn, J. (1999) 'Homicides by people with mental illness: Myth and reality', *British Journal of Psychiatry*, 174, 9–14.

Taylor, T. *et al.* (2010) 'Meeting the needs of women in mental health rehabilitation services', *British Journal of Occupational Therapy*, 73(10): 477–80.

Telford, R. and Faulkner, A. (2004) 'Learning about service user involvement in mental health research', *Journal of Mental Health*, 13(6): 549–59.

Tennant, R. *et al.* (2007) 'The Warwick–Edinburgh Mental Well-being Scale (WEMWBS): Development and UK validation', *Health and Quality of Life Outcomes5:63 doi 10 1186/1477-7525-5-63*.

Tew, J. (2011) *Social Approaches to Mental Distress*. Basingstoke: Palgrave Macmillan.

Tew, J. (2012) 'Recovery capital: What enables a sustainable recovery from mental health difficulties?', *European Journal of Social Work*, doi:10. 1080/13691457

Tew, J. *et al.* (2012) 'Social factors and recovery from mental health difficulties: A review of the evidence', *British Journal of Social Work*, 42(3): 443–460.

Tew, J. *et al.* (2013) *Whole Family Approaches to Reablement in Mental Health: Scoping Current Practice*. Birmingham: Family Potential Research Centre.

Tew, J., Gell, C. and Foster, S. (2004) *Learning from Experience: Good Practice in Service User and Carer Involvement in Mental Health Education*. London: National Institute for Mental Health/Higher Education Academy.

Tew, J., Holley, T. and Caplen, P. (2011) 'Dialogue and challenge: Involving service users and carers in small group learning with social work and nursing students', *Social Work Education*, doi: 10.1080/02615479.2011.557429

Thomas, N. *et al.* (2009) 'Changing from mixed-sex to all-male provision in acute psychiatric care: A case study of staff experiences', *Journal of Mental Health*, 18(2): 129–36.

Thomas, R. and Corney, R. (1993) 'The role of the practice nurse in mental health: A survey', *Journal of Mental Health*, 2, 65–72.

Thomson, L., Galt, V. and Darjee, R. (2004) *An Evaluation of Appropriate Adult Schemes in Scotland* (Scottish Executive Research Findings 78/2004). Edinburgh: University of Edinburgh.

Thornicroft, G. (2006a) *Shunned: Discrimination against People with Mental Illness*. Oxford: Oxford University Press.

Thornicroft, G. (2006b) *Actions Speak Louder: Tackling Discrimination against People with Mental Illness*. London: Mental Health Foundation.

Thornicroft, G. *et al.* (2002) 'What are the research priorities of mental health service users?', *Journal of Mental Health*, 11(1): 1–5.

Thornicroft, G. *et al.* (eds) (2011) *Oxford Textbook of Community Mental Health*. Oxford: Oxford University Press.

Thornicroft, G., Parkman, S. and Ruggeri, M. (1999) 'Satisfaction with mental health services: Issues for ethnic minorities', in D. Bhugra and V. Bahl (eds), *Ethnicity: An Agenda for Mental Health*. London: Gaskell.

Tiemans, B., Ormel, J. and Simon, G. (1996) 'Occurrence, recognition and outcome of psychological disorders in primary care', *Psychological Medicine*, 153, 636–44.

Tien, A. Y. (1991) 'The distribution of hallucinations in the population', *Social Psychiatry and Psychiatric Epidemiology*, 26, 287–92.

Tienari, P. *et al.* (2004) 'Genotype-environment interaction in schizophrenia spectrum disorder: Long-term follow-up study of Finnish adoptees', *British Journal of Psychiatry*, 184, 216–22.

Time to Change (2011) *Annual Report 2011*. London: Time to Change.

Timmins, N. (2012) *Never Again? The Story of the Health and Social Care Act 2012*. London: King's Fund.

Titmuss, R. M. (1968) *Commitment to Welfare*. London: George Allen & Unwin.

Todd, Lord A. R. (1968) *The Todd Report: Royal Commission on Medical Education*. London: HMSO.

Tudor Hart, J. (1988) *A New Kind of Doctor*. London: Merlin Press.

Turner, R. and Roberts, G. (1992) 'The Worcester Development Project', *British Journal of Psychiatry*, 160, 103–7.

Tyrer, P. (2011) 'Has the closure of psychiatric beds gone too far? Yes', *British Medical Journal*, 343: 7457.

Tyrer, P. and Steinberg, D. (2003) *Models for Mental Disorders: Conceptual Models in Psychiatry*. Chichester: Wiley.

Tyrer, P. *et al.* (2006) 'The Bed Requirement Inventory: A simple measure to estimate the need for a psychiatric bed', *International Journal of Social Psychiatry*, 52(3): 267–77.

Ungerson, C. (1987) *Policy Is Personal: Sex, Gender and Informal care*. London: Tavistock.

Union of Physically Impaired Against Segregation (UPIAS) (1976) *Fundamental Principles of Disability*. London: UPIAS.

Ustun, T. B. *et al.* (1999) 'Multiple-informant ranking of the disabling effects of different health conditions in 14 countries: WHO/NIH Joint Project CAR Study Group', *Lancet*, 354, 111–15.

Valios, N. (2000) 'Appeal court broadens definition of disability', *Community Care*, 22–28 June, 11.

Valuing People Support Team (2004) *Green Light for Mental Health* (parts A and B). London: Valuing People Support Team/DH.

Vaughan, P., Kelly, M. and Pullen, N. (2000) 'Services for mentally disordered offenders in community psychiatry teams', *Journal of Forensic Psychiatry*, 11(3): 571–86.

Vaughan, P. J. (1999) 'A consortium approach to commissioning services for mentally disordered offenders', *Journal of Forensic Psychiatry*, 10(3): 553–66.

Vaughan, P. J., Kelly, M. and Pullen, N. (2001) 'The working practices of the police in relation to mentally disordered offenders and diversion schemes', *Medicine, Science and the Law*, 41(1): 13–20.

Vaughan, P. J. and Stevenson, S. (2002) 'An opinion survey of mentally disordered offender service users', *British Journal of Forensic Psychiatry*, 4, 11–20.

Wade, D. and Halligan, P. (2004) 'Do biomedical models of illness make for good health-care systems?', *British Medical Journal*, 329, 1398–401.

Wahl, O. F. (1995) *Media Madness: Public Images of Mental Illness*. New Jersey: Rutgers University Press.

Wallcraft, J. and Bryant, M. (2003) *The Mental Health Service Users Movement in England*. London: Sainsbury Centre for Mental Health.

Wallcraft, J. and Michaelson, J. (2001) 'Developing a survivor discourse to replace the "psychopathology" of breakdown and crisis', in C. Newnes, G. Holmes and C. Dunn (eds), *This Is Madness Too*. Ross on Wye: PCCS Books.

Walsh, E. and Fahy, T. (2002) 'Violence in society', *British Medical Journal*, 325, 507–8.

Walsh, E., Buchanan, A. and Fahy, T. (2002) 'Violence and schizophrenia: Examining the evidence', *British Journal of Psychiatry*, 188, 490–5.

Walsh, J. *et al.* (2011) 'Perception of need and barriers to access: The mental health needs of young people attending a Youth Offending Team in the UK', *Health and Social Care in the Community*, 19(4): 420–8.

Walshe, K. *et al.* (2004) 'Primary care trusts: premature reorganisation with mergers, may be harmful', *British Medical Journal*, 329, 871–2.

Walton, P. (2000) 'Psychiatric hospital care: A case of the more things change, the more they remain the same', *Journal of Mental Health*, 9(1): 77–88.

Wanless, D. (2002) *Securing Our Future Health: Taking a Long Term View*. London: DH.

Ward, R., Pugh, S. and Price, S. (2010) *Don't Look Back? Improving Health and Social Care Service Delivery for Older LGB Users*. London: Equality and Human Rights Commission.

Warner, L. and Ford, R. (1998) 'Conditions for women in in-patient psychiatric units: The Mental Health Act Commission 1996 national visit', *Mental Health Care*, 1(7): 225–8.

Warner, L. *et al.* (2000a) 'Could this be you? Evaluating quality and standards of care in the inpatient psychiatric setting', *Mental Health and Learning Disabilities Care*, 4(3): 89–92.

Warner, L. *et al.* (2000b) *National Visit 2: A Visit by the Mental Health Act Commission to 104 Mental Health and Learning Disability Units in England and Wales – Improving Care for Detained Patients from Black and Minority Ethnic Communities (Preliminary Report)*. London: Sainsbury Centre for Mental Health.

Warner, R. (2004) *Recovery from Schizophrenia: Psychiatry and Political Economy* (3rd edn). New York: Routledge.

Warner, R. *et al.* (1993) 'The effects of a new mental health service based in primary care on the work of general practitioners', *British Journal of General Practice*, 43, 507–11.

Watson, A. (1997) *Services for Mentally Disordered Offenders in the Community: An Inspection Report*. London: DH.

Wearden, A. J. *et al.* (2000) 'A review of expressed emotion research in health care', *Clinical Psychology Review*, 20(5): 633–66.

Webb, Y. *et al.* (2000) 'Comparing patients' experience of mental health services in England: A five-trust survey', *International Journal of Health Care Quality Assurance*, 13(6/7): 273–81.

Webbe, A. (1998) 'Ethnicity and mental health', *Psychiatric Care*, 5(1): 12–16.

Webber, M., Treacey, S., Carr, S., Clark, M. and Parker, G. (2014) 'The effectiveness of personal budgets for people with mental health problems: a systematic review', *Journal of Mental Health*, 23(3): 146–55.

Webster, C. (2002) *The National Health Service: A Political History*. Oxford: Oxford University Press.

Weich, S. *et al.* (2011) 'Mental well-being and mental illness: Findings from the Adult Psychiatric Morbidity Survey for England 2007', *British Journal of Psychiatry*, 199, 23–8.

Weinberg, A. and Huxley, P. (2000) 'An evaluation of the impact of voluntary sector family support workers on the quality of life of carers of schizophrenia sufferers', *Journal of Mental Health*, 9(5): 495–503.

Welsh Government (2010) *Mental Health (Wales) Measure 2010*. Cardiff: Welsh Government.

Welsh Government (2012) *Together for Mental Health – A Strategy for Mental Health and Wellbeing in Wales*. Cardiff: Welsh Government.

White, E. (1990) 'The work of the Community Psychiatric Nurses Association: A survey of the membership', *Community Psychiatric Nursing Journal*, 10, 30–5.

White, E. (1993) 'Community psychiatric nursing, 1980–1990: A review of organisation, education and practice', in C. Brooker and E. White (eds), *Community Psychiatric Nursing: A Research Perspective* (vol. II). London: Chapman & Hall.

Whittle, M. C. and Scally, M. D. (1998) 'Model of forensic psychiatric community care', *Psychiatric Bulletin*, 22(12): 748–50.

WHO (1999) *The World Health Report: Making a Difference*. Geneva: WHO.

WHO (2001) *World Health Report 2001: Mental Health, New Understanding, New Hope*. Geneva: WHO.

WHO (2004) *WHO Guide to Mental and Neurological Health in Primary Care*. London: Royal Society of Medicine Press.

WHO Europe (2008) *Policies and Practices for Mental Health in Europe*. Geneva: WHO.

WHO/WONCA (2008) *Integrating Mental Health into Primary Care: A Global Perspective*. Geneva: WHO.

Widgery, D. (1991) 'GP mourns the dying East End', *GP Magazine*, July, 32.

Wilkinson, R. and Pickett, K. (2009) *The Spirit Level: Why Equality Is Better for Everyone*. London: Penguin.

Willis, J. (1995) *The Paradox of Progress*. Abingdon: Radcliffe Medical Press.

Wilson, M. and Francis, J. (1997) *Raised Voices: African-Caribbean and African Users' Views and Experiences of Mental Health Services in England and Wales*. London: Mind.

Wilson, T. and Holt, T. (2001) 'Complexity science: Complexity and clinical care', *British Medical Journal*, 323, 685–8.

Winchester, R. (2001) 'Pushed to breaking point', *Community Care*, 7–13 June, 18–20.

Wolfensberger, W. (1972) *The Principle of Normalization in Human Services*. Toronto: National Institute on Mental Retardation.

World Health Organization (WHO) (1978) *Alma Ata, Global Strategy for Health for All by the Year 2000*. Geneva: WHO.

Wright, A. F. (1995) 'Continuing to defeat depression', *British Journal of General Practice*, 45, 170–1.

Wright, S. *et al.* (2000) *Thematic Review of NHS R&D Funded Mental Health Research in Relation to the National Service Framework for Mental Health*. London: Institute of Psychiatry.

Zubin, J. and Spring R. (1977) 'Vulnerability – A new view schizophrenia', *Journal of Abnormal Psychology*, 86(2): 103–24.

Index

Printed and bound by CPI Group (UK) Ltd, Croydon, CR0 4YY